THUGS

THUGS

HOW HISTORY'S MOST NOTORIOUS DESPOTS TRANSFORMED THE WORLD THROUGH TERROR, TYRANNY, AND MASS MURDER

MICAH D. HALPERN

THOMAS NELSON
Since 1798

NASHVILLE DALLAS MEXICO CITY RIO DE JANEIRO BEIJING

Published in Nashville, Tennessee, by Thomas Nelson. Thomas Nelson is a trademark of Thomas Nelson, Inc.

Thomas Nelson, Inc., titles may be purchased in bulk for educational, business, fund-raising, or sales promotional use. For information, please e-mail SpecialMarkets@thomasnelson.com.

Library of Congress Cataloging-in-Publication Data

Halpern, Micah D.
    Thugs: How history's most notorious despots transformed the world through terror, tyranny, and mass murder / Micah D. Halpern.
        p. cm.
    ISBN 10: 1-59555-073-9
    ISBN 13: 978-1-59555-073-6
    1. World politics—Miscellanea. 2. Despotism. 3. Totalitarianism. 4. Mass murder. I. Title.
    D32.H36 2007
    321.9092'2—dc22

                                                        2007013037

Printed in the United States of America
07 08 09 10 11 QW 8 7 6 5 4 3 2 1

There is one safeguard known generally to the wise,
which is an advantage and security to all, but
especially to democracies against despots—suspicion.
—DEMOSTHENES

Rebellion to tyrants is obedience to God.
—THOMAS JEFFERSON

When I despair, I remember that all through
history the ways of truth and love have always
won. There have been tyrants, and murderers,
and for a time they can seem invincible, but
in the end they always fall. Think of it—always.
—MAHATMA GANDHI

CONTENTS

CONTENTS

CONTENTS

CONTENTS

It is my hope that by reading this book, you will be entertained in addition to being informed. *Thugs* is a popular history. It is about legacy and continuity. It is about the horrors that shaped history and the perpetrators of those horrors. It is an accessible entrée into the lives and careers of some of the world's most powerful leaders.

So who made the cut? How did I decide who was in and who was out? Who was despotic enough, demonizing enough, ruthless, barbaric, merciless enough? And was that even my criteria?

My guiding principle was that many of these leaders cared not a whit about the values and ideals that I and my world—the free and democratic world—hold dear. These are leaders who used their power for the purpose of furthering their own personal and political goals. *Thugs* is a peek into the private lives of the rich and infamous. It is a glimpse into the political aspirations of the biggest and most notorious of egos.

Unfortunately there are many despots, dead and alive, to choose from. I chose to write about leaders not because they were necessarily worse than others but because of the way they impacted history. I chose people for the roles they played, not merely for the barbaric acts they performed. Brutality alone was not enough to warrant a place in *Thugs*. I wanted characters about whom there was controversy. Controversy centering on their place in history. Controversy about the role they played during their own historical period and in their own country. They are people who arouse controversy in academic circles and are the subjects of popular debate.

I wanted characters that were a blight on society, and I wanted to know what made them tick. Were they aggressive and did what they thought necessary to advance and change their country, their culture, their people? Were they immature leaders who did not and could not really manage the mantle of leadership? Or were they simply possessed by their own superhuman egos?

Some of the characters are far worse than others. Some easily fit into what could almost be a universal model for a thug or a tyrant: Hitler, Mussolini, Stalin. Others could be considered great leaders, but they were also authoritarian rulers: Genghis Khan, Mao Tse-Tung. There are those who were undeniably great leaders, but who were also classic dictators: Alexander, Caesar. And then there are those who committed acts so heinous that their pristine reputations are tainted, altering their places in popular history. That's how King David wound up on my list. The second king of Israel consorted with a married woman (Bathsheba), and then ordered the death of that woman's husband (a warrior fighting in the king's own army).

The lives and proclivities of some of these otherwise ruthless people will make you laugh because they're just plain funny. King Farouk was a collector. He had the largest collection of pornography in the world. He also had a rare coin collection that rivaled his porn collection. In order to feed his coin-collection habit, the king stole money. He was a master pickpocket.

Some were just pitiful. Bashar Assad wanted to live out his life far away from home as an English gentleman and an ophthalmologist. But then his playboy brother—the son who was supposed to take over the reins from his father—went and got himself killed. So Bashar was plucked from his life in England and given a crash course in Syrian politics and the art of ruling. Call it despot training 101. His coursework was completed with the death of his father. The rest was on-the-job training.

And then there are those who were so absolutely self-absorbed that they had no idea history would show them in a bad light. Nicholas of Russia couldn't see that when he went to the front to fight alongside his men and bolster their spirits, he was essentially giving up—no, throwing away—the throne. He thought he was doing the right thing. He thought he was inspiring his troops. Instead he left the entire country and all the decision-making authority in the hands of his German-born wife so that he could go fight a war against his enemy—the Germans.

Some thugs are actually larger than life. They are mythic characters with mythic proportions. They are the answers on *Jeopardy* and the questions on *Millionaire*. Their stories tell themselves, and our knowledge of their lives is intertwined with lore. Those rulers made it onto my list because I want them to be seen in their proper context—not as masquerade party figures but as the despots and authoritarian leaders they really were. So you will read about Cleopatra. Not because she was so beautiful (though she probably wasn't) or because she was inherently evil. Cleopatra is on the list because she was considered by the Egyptians to be a god. As a god, Cleopatra had the power of life and death. And through her power and charm she manipulated her relationship with Julius Caesar and the entire empire of Rome.

The model of an authoritarian leader is predominately that of a man. This is not a sexist statement; it is a historical fact. Few women are deserving of the title "thug," and there are several good reasons for that. Even if they had traits that would have defined them as despotic, dastardly, demonic, cruel, and brutal, most women kept that side of themselves to themselves. Their public persona was less severe to the public eye. Certainly women have occupied seats of power, but historically they are less brutal in the application of their power than are men.

So why write a book about these men (and few women) who have already made their mark in modern history texts? To counteract the apparent desire to creatively rewrite some of this history. The reason for these creative rewrites is very simple: People do not like to see their leaders described as monsters. They do not like to read about the horrific atrocities the founders of their worlds perpetrated. They do not want to be blamed, even hundreds of years later, for creating and unleashing monsters onto the world. So great stories are often made up to soften the evil doings of the past—stories that have very little to do with history but that make the awful a little more palatable and acceptable. It's a natural response.

Without the sugarcoating, it would be hard for many countries to display national pride. Even Americans feel the need to stretch the truth just a little to fabricate a bit of history and lore. There is little doubt George Washington did not cut down that cherry tree, and in all probability, he was not that honest. That was certainly the case concerning his matrimonial promises. But Americans need to believe those stories and pass them on from generation to generation. The great myths of a society and a culture are built on these stories. So sometimes we whitewash our leaders, and that's okay, as long as we know what we are doing.

History is a powerful political tool. And while I am not a believer in that old adage coined by Harvard's George Santayanah about the doom awaiting those who do not learn from history, I am respectful of history.

The politically motivated would have us rewrite history. Then there are historians who, by my observation, simply have an axe to grind. When writing about these despotic leaders, some historians feel the need to vilify their subjects while others paint them almost as saints. Some have written official "objective" histories while others have written extremely critical works. The truth is somewhere in between, and we need to know and remember that.

I found this study fascinating. It is a look at the motives and operational styles of the most vile and heinous movers and shakers of Europe, the Middle East, and Asia—three great regions that influenced the world in ancient times and continue to wield great influence today. To take this book further afield, venturing into South America and Africa, would have expanded the field too far and required a different lexicon. I'm saving that for another time. But for a look at the origin of various titles and descriptive words used of leaders in this work, I have included an appendix of etymology.

I have attempted an accessible accounting of some of the most outstanding activities and foibles of a select group of extraordinary world leaders from across the ages. I have chosen to write in an approachable and, I hope, engaging style. For those who wish to delve deeper into the personalities presented here, I have included a list of recommended reading.

My hope is that this book will be a catalyst to conversations about thugs, both past and present. Let's bring discussion and debate about these leaders and their actions into the mainstream. Let's explore our history together, openly.

Thugs is about dictators and despots and demons. About monsters and maniacs and their merciless acts. *Thugs* is about people.

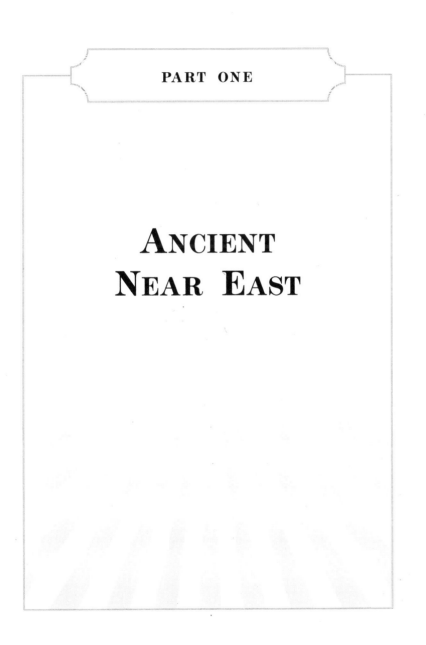

PART ONE

ANCIENT
NEAR EAST

The Ancient Near East is referred to as the cradle of civilization because that's where it all began.

The history of the region is replete with dictators and kings. Some of those kings were despots; others were cutting-edge pace setters. The Near East was both the center of culture and the center of ruthlessness. Most ancient leaders left their footprints in the desert sand.

It was home to the Bible and the Koran. Both holy books understood the power of leaders and the importance of justice and righteousness. The prophets in the holy books corrected the ways of the people and explained the ways of leaders who so often thought themselves above the law.

No other place on earth has seen such pendulum swings. It was in Ur Qasdim that monotheism began. One of monotheism's greatest contributions to the world was stopping human sacrifice. Abraham came from Ur Qasdim. And so did Saddam Hussein. In Abraham's time, human life and human dignity were highly regarded and considered holy. But the Butcher of Baghdad forgot the lessons of the forefather Abraham, or maybe he just chose to reject them.

The history of the leaders, dictators, and kings of the Near East reveals the great heights humanity is capable of reaching and the unimaginable lows to which we have stooped.

1

HAMMURABI
The First Lawmaker

Born: Circa 1810 BCE
Died: Circa 1750 BCE
Ruled: 1792–1750 BCE

Innocent until proven guilty. Today it is a given. Today it is an expected and naturally assumed part of law. But until Hammurabi, the Emperor of Babylon, codified ethical behavior and lawlessness ruled.

Hammurabi, the sixth king of Babylon, was one of the empire's best-known leaders. It was he who expanded and transformed Babylon into a monarchy, creating the Babylonian Empire and turning himself into its first emperor. The name Hammurabi translates into "the kinsman is a healer." Apparently, his parents had different aspirations for their son than he had for himself. This Hammurabi was a conquering warrior. His exploits included capturing and destroying the kingdoms of Sumer and Akkadian, ousting them from influence, ending their control over the world, and furthering his own. Sumer and Akkadian were, in their day, as powerful as the United States is today.

Although he was a masterful conqueror whose army successfully destroyed enemies and neighboring societies, Hammurabi's crowning glory was not his military achievements. It was the code of law, ethics, and conduct that he composed and enacted. It was the Code of Hammurabi.

Written on a *stela*—a large eight-by-eight-foot black basalt stone that stood in a public place so it could be easily seen by everybody—the code was like a big billboard. Unfortunately, while everyone could see the stela, few people at that time could read it. Illiteracy was rampant. But everyone knew what it said. The stela was considered prime plunder and was stolen by warring enemies of the Babylonians. It was probably taken to the city of Susa where, in the early twentieth century, it was rediscovered. Today Hammurabi's code is safely ensconced in Paris at the Louvre Museum.

Once laws were literally written in stone, they were to be taken seriously. Hammurabi codified 282 laws covering all aspects of life. He dealt with family rights and children's rights and the rights of slaves. He set down rules of conduct in both business and personal affairs. But the greatest contribution of the code is not the specifics of the laws that were written but the fact that the laws were written at all.

Hammurabi's code proves to us that he was not merely a conquering king and vanquishing emperor. He was a ruler who was dedicated to justice. And he was a dictator. Who else could and would set down those laws? Hammurabi's legal system was so developed that he even thought to codify a law defending a woman falsely accused of adultery.

Code #132: If the finger is pointed at a man's wife about another man, but she is not caught sleeping with the other man, she shall jump into the river for her husband.

RAMESES II
God of Egypt

Born: Circa 1303 BCE
Died: Circa 1225 BCE
Ruled: 1292–1225 BCE

Pharaoh is the name given to all the great kings of Egypt.

All Egyptian kings in the Bible were called pharaoh. In Genesis Joseph served Pharaoh, king of Egypt. And in Exodus Moses was raised by the daughter of Pharaoh, king of Egypt. Yet the two lived during very different periods. It was a title-turned-name that they all carried. The word *pharaoh* comes from the ancient Egyptian *pr-aa*, which means "the great house." The pharaohs were more than mighty and masterful men. They were also considered to be gods, both in their lifetimes and after their deaths.

They were the rulers of the crescent-shaped Nile River, the most fertile region in the world. The symbol of the society in which the pharaohs lived was the fertile crescent, and to this day the crescent-shaped moon is one of the great symbols of Islam. When you fly above Egypt today you can see just how important the Nile River is. It carves a green semi-moon into the barren desert.

The pharaohs of the biblical books of Genesis and Exodus are typical of Egyptian history. They adopted and adapted surrounding culture. So when the Bible describes Joseph rising from prisoner to court adviser second only to Pharaoh, it shows just how open they were to outside culture.

The pharaohs were absolute rulers with absolute control. And yet, there were pharaohs who were deposed and even some who were assassinated.

Rameses II was by far the most influential of the pharaohs. He was also the most notorious. Rameses, son of Pharaoh Seti I and Queen Tuy, ascended the throne at about twenty years old at the request of his father, who was getting on in years. Rameses was not heir to the throne; he usurped it and proceeded to rule for sixty-seven years during the nineteenth dynasty in the twelfth century BCE. Pharaoh Rameses II was the second-longest ruling of the pharaohs, and during his reign he fathered more than a hundred children.

This king was given many titles, including Rameses the Great and Son of Ra, the Egyptian sun god. He was a bold leader who envisioned uniting the upper and lower sections of Egypt. While he was a great warrior, Rameses was also a peacemaker. Under his domination, Egypt stretched from northern Syria through large parts of Africa.

Architecture was Rameses' passion. He built and he built and he built, more than any other pharaoh before or after him. Rameses built great monuments honoring himself and paying tribute to his own exalted powers. The tomb of his beloved wife Queen Nefertari is believed to be the most beautiful of all the tombs uncovered in Egypt. He expanded and improved the monuments in Luxor and Karnak. He erected a mortuary at Thebes and constructed numerous colossal temples in tribute to the gods.

Rameses' Abu Simbel temple towers above all else in glory and splendor. It looms larger than large with four humongous columns displaying four different images of Rameses the Great nestled among the gods. The temple was called the House of Rameses, Beloved of Amun.

Rameses II was a dynamic warrior. His army employed large numbers of mercenaries, and under his reign the slave population increased dramatically.

And when war and acquisition did not go his way, Rameses became resourceful, wily, and wise. He is probably the first ruler ever to draft and implement an international treaty. Architecture aside, creating the concept of a peace treaty and then implementing and standing by the treaty is one of the greatest gifts this pharaoh gave to future civilizations.

Egypt was forever battling the Hittites in the north. After a prolonged battle at Kadesh, which is located in today's Syria, Rameses suffered what he considered a significant defeat. He feared this one defeat would limit the future growth of his empire, so he signed a treaty with the Hittites. Included in the treaty was a clause common for the time. Pharaoh Rameses II would marry the daughter of the Hittite king, thereby assuring that both sides would adhere to the treaty. The deal was done; the marriage took place. Rameses had another wife.

Along with jewels, baubles, coins, and food, it is believed Rameses was buried with two of his most-loved possessions: his favorite horse and his favorite wife. Not surprisingly, the tomb of Rameses II was robbed many times. By the time it was uncovered, archaeologists found it empty and barren. But that is not the end of the most powerful pharaoh in history. The mummy of Rameses II was found and is considered by experts to be one of the best-preserved mummies ever discovered.

DAVID
The Shepherd King

Born: Circa 1005 BCE
Died: Circa 965 BCE
Ruled: Circa 1011–971 BCE

David. The slight young boy who slew the great giant.

For Jews, David was king—the monarch who set up his capital in the city of Jerusalem.

For Christians, David is considered to be the progenitor of the Messiah.

For Muslims, David is one of the prophets of Islam.

David, son of Jesse, first came to fame as a musician. He was a simple shepherd boy who played the lyre with great grace and dexterity and had the ability to soothe the troubled soul of Saul, the first king of Israel.

King Saul was suffering from severe depression, and David was brought in to play music and sing songs (called psalms) that he composed for the king. The psalms were intended to relieve the tremendous stress and pressure bearing down on Saul.

Israel was at war with the Philistines. The future looked very bleak. Today, we would call it a media ploy and label it a hoax. It was a game of intimidation. Day after day Goliath, the great symbolic warrior of the Philistines, would goad Saul by asking if there was no one in all of Israel brave enough to fight him. Goliath would enter the valley called Ella that separated Saul's army and the army of the Philistines. Each army would be poised for battle on their mountain top, and Goliath would call out again and again to the king of Israel.

There was a lull in battle. Saul was trying to regroup and strategize but was overcome by depression. The more Goliath taunted, the greater the depression grew. Even the pleasant songs of little David could not raise Saul's spirits. Like in so many great myths about great leaders, the boy took up the challenge.

Saul tried to cloak little David in his own royal armor, but the armor was too bulky for the boy. So wearing only the clothes of a shepherd and clutching five smooth stones that he picked up in the *wadi*, or riverbed, David faced the giant.

Goliath shouted up at Saul, "You sent a boy to do a man's work"—an expression that remains in our lexicon even today.

David placed four of the stones in his pouch, put one in his sling and took aim. He found the one chink in Goliath's armor—the one hole, the unprotected spot in the center of his forehead—and the giant was felled. It was a great victory. David took Goliath's sword and, with the giant's own blade, decapitated him. The army of Israel rushed down the hill, and the Philistine army ran back in the direction of the sea.

So begins the saga of one of history's first benevolent dictators—a true ancient thug.

David's glory is now part of history. He became part of Saul's family and the commander of Israel's armies. He was the best friend of Saul's son Jonathan and was given Saul's second daughter, Michal as his first wife. Seven more wives and a host of mistresses would follow.

This is the kind of story that great history is made of.

David's greatness and popularity were on the rise. He was anointed king by the prophet. Then, after Saul's death, David became king of Judea while Saul's son Ish Bosheth was anointed king of Israel. Judea was in the south, and the city of Hebron was chosen by David to be his capital. Israel, in the north, was its own state. Soon after, Ish Bosheth was assassinated, meeting the same fate as his father. When the death of Ish Bosheth was announced to David (the assassins personally delivered the ruler's head thinking they would receive a reward), David flew into a rage, killing the assassins just as he had killed Saul's murderer.

The elders of Israel then came down to Hebron and asked David the Beloved to extend his rule over all twelve tribes of Israel. And he accepted.

In addition to being a wonderful musician and a brilliant warrior, David was an astute politician. After assuming kingship of all Israel, David moved his capital from Hebron just a little farther north to the city of Jerusalem. Jerusalem was neither in the north nor in the south of Israel; it was a city controlled by the Jebusites. By relocating to Jerusalem, David avoided angering his southern constituents who would have accused him of abandoning them.

He also placated his new northern constituents by not ruling them from the South. Think of Jerusalem as Washington, D.C., which is neither North nor South. It is below the Mason–Dixon line, which runs along Pennsylvania and Maryland.

Even the best politicians have enemies. David's own son Absalom, rose up in rebellion against his father. When their two armies clashed in battle, Absalom caught his curly locks in the branches of an oak tree and could not untangle himself to run free. A general in David's army, thinking he would please his king, killed Absalom. Rather than rejoice at the death of his enemy, David lamented the loss of his beloved son.

David was a successful monarch. He expanded the borders of Israel and successfully brought Israel into international recognition. He was a great planner. He had a creative side. He was a poet. He wrote the psalms—poetry with a magical quality and profound philosophy that transcends translation.

But David, king of Israel, had a tragic flaw. He lusted. So much so that he used the power of his position as commander in chief of the army to have the husband of his lover murdered.

In ancient cities the highest building belonged to the king. It was the most secure and offered the best vantage point. From his palace David could look down and see the entire city. And that is how he spied the lovely Bathsheba sun bathing on her rooftop. The king was overcome with desire.

David and Bathsheba conceived a child. At the time, Bathsheba's husband, Uriah, was a Hittite mercenary—an officer commanding part of David's army. Uriah was far from home and could not have impregnated his wife. In order to cover up his indiscretion, David had Uriah brought back from the front for a conjugal visit. But out of guilt Uriah refused to go home. He would not allow himself the comforts of home while his men were embroiled and suffering in battle.

David sent Uriah back to the front. Without knowing it, Uriah was carrying his own death notice. David had given him a message to take back to the front instructing that Uriah should be put directly in the line of fire and that everyone else should pull back.

After Uriah's death the prophet Nathan appeared before David and offered him a parable. The prophet told of two men: one who had a large flock, the other who had only one sheep. The rich shepherd stole the one sheep from the poor shepherd and brought it to slaughter to feed a guest. David was enraged. How dare the prosperous man behave in that manner; how evil!

"You," said the prophet Nathan to David, king of Israel, "you are that man."

4

CYRUS
The Enlightened Dictator

Born: Circa 580 BCE
Died: Circa 529 BCE
Ruled: 559–529 BCE

Cyrus was the greatest ruler of Persia. Long before the famous Alexander, Cyrus crowned himself with the title "The Great." It was a title he deserved to hold.

Cyrus was the founder and mythical leader of an entire civilization. In a rare combination of benevolence and battle, he succeeded in bringing the tribes of Mede and Persia together, forging one large society under his domination. Unlike his contemporaries, Cyrus the Great was tolerant of different religions, languages, and cultures. Under Cyrus, Persia was the greatest power of the region.

His early life reads like a mythological tale. It is the story of a child who was rejected by his parents and later returned to erect an entire civilization. When hearing about Cyrus, the stories of Oedipus Rex and of Romulus and Remis immediately come to mind, although historically, Cyrus lived first. In all likelihood, it is precisely because of his birth and early years that Cyrus was so determined to conquer the two tribes and forge them into one.

The son of a Persian king and a Mede princess, the child was given the name Cyrus II after his grandfather, Cyrus I of Anshan. Cyrus is a rather strange and unusual name, especially as it relates to the original languages of the time. It is probably the Latinization of the Greek word *korus* or *khor*, which mean "sun." So Cyrus (or Khorush or Koresh, as he is called in the Bible) means "having the qualities of the sun." At his birth, Cyrus's parents dreamt that their child would be like the sun. His grandfather had another dream.

The story goes that shortly after the birth of the boy, Cyrus's grandfather, Astyages—ruler and great conqueror—had a dream. The dream was interpreted by an oracle to mean that this newly born grandson would grow up to revolt against his grandfather and take over the kingdom. So the grandfather ordered that baby Cyrus be slaughtered.

Fortunately for Cyrus, and for history, the loyal and trusted man charged with carrying out this inhumane order could not do so. He passed the order to a simple herdsman who, in turn, was unable to kill the baby. As fate would have it, the herdsman's wife had just given birth to a stillborn baby boy. The children were swapped. The herdsman returned with a dead baby, and that child was brought as proof to the king of Cyrus's murder. The herdsman took Cyrus and raised the boy as his own child.

Eventually, the truth unfolded. Grandfather Astyages was outraged and ordered that the son of his trusted and loyal aide (the man originally given the kill order) be beheaded. Cyrus went on not to rule his grandfather's kingdom but to create and rule a grand empire, leading Persia into new glory.

Almost everything we know about Cyrus comes from the Roman historian Herodotus and is confirmed by numerous archeological finds attesting to the grandeur and greatness of Cyrus.

Cyrus conquered the entire Iranian plateau. He launched campaigns into Egypt and Assyria in the north. He conquered Mede. But his greatest contribution was conquering the Babylonian Empire, unseating them as a world power. With this conquest, Cyrus the Great established Persia as the most significant culture and power in the world.

The Babylonians had sacked Jerusalem, destroyed the temple, and sent the Jews into exile. But Cyrus—the lover of language, culture, and religion—allowed the Jews reentry and even permitted them to rebuild their temple. With all his conquests, it was the title king of Persia that Cyrus wore most proudly. So was he really a thug, a despot, a dictator? He was. In those days, the only way to preserve your role as king was to assume one of two roles: tyrant or benevolent dictator. Cyrus's decision to rule with benevolence was a calculated and clearly effective form of leadership. But he still possessed the ability to intimidate his enemies and to ruthlessly kill and eliminate all opposition to his authority.

The final breaths of Cyrus's the emperor and king of Persia, were much less dramatic than his birth. Cyrus' final adventure was to a far-off land—probably today's Khazakhstan—where he died in a battle against a nomadic tribe, the Massagetes. Babylon learned of Cyrus's death in battle in the winter of 530 BCE.

Letters dated the "first year of the reign of King Cambyses" show that Cyrus had appointed his son, Cambyses, as his successor. The father left his son advice for ruling, telling him to offer "his blessing on those who should remain on friendly terms with one another, and a curse upon those who first did wrong."

Cyrus the Great died three days after being wounded in the battle.

5

DARIUS

The Benevolent Dictator

Born: Circa 549 BCE
Died: Circa 486 BCE
Ruled: Circa 521–486 BCE

Darius the Great was a revolutionary.

He was a success of Cyrus. He modeled himself on the original; the first great leader of Persia. He had large boots—or probably sandals—to fill, and he filled them well. Darius embraced the reforms that had been brought to the ancient world by Cyrus and took them one large step further.

The values that Darius held personally were incorporated into his style of governance. This ruler of the Persian Empire was a true benevolent dictator. His greatest contributions were the organization of government and the expansion of rights. He instituted a legal system that set down rules of evidence, limited slave sales, and acknowledged and dealt with the issues of deposits, bribery, and assault.

In his personal life, Darius of Persia was organized and lived by a series of ethics. And that is the way he ruled. Under his tenure, wars were no longer fought merely for the thrill of conquest or the machismo of battle. Wars were calculated ventures undertaken to gain necessary, natural frontiers or to quiet infidels and squelch enemies.

For Darius, wars were tactical. Governing was paramount. He battled and took over many neighboring societies when it was necessary, and then he imposed his values and cultures on them. It was that combination of warrior and humanitarian that made Darius so feared and so respected.

He organized his army and instituted a draft. He introduced the notion of a pay scale for soldiers. He created a training regimen so that soldiers would be better capable of fighting and achieving their military goals. Soldiers became professionals; employed workers, they were no longer guns for hire.

A government is only as good as the people it represents. When the people are satisfied, the people are happy. That means the government is doing its job, and Darius was very good at keeping his people happy and his government offices well managed. He improved the lives and livelihoods of his people by delivering to them the services they needed and by staying out of their way.

Certainly there was tension. Certainly there was corruption. Until Darius's reforms were put into place, the coveted positions of governor were handed down from father to son. Insurrection and deviance from the rules of government by anyone was met with punishment.

For the period in which he lived, Darius was almost the ideal benevolent dictator. Almost.

He divided the Persian empire into twenty provinces and gave each one pseudo-independence. Each province followed its own laws, answered to its own elite, and practiced its own customs. The prime responsibility of each provincial government was to maintain law and order and to pay tributes—taxes and monetary retribution—to the central government.

Government functions with ease when there is almost no need for commitment or participation from the people, and when the leadership is honest and committed to improving society. But even when times were hard and tributes due the emperor of Persia placed an undue burden on the local governments, Darius demanded his payment. As advanced as he was in many areas, Darius had no real understanding of economic cycles. It was simple: if the tributes were not met then heads would roll. The money Darius received went not exclusively to line his palaces with gold or adorn his women; much of the money went into government coffers and was used for building. Darius was a financier.

Well-built cities and majestic buildings were a major dimension of Darius's legacy. He built a new capital city called Persepolis. And not one stone, not one corner of the edifice, was built by slaves. Darius used only paid workers for his building. He dug a canal from the Nile to the Suez. He built a labyrinth of interstate highways crisscrossing the empire. The highways had rest stops and guard towers to protect travelers. Inns were built along the road to provide lodgings and food. Maybe it was because of the criminal system that Darius initiated and the severe punishments that came with breaking the laws he instituted, or maybe it was because of the sense of culture he imbued in his subjects, but there was virtually no wayfarer crime. There were no road pirates.

Darius was a monotheist, which is one reason he let the Jews continue to rebuild their temple. Yet despite his monotheism, he had a tolerance for other religious practices and even for paganism. His tolerance served him well because the vast majority of the people whom Darius and his warriors conquered were pagans. Darius neither asked nor forced his conquered subjects to convert, although he certainly had the power to do so.

He was curious. He sent out exploration teams and attempted to trade across the world. He used the sea as well as land for transport, and he expanded his trade the world over. But, like many people and even cartographers of his time, Darius had no grasp of geography.

Darius made a critical error in geography, and it was that error that soon brought Darius the Great and his entire empire to ruins. Darius crossed the Bosporus River and then the Danube River, entering Europe on his way to secure and solidify his border. He thought the Black Sea was much closer than it really was. The resources and manpower needed were too great. Although his conquest was successful, the region was too vast to be properly policed. Darius was weakened.

The Persian Wars soon followed. Then came insurrections in Egypt. For Darius and his empire, it was the beginning of the end.

6

CLEOPATRA
Hollywood's Not So Beautiful Beauty Queen

Born: 69 BCE
Died: 30 BCE
Ruled: 51–30 BCE

"For (as they say) it was not because [Cleopatra's] beauty in itself
was so striking that it stunned the onlooker, but the inescapable
impression produced by daily contact with her: the attractiveness
in the persuasiveness of her talk and the character that surrounded
her conversation was stimulating. It was a pleasure to hear the
sound of her voice, and she tuned her tongue like a many-stringed
instrument expertly to whatever language she chose."
(FROM PLUTARCH'S *LIFE OF MARK ANTONY*)

Cleopatra was the last of the Egyptian pharaohs. That is almost the only statement that can be made unequivocally about this queen of the Nile. Cleopatra was a remarkable woman who used her wit and her cunning, her womanly ways and brilliant mind, to woo and wed her way through countless lovers and husbands across distant continents and then to dispose of them. Historians have never quite come to an agreement on the details of this woman's life.

Hollywood has been kinder to the mysterious Cleopatra than were her contemporaries. One thing is for sure: Cleopatra was as large a legend in her own lifetime as she is today.

Cleopatra was the third daughter of Ptolemy XII. In 51 BCE, when she turned seventeen and after the deaths of her sisters, she was chosen by her father to share his throne. Cleopatra was charming and charismatic, and when her father died a few months later, she was left alone as Egypt's leader. But Egyptian law does not recognize a female ruler, so she was forced to find a suitable male. Cleopatra chose her younger brother, Ptolemy XIII, making him both her husband and her co-regent in Egypt. Meanwhile, Egypt was crumbling at Cleopatra's feet.

For two centuries, Egypt—a society that saw itself as the world's greatest culture—had treaties and cultural exchange with Rome. Throughout his reign, Ptolemy XII paid enormous monetary tributes to Rome to keep them from meddling too much in local affairs. Now Egypt was losing luster and strength in direct relation to the rise of the Roman Empire, which was slowly taking control of Cleopatra's domain. As Rome became greater, Egyptians found it more difficult to accept their new status.

Cleopatra truly loved her country. She adopted the religion of Egypt and was the only pharaoh to speak the language of the Egyptians. Cleopatra understood that Egypt was waning. She realized that her personal future and the future of the country she loved could only be guaranteed through a close link with Rome.

Cleopatra was desperate. She needed to return Egypt to power. She needed to maintain her dynasty. She needed the help of Julius Caesar.

Imagine you are Julius Caesar—the most powerful person in the world. You have arrived in Alexandria, Egypt, from Rome. You are staying in a royal palace and you receive a present. It is a tightly rolled oriental carpet.

You have the carpet unfurled and inside is Cleopatra, the twenty-two-year-old pharaoh of Egypt. Some accounts describe Cleopatra as beautiful; some say she was truly unattractive and even masculine. Everyone calls her a seductress.

Even for a woman given to drama and extravagance, this was truly one of the most dramatic entrances ever made and one of the most expensive gifts ever given. Cleopatra's seductive talents matched her enormous ego and sense of power. The sex symbol of the ancient world was a cold and calculating woman with whom scores of powerful men fell in love.

Caesar had come to Alexandria to conquer the city. Cleopatra came to Caesar to enlist his help in her battle for sole regency over Egypt. She wanted Caesar's help in the power struggle that she was waging against Ptolemy XIII. The entire carpet escapade was planned so that Cleopatra could get to Caesar before her brother got to him. It worked. By the time Ptolemy XIII arrived in Alexandria, Caesar had already fallen in love with Cleopatra.

Now Cleopatra, armed with Caesar's army, was able to defeat Ptolemy XIII. The battles of Alexandria had their consequences: the great library was burned and some books were damaged, but many were able to be salvaged. Most important, Cleopatra had her throne, and Cleopatra had her man. Then she married an even younger brother, Ptolemy XIV, who at age twelve was no threat to the diabolical Cleopatra even though he bore the title co-regent of Egypt.

Julius Caesar, Cleopatra, and Ptolemy XIV traveled up and down the Nile and throughout Caesar's empire. During one of their trips, this time to Dendara in 47 BCE, Cleopatra was worshipped as a god. Rather than feeling emasculated, Caesar was infatuated with Cleopatra's status.

Cleopatra could not marry Caesar; Roman law forbade it. Caesar was married and bigamy was forbidden under Roman law. Being lovers, however, was acceptable, and Cleopatra bore a son believed to be the son of Caesar. She named him Ptolemy Caesar and nicknamed him Caesarion (little Caesar). Depending on which sources are referenced, the Romans either despised or revered the queen of Egypt. But regardless of the Romans' opinion of the queen, the union between Cleopatra and Caesar brought peace between Egypt and the Roman Empire. The couple resided in Rome with their child in a great palace built in their honor.

But not for long. Caesar was assassinated by a group of conspirators, including Roman senators, on March 15, 44 BCE—a day now known as the Ides of March. Little Caesar was not an eligible contender to the legacy of Caesar, as illegitimate children were forbidden from being legitimate heirs according to Roman law. Cleopatra returned to Egypt from Rome, along with her son and her brother, Co-regent Ptolemy XIV.

Shortly after their return, Ptolemy XIV was murdered—probably by Cleopatra, and probably so that she could replace him with her infant son who was a viable ruler under Egyptian law.

The death of Caesar left Rome with a gap in its leadership. Tensions were rising, and a rivalry grew between Marc Antony and Octavian, both of whom hoped to rule Rome. Meanwhile, Egypt, having been abandoned by its leadership as Queen Cleopatra cavorted around the world, was suffering miserably from famine and plagues.

Cleopatra cast her lot with Marc Antony, and he called for her to come to Turkey. She took his breath away, and the two became lovers. Their relationship saw the birth of twins: Cleopatra Selene, which means "moon," and Alexander Helios, which means "sun."

One of the most famous legends of Cleopatra's cunning and maipulations is a wager she made with Marc Antony. Cleopatra bet that she could cater the most expensive banquet in history. As Marc Antony watched from his divan, Cleopatra took off one priceless pearl earring, ground it up, poured it into a wine chalice, and drank. In shock, Marc Antony acknowledged that Cleopatra had won the bet.

Antony gave his mistress many presents, which irked his wife, Octavia. Octavia was the sister of Antony's rival for power, Octavian. So while Cleopatra was given presents, Octavia was given a divorce. The presents included large pieces of Roman land, which led the people of Rome to despise Cleopatra more and more. And he paid Cleopatra the ultimate compliment by putting her name and face on the silver denarii, a Roman coin.

Octavian declared war on Marc Antony on September 2, 31 BCE. Octavian's Admiral Agrrippa defeated Antony's forces in Actium, which we now call Greece.

Cleopatra was taken captive, a spoil of the war.

Cleopatra ruled Egypt from 51–30 BCE as queen and pharaoh. Ascending the throne at age seventeen, she ruled until committing suicide at the age of thirty-nine. Who died first, Antony or

Cleopatra? The stories vary. Some have it that Antony killed himself after learning of Cleopatra's death. Some say it was the other way around: Cleopatra killed herself after hearing of Antony's death. Cleopatra died as dramatically as she lived. Imprisoned, she snuck an asp into a basket of figs and then lay down on a bed of gold to die, her dead and dying maidservants at her feet. Cleopatra had determined that she preferred to die, poisoned by a snake, than to live out her life a prisoner of the Romans.

She was as cunning in death as she was in life: Egyptian religion declared that their queen, killed by the sting of an asp, would be forever immortalized.

7

HEROD

The Man with an Edifice Complex

Born: 73 BCE
Died: 4 BCE
Ruled: 37–4 BCE

History records the lives and tyrannical rule of many men named Herod, but only one merits the title Herod the Great.

Herod the Great was arguably one of the greatest builders in the history of the world. His architectural triumphs rival the edifices of Pharaoh Rameses II and the Great Wall of China. Herod's fortresses, cities, temples, and monuments were truly wondrous. Those that still stand are marvels even in our time.

Herod was a man given to extremes. He loved his wives (there were probably ten in all) and his many children dearly. He literally moved mountains for them. He literally knocked mountains down, hollowed them out, created others and even flattened mountains all to build a great edifice. That is how he architecturally 'made room.' Herod expanded the upper plateau of Mount Moriah in order to have the large space he needed to erect his expanded new version of the Second Temple.

In a final act of love and caring, Herod had his wife Miriamne (Miriam) pickled. Pickled. And not just in any pickling spice. Herod chose a spice that would reflect his love and her delicacy. Driven into a crazed act of jealousy because of his belief that his wife had betrayed him with another man, Herod pickled his wife in honey. Why honey? To preserve her sweetness. All other pickling agents are sour and bitter, like vinegar and alcohol. Honey is the sweetest of all pickling spices and most appropriate for the woman Herod loved so very, very much. He also pickled two of his sons, Aristobulus and Alexander.

The story of Herod's rise to leadership is a great one. It eventually includes his ascension to the throne as king of Judea under the Romans, an empire Herod dominated for thirty-three years, from 37 BCE until his death in 4 BCE.

Herod was an extremely paranoid man, wary of everyone who had claim to the throne, including his wife and sons. While Jewish identity is matrilineal, Jewish leadership—especially during the Greek and Roman periods—was determined patrilinealy. Jewish leaders were the priests, and the priesthood (most importantly the position of high priest) was handed down from father to son. The reason Herod so jealously and brutally protected himself and his rule was that he could never naturally assume the priesthood and the throne. He was the product of pagan Idumean parents who were forced to convert to Judaism.

Miriamne was more closely linked in lineage to priestly leadership than Herod was. Herod was an appointed ruler—appointed by the great Marc Antony and Octavian, but an appointee never-theless. His wife and their five children were born into leadership.

Mariamne was the granddaughter of Hyrcanus—the last of the priestly kings and a victim of Herod's oft-bloodied sword. Mariamne was Jewish royalty; she was the last of the Hasmoneans, also known as the Macabbees. Historically, it is somewhat ironic. The Maccabbees took power after a fight against corruption only to become so corrupt themselves that they forced the conversion of their last king. That king was Herod—a man nowhere close to the high class of the priests.

In 38 BCE, Herod married Mariamne and appointed her brother Aristobulus to be high priest. Aristobulus was a popular high priest. It's not that he was very successful. He wasn't a failure, either. But he was popular, so in 29 BCE, Herod had Aristobulus drowned. (That was the same year Herod murdered and pickled his wife.)

A year later, in 28 BCE, Herod also assassinated his mother-in-law Alexandra. Scores of other Jewish priests were assassinated under his orders. So jealous was he of his own sons by Mariamne, Aristobulus and Alexander, that he ordered their deaths as well. A third son died a young but natural death, and Herod's two daughters were of little threat to their menacing, maniacal father.

Macrobius, a biographer of Augustus who was present as Herod declared that his sons were to be assassinated, is attributed with coining the phrase, "It is better to be Herod's swine than his son."

Herod was an egotist and megalomaniac of the highest order. The great historian Heinrich Graetz called him "the evil genius of the Judean nation." He used Judea and the Jews as a fulcrum to achieve his great dream of fame and fortune. As ruler of Judea he was all-powerful. He built edifices as enormous as his ego. Through tapestries and stone, marble and gold, he created his own place in history. And for the Jews of Judea, Herod's reign was an enormously prosperous period economically and culturally—even religiously.

The concept of separation of church and state did not exist during Herod's lifetime. But Rome had learned a lesson about the Jews when they were under Greek rule: Jews would not abandon their religion. The Romans practiced a form of idol worship that included posthumously deifying rulers. They knew the Jews would have no part of their religion. Rather than attempt to force them to convert, the Romans decided that Jews could follow their own religion, as long as they paid for the privilege. The Jewish tax was called *fiscus judaicus*. The arrangement worked splendidly for Herod.

Judea was prime real estate; it was the center of many major trade routes. The region was known for exceptional olive oil, which in that time was used not only for cooking but also as fuel for light. Judean wine was famous, and dates, used as a sweetening agent, were in demand. The spice trade from Yemen and Arabia came through Judea on its way to Rome. Economically, Judea was well-off. Rome was happy. And Herod could concentrate on his true passion for building.

Perched high above the Dead Sea, Herod built the great desert fortress of Masada. The fortress lacked no amenity: it included winter and summer palaces, a synagogue, bath houses, and even had a water system allowing agriculture to blossom high on a desert mountain. He built Herodion—a man-made, flat-topped mountain—which was visible for miles around and served as Herod's eventual burial place. He constructed the glorious building around

Maccepella, known as the Tomb of the Patriarchs, in Hebron. And in honor of Augustus, he built the Mediterranean port city Caesarea, which rivaledthe grandeur of almost any Roman city. Caesarea would become the administrative seat of Rome in Judea. It was there that Herod constructed a man-made harbor, amphitheaters, and hippodromes for the sporting games that were held not only in Rome but also in Judea. Herod's mastery of building skills was awe-inspiring, and most of the structures he built in Caesarea—like in Masada—still stand today.

Under Herod, Jerusalem became one of the greatest cities in the world. The rabbis, scores upon scores of whom were put to death by Herod's decree, were no great fans of the ruler. And yet the Mishna, one of the greatest Jewish religious compilations composed during this period, describes the splendor and beauty of Jerusalem. It is written in the Mishna that "anyone who has not seen Herod's Jerusalem has not seen a beautiful city." Herod built a fortress at the most vulnerable point of Jerusalem. Called Antonia's Fortress, it is named after Herod's friend and ally Marc Antony. He built a remarkable wall around the city, the entrance of which was adorned with three spectacular towers representing the family he assassinated—his wife and their two sons.

Then Herod turned his attention to the temple, the most holy of Jewish sites that had been destroyed in 586 BCE by the Babylonians.

Initially it was rebuilt as a cheap replica of the first. But Herod took the temple to new heights, expanding and improving it. Devising an incredibly complex and precise system of transportation, pulleys, and cranes, he used rocks as large as two hundred tons (the average rock size used was about twenty tons; the smallest was seven tons) to craft one of the most beautiful buildings in the world. The temple was large enough to hold all the Jews of Judea, and all those living throughout the Roman Empire, three times a year when they gathered to offer sacrifices in honor of the Jewish holidays. The rabbis said, "He who has not seen the Temple of Herod has not seen a beautiful building."

It took at least ten thousand men at least ten years just to build the retaining wall around the temple. There was so much gold in the temple that it was blinding. The marble was laid as if to look like the rippling water of the sea.

But Herod's beautiful temple was blighted. At the entrance, he placed a huge Roman eagle. The site of the eagle was so Roman, so pagan, so repugnant to the Jewish religion that a group of rabbinic students destroyed the statue. Herod's response was to have them dragged before him in chains and burned alive.

Herod was a builder of majestic proportions. He cared more about his edifices than he did about the people he ruled. He poisoned, pickled, burned, and brutally murdered thousands upon thousands of his subjects. The best way to survive in Herod's world was not to marry him but to work for him. If you survived the hazards of hauling, you were well fed and cared for.

Yet another popular adage from Herod's reign is the saying that "Herod is much better to his workers and his slaves than to his family."

In the end, the man who brought so many others to violent deaths died naturally. Even with his final, dying breaths, Herod—true to himself—ordered the deaths of others.

The last moments of Herod's life are recorded by Josephus:

In the hot springs of Callirrhoe, east of the Dead Sea, the king sought relief from the sickness that was to bring him to the grave. When the end drew near, he gave orders to have the principal men of the country shut up in the hippodrome at Jericho and slaughtered as soon as he passed away, that his grave might not be without the tribute of tears. This barbarous command was not carried into effect; but the Jews celebrated as a festival the day of his death, by which they were delivered from his tyrannical rule. (*The Jewish War* 1:38)

8

PONTIUS PILATE
He Washed His Hands of the Whole Affair

Born: First century CE
Died: After 36 CE
Ruled: 26–36 CE

The Ethiopian Orthodox Church calls him Saint Pontius Pilate. Christians claim that he ordered and implemented the crucifixion of Jesus.

An inscription near a Judean temple excavated in 1961 near Caesarea bears the name of Pontius Pilate. Translated, the inscription reads, "Tiberium Pontius Pilate, prefect of Judea." Tiberium is for Tiberius, the Roman emperor. There was probably a temple erected for and named after the emperor during the time that Pontius Pilate was the prefect of the region. Pilate was probably present at the opening ceremony, explaining why his name was entered into the inscription. From this we know that he was a genuine historical character. But we still do not know his actual title. While in Caesarea he is referred to as a prefect, he is otherwise referred to as a procurator.

Both *prefect* and *procurator* mean "governor," but the titles are not interchangeable in Roman tradition. A prefect is a more exalted form of governor than is a procurator.

One thing can be said with certainty about Pontius Pilate: very little we know about him is certain. And what we know paints the portrait of a cruel, manipulative, insensitive man who had only limited power and wielded it for evil.

Legend and lore surround Pontius Pilate. The little hard information we have comes from the Christian Bible, Josephus, and the writings of some of the early church fathers and centers only around the time he spent in Judea. Very little is known about him before he came, and very little is known after he left. According to legend, Pilate was the illegitimate son of Tyus, king of Mayence. He was sent to Rome as a hostage, and while in Rome committed a murder and was arrested. Pilate was banished to Pontus and given the responsibility of controlling and settling down the tribes. That is how he came to be called Pontius Pilate—he was Pilate of Pontus. According to other legends, the boy Pilate was born in Fortingal, which is in Pertshire, Scotland. Or maybe he was from Spain. Or perhaps Forschheim, just outside of Hausen, Germany.

Wherever and under whatever circumstances he really was born makes no difference. What matters is that Pontius Pilate did exist. He was real, he held a position of some importance in Judea, and he paved the way for the crucifixion of Jesus. What matters is that Pontius Pilate played one of the most infamous roles in history.

The Christian Bible depicts Pilate as a somewhat pitiful character. He could not make a real decision about the fate of Jesus. He is described as vacillating back and forth and finally turning to the mob for direction, asking them how he should proceed. Pilate then calls for the chalice.

"Cup bearer, cup bearer," he calls. And the cup bearer comes with a chalice filled with water. The servant pours the water over Pilate's hands, as was the custom of the day.

Pilate then says, loudly enough for the people to hear, "I wash my hands of the whole affair." In other words, Jesus' crucifixion is not his responsibility but the responsibility of the Jewish mob that called for Jesus to be killed. The Gospel of Matthew records Pilate's words to mean, "I am innocent of this man's blood; you will see."

Other sources do not agree with the Christian Bible's depiction of a passive, pitiful, indecisive man. According to Josephus, it seems that Pilate was sent to Judea expressly to put down the Jewish uprising. It seems that the Jewish revolt was trying the patience of Rome. The Jews were a thorn in the emperor's side. Pilate had experience dealing with insurrections in the outer regions of the Roman Empire, so it was thought that he could handle the Jews of Judea.

We know Pontius Pilate is a character who clearly and deliberately agitated the Jews by desecrating the temple. That got him into trouble with the emperor.

Josephus describes one of the incidents involving Pilate, the temple, and the Jews.

On one occasion, when the soldiers under his command came to Jerusalem, he made them bring their ensigns with them, upon which were the usual images of the emperor. The ensigns were brought in secretly by night, but their presence was soon discovered. Immediately multitudes of excited Jews rushed to Caesarea to petition him for the removal of the obnoxious ensigns. He ignored them for five days, but the next day he admitted the Jews to hear their complaint. He had them surrounded with soldiers and threatened them with instant death unless they ceased to trouble him with the matter. The Jews then threw themselves to the ground and bared their necks, declaring that they preferred death to the violation of their laws. Pilate, unwilling to kill so many, succumbed and removed the ensigns. (*The Jewish War* 2:169–74)

He also describes another incident:

At another time he used the sacred treasure of the temple, called corban, to pay for bringing water into Jerusalem by an aqueduct. A crowd came together and clamored against him; but he had caused soldiers dressed as civilians to mingle with the multitude, and at a given signal they fell upon the rioters and beat them so severely with staves that the riot was quelled. (*The Jewish War* 2:175–77)

Philo, a contemporary of both Jesus and Pilate, records that on another occasion Pilate dedicated some gilded shields in the palace of Herod Antipas in honor of the emperor. On these shields there was no representation of any forbidden thing, but simply an inscription of the emperor's and donors' names. The Jews petitioned him to have them removed. When he refused, they appealed to Tiberius, who sent an order that the shields should be removed to Caesarea.

Pontius Pilate created so much resentment and fomented such unrest that Emperor Tiberius was constantly being bombarded by complaints. Pilate expropriated temple funds for the building of an aqueduct. He gratuitously massacred Samaritans. The discord suggested to the Roman Senate that the arrogant Pilate needed to be recalled, tried, and punished for misusing his authority. In the end, Pontius Pilate was sent back to Rome and prosecuted for his acts of cruelty and oppression.

There is a cloak of mystery surrounding Pilate's death. According to one legend, he committed suicide at the request of Emperor Caligula. Eusebius wrote that Pilate was exiled to the Vienne on Gaul, which is today's France, and that it was there he committed suicide. Another legend has him converting to Christianity before his death.

The most enthralling of all legends recounts that the body of Pontius Pilate was thrown into the Tiber River. But the evil spirit of Pontius Pilate was so disruptive to the gentle waters that his body was removed and dumped into the Rhone. The Rhone, too, rejected Pilate, and so once again the body was removed. This time it was sunk into the Lausanne lake where it was again rejected.

In the end, the true resting place of Pontius Pilate is shrouded in mystery. Some Eastern traditions even assert that he committed suicide for guilt over his role in the crucifixion of Jesus.

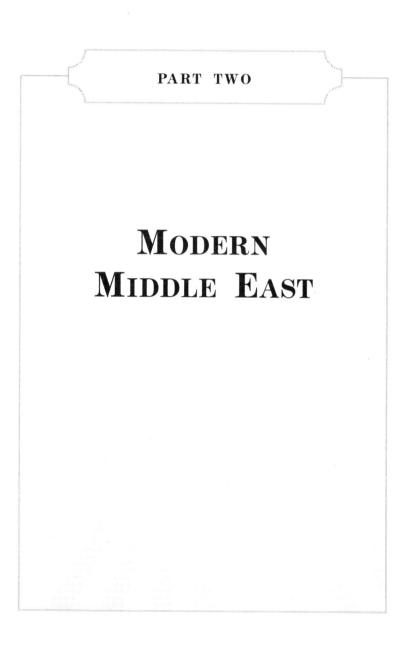

PART TWO

MODERN MIDDLE EAST

Chronologically, the Middle East has entered the twenty-first century. Philosophically and governmentally, it is bogged down in early history.

The Middle East of today is a conglomeration of contiguous countries spanning three continents—a little bit of this and a little bit of that. A little bit of North Africa (Egypt), a little bit of Asia (Jordan), and even a little bit of Europe (Turkey). There are a few blatant exceptions, but for the most part, these countries are linked not only by land but also by style of government, religion, culture, and history. Israel, of course, is the most obvious exception to the rule. Turkey is the other exception. The modern Middle East is a study in contradictions.

Emotions run high in the modern Middle East. And oil, in some countries, flows well. That oil has created some of the wealthiest dictators in the world. The Middle East has a vernacular of its own. Freedom and equality are terms that are bandied about in the region, but their reality is hardly recognizable from the Western portion of the modern world.

Many Middle Eastern countries are still ruled by kings. Others are ruled by colonels. Some rulers call themselves monarchs, and some have the audacity to insist that they be called president, or better yet, president for life. The change that takes place often comes about through military coup or fixed elections with candidates receiving 99 percent of the vote. Power is wrestled away from a king and passed on to a soldier. Promises to liberalize a society are freely made, but only rarely carried out. Some leading characters are comical; many are dangerous. Most rulers in the modern Middle East are men who have left a huge impression of oppression on the societies that they have led.

The region is rife with conflict and ripe for despots and thugs. To understand modern Middle East dictators is to understand the modern Middle East.

1

ABDULLAH I
From Desert Wanderer to King

Born: 1882
Died: 1951
Ruled: 1921–1951

The first king of Jordan was actually born in Arabia in the Muslim holy city Mecca in the year 1882. Abdullah ibn Husayn (Abdullah, son of Hussein) was born of the prominent Hashemite family. He was the son of Sharif Husayn ibn Ali, the ruler of Hijaz.

Abdullah, like his father and brother, was a fighter—a sword-carrying, head-dress wearing, classic twentieth-century-Arab warrior. War was a way of life, providing not only their survival but also allowing them to thrive. It was how, in 1917, Sharif transformed himself from ruler of Hijaz to king of Hijaz and appointed his son Abdullah to be foreign minister.

Together, father and sons led their private militia in successful attacks against the Ottoman Empire of Turkey and other enemies of Great Britain. In response to their initiative and military prowess, the sons were rewarded by the British. Abdullah was given a major plot of land to rule and was named the emir of Trans-Jordan. His brother Faisal was rewarded with the position of king of Iraq.

The land of Jordan belonged to the Ottoman Empire at the beginning of the nineteenth century. After World War I, the area was under Syrian rule until it finally came under the jurisdiction of Great Britain and was renamed Trans-Jordan. It was Trans-Jordan that the British placed under the rule of Abdullah ibn Husayn in July of 1921.

At the time, Abdullah, who held a British passport, was very pro-Western and pro-British. He accepted the position of emir of Trans-Jordan with one caveat: no more Jews would be allowed to immigrate to Trans-Jordan. The British acquiesced, and Emir Abdullah was true to his word.

Over time Abdullah's allegiance and attitude toward the West changed. In World War II, he led his fighters into battle against the Allied powers and their allies in the region, his former friends and sponsors. In May of 1946, Trans-Jordan gained its independence from the British, and Emir Abdullah of Trans-Jordan became the first king of the Hashemite Kingdom of Jordan.

The king's attitude toward Jews never wavered; it only strengthened. In 1948, after the partition of Palestine and when Israel declared itself a state, Abdullah led his forces against the new nation. His attitude toward Israel was no secret, and he was a highly trained military leader. His British-trained Jordanian soldiers were the most professional of all the Arab armies. It was a dynamic, winning combination for the United Arab Forces. Abdullah was given the position of commander in chief of the United Arab Forces, now called the Arab League. The league was created in an attempt to unify splintered Arab countries by pitting them against a common enemy: Israel.

The outcome of the 1948 war was a terrible blow for the Arab world and for Abdullah. His primary objective was to eliminate the world of Jews and to see to it that a Jewish state was never created. He failed. Israel declared statehood in May of 1948. In the early part of 1950, Abdullah entered into a nonaggression pact with Israel.

Abdullah was very practical in his understanding of the region and the limits of his power. He knew he was not a native of the area and that both his positions, first as emir and then as king, were by virtue of the British and their colonial control. He knew that the Israelis were there by force of might and determination. The war taught him that they were not about to be intimidated, and certainly, they were not about to be moved.

So he embarked on a series of meetings with Israeli leaders, creating a basis of understanding. Negotiations surrounding the pact between Israel and the Hashemite Kingdom were, of necessity, top secret. There are tales of Israel's first prime minister, David Ben Gurion, donning Arab *galabiyeh* and *kaffayeh* for talks with the king. Modern Israeli lore is full of humorous stories about Golda Meir, the Milwaukee-born school teacher who became Israel's fourth prime minister. As Ben Gurion's foreign minister, Meir could be found dressing up as an Arab male, crossing the border for talks in the royal palace with Abdullah, and then being whisked back home.

By the spring of 1950, Abdullah, true to form, succeeded in

occupying the West Bank of the Jordan River—the area retaken by Israelis in the Six Days' War of 1967. It is that area that has been the focal point of Middle East conflict and world attention. Palestinians claim it as their land; Israelis claim it as their land. In truth, it belonged to the Jordanians who by now have no interest in claiming the area.

Abdullah also tried, and ultimately failed, to create a United Arab Federation, preferably placing himself and his Hashemite Kingdom leaders as rulers. His dream was to unite Arabs across the region in a loosely bound federation sharing government, vision, and foreign policy. His goal was to form one country composed of Jordan, Iraq, and Syria. He was successful in creating a federation between himself and his brother, Faisal, in Iraq, but creating a federation with your brother is easy. After Faisal was deposed, the entire concept of a United Arab Federation collapsed.

Despite his failures, Abdullah was very good at securing land. He was excellent at training and maintaining a strong military—lessons he learned at his father's knee. But Abdullah was much weaker and much less interested in nation building and in creating and providing an infrastructure for his new country. During his tenure, Jordan developed very little industry and almost no foreign trade. The king was wealthy; his country was abysmally poor.

Abdullah was assassinated on the steps of the al-Aqsa Mosque on top of the Temple Mount in Jerusalem. Abdullah would often go to the al-Aqsa Mosque to pray, bringing his beloved grandson Hussein with him. On that fateful day, July 20, 1951, the young Prince Hussein accompanied his grandfather to the steps of the Mosque. They were together when the shots of the assassin rang out. In a scene out of the movies, the king was felled, but his grandson survived because of a gift given to him by his doting grandfather—a medal. One of the assassin's bullets bounced off the medal. Had the medal not been there to protect the boy who would one day soon take his grandfather's place as the ruling monarch of Jordan, it would have punctured his heart.

Being witness to the murder of his grandfather became one of the most pivotal and significant events in the life of Hussein. Abdullah's son—Hussein's father—was crowned king of the Hashemite Kingdom of Jordan, but his reign was short-lived. He was determined to be unbalanced, mentally ill, and unfit for leadership. The mantle of leadership passed to sixteen-year-old Hussein, just the way Abdullah would have wanted it.

2

FAROUK
The King of Porn

Born: 1920
Died: 1965
Ruled: 1936–1952

Farouk was king of Egypt from 1936 until he was ousted in 1952. But the title king before his name is not what made Farouk famous. He is better known for his avarice and greed, for his royal nepotism, and for having what was arguably the largest collection of pornography in the world.

Even larger than his porn collection was his numismatic collection. Yes, King Farouk loved coins. His obsession was so great that by 1952, when a silent coup forced his departure from Egypt, Farouk left behind the most valuable coin collection in the world. The collection was so heavy that Farouk could not take it with him, but neither did the Egyptians want to keep it. After much haranguing, arguing, and pleading, the decision was made to auction off the King Farouk numismatic collection.

Sotheby's published a multivolume catalogue written by Baldwin & Co. with the descriptions of 8,500 coins. The collection was so large that the auction house decided to separate the coins into lots, combining rare and less-rare coins in each lot. The proceeds of the sale went to the state.

A coin sale. What an apt symbolic end for Farouk. While most of the Egyptian citizenry begged for a few coins to survive, the king hoarded thousands of coins for amusement.

Farouk was born in Cairo on February 11, 1920. Sixteen years later Farouk's father, Ahmed Fouad I, died, making Farouk king of Egypt. According to Egyptian law, however, a boy of sixteen is considered too young to be given royal authority, so Farouk was forced into the position of king in waiting. A regency council ruled Egypt for two years and then, on his eighteenth birthday, the full title and power of king became his.

Farouk was not a stellar leader. He was callous and uncaring. He failed at almost every test of character and import as king. He was a child in the robes of a king; every whim was a demand that needed to be fulfilled.

Not only was he immature and childish, Farouk was also foolish. In 1940, as the rest of the world was taking sides in World War II, the king of Egypt decided that his country would remain neutral. Not only was that a silly decision, it was an impossible decision. Egypt had an intact treaty with Britain and was full of advisors from Italy. That was problematic since Great Britain and Italy were enemies during the war.

In 1942, Britain forced King Farouk to appoint a pro-British prime minister. It was the beginning of the end for Farouk in his role as king. It was a move that belittled King Farouk's power and authority in the eyes and minds of his countrymen. It was pivotal in the decision to create a movement to oust England from Egypt and also, more importantly, to remove Egyptian royalty from high posts.

Farouk held on for a couple of years, and it was during this period, when his power and personality were most challenged, that his greatest contributions to the Arab world were made. In 1945, King Farouk of Egypt was a key player in the establishment of the Arab League. The objective of the Arab League at the time was to try to unite the divided and splintered Arab world. It's a role the league still attempts to fulfill today. Though much of the Arab world remains fractured, the myth of Arab unity is still maintained in the Arab League—particularly in Egypt, which is the Arab League's seat and home to Pan Arabism.

In 1950, in a misguided attempt to regain control of his country and his people, Farouk implemented general, national elections. By 1952, after a silent coup led by the Free Officers, Farouk was deposed. In a case of history repeating itself, he placed his infant son, Ahmed Fouad II, as ruler of Egypt. He then ran away with his family to Italy. From there, Farouk made his way to Monaco where he became a citizen, and then he went back to Rome.

As king, Farouk overemphasized his own pleasure at the expense of his people. He was also a pilferer—a petty, and not so petty, thief. As royalty, Farouk mingled with leaders from around the world, offering him the opportunity to steal from the most powerful and famous names of his generation. He stole a ceremonial sword from the shah of Iran and a pocket watch from Winston Churchill. He was even known to pickpocket commoners when he had occasion to mingle with his own subjects. Farouk became a very skilled thief and was most often referred to in international circles by the nickname "the Thief of Cairo."

King Farouk was larger than life; he was a real-life caricature. In fact, David Suchet—the actor who played the world-famous detective Hercule Poirot—said that he decided to have his character sport a thick handlebar mustache just like King Farouk.

During his reign as king of Egypt, and even afterward, Farouk was a man of excess. He was a glutton, and his appetite for food was world famous. There are stories of his feasting ravenously on meats and wines and cakes. A small man—well, not quite—Farouk was described as a "stomach with a head" when he reached a weight of three hundred pounds. Farouk died in Rome on March 18, 1965, while eating. The former king, the playboy, the pilferer, the money collector, the man who misunderstood and scorned his subjects, collapsed into his meal.

3

GAMAL ABDEL NASSER
Twentieth Century Arab Visionary

Born: 1918
Died: 1970
Ruled: 1956–1970

Gamal Abdel Nasser was a proud Egyptian.

And he hated the British. He hated them partly because, as an adolescent, he was expelled from school for leading one of many anti-British demonstrations and riots. The events were held in an attempt to end British involvement in his homeland. And his attitude wasn't helped much when he received a wound to his head by British forces.

But he didn't just hate the British. He hated the French, and he disliked the Americans.

He hated the Israelis. He felt humiliated by them when the Israeli army trounced the Egyptian army in the war that came to be known as the Six Days' War because it was over so quickly. When the dust cleared, all that remained was a pile of boots kicked off by Egyptian soldiers as they ran for their lives in hasty retreat.

He hated the Egyptian royal family for being weak and corrupt, and for weakening Egypt. He hated them for bowing to British influence.

He loved Egypt, and he loved the Arab world. And Nasser worked hard to restore pride, independence, self-sufficiency, and sovereignty to his people.

From the time of his birth on January 15, 1918, in the Egyptian port city of Alexandria, until he had them thrown out and deposed in 1952, Egyptian citizen Gamal Abdel Nasser lived under the rule of a monarchy. It was a monarchy that allowed for British involvement in most of Egypt's foreign affairs. The thinking was that the royal family was willing to let the Brits call the shots, as long as the Brits allowed the royal family to make internal decisions and maintain their wealth and position.

Nasser did not agree with the monarchy. He was part of the anti-colonial campaign to boot Britain from Egypt. He was an anti-British activist in grade school, in secondary school, in law school, and during his tenure at the Egyptian Royal Military Academy. Almost everyone involved in the campaign saw the fault not in England as much as in the weakness of the Egyptian royal family. Nasser was no exception.

In 1942, the situation changed. That was the year the British strong-armed King Farouk of Egypt to accept a government that was headed by Nahas Pasha, a man of their choosing. Pasha was a British lackey who assumed the position of prime minister of Egypt. For Nasser and for other nationalists, it was the straw that broke the Egyptian camel's back. British intervention was no longer limited to foreign affairs. The monarch had allowed the British to trespass on domestic political agendas.

When the Arab-Israeli war broke out in 1948, Egypt was dealt a humiliating defeat that was blamed on the royal family. They were accused of providing defective, out-of-date weapons to Egypt's army that were obtained in deals that sacrificed the lives of soldiers but lined their own pockets.

Nasser, an instructor at the Egyptian Army Staff College, founded a secret organization of officers in the Egyptian army called the Society of Free Officers. The society eventually orchestrated the coup that on July 23, 1952, in a bloodless rebellion, deposed the royal family headed by King Farouk.

When the royal family was ousted, General Neguib took over, and Nasser was his second in command. But that soon changed. Two years later, with the help of the Society of Free Officers, Gamal Abdel Nasser took over as the first president of Egypt on November 17, 1954.

The Suez Canal was a point of contention between the Egyptians and the British for many years. Built in 1869 in Egypt by Egyptian workers, the canal was under joint British–French control. Forty percent of all revenues went to the British. The royal family had quietly acquiesced to the arrangement, but the Egyptians reaped few benefits from this monumental engineering feat.

In 1956, out of arrogance and spite, Nasser nationalized the Suez Canal. It was an act of defiance aimed at eliminating foreign dominance on Egyptian soil. Britain and France were insulted. They responded by declaring war on Egypt. The United States intervened, siding with Egypt and saying that the Egyptians had a valid point.

Nasser was a military warrior as well as a political leader. He successfully defeated the British and French efforts to reclaim their property, and they stood down.

Nasser had a vision for his country, for his countrymen, and for the Arab and Muslim world. There were five points on his agenda: fighting poverty, improving education, activating nationalist spirit, developing infrastructure, and inspiring national pride and identity.

The successful conclusion to the conflict with Britain and France was a huge political success not only in Egypt but also around the Muslim world. Here was an Arab leader who showed up the West, who stood up to major international powers and taught them not to exploit an Arab country. The Egyptian president was a true hero in Muslim eyes.

But now Egypt faced a bigger issue—a problem so big that it had been around since the days of Euclid and worsened with time. The problem was the annual flooding of the Nile River.

Nasser went about creating an enormous project. He decided to build the Aswan Dam. Now not only would the Nile not flood, it would be the source for a hydroelectric power plant that would help solve the problem of expensive electricity and bring jobs and a better economy to Egypt. But where would he get the resources? Britain and France had just been booted out of his country. The United States had supported Egypt in the feud, but they also supported the enemy Israel. Nasser approached the Soviet Union. It was a perfect team. Even though they had neither cultural nor religious links, they had a mutually beneficial relationship. The Egyptians had their money; the Russians had access to the Mediterranean Sea. The dam was completed in 1962, and Egypt was on its way to becoming a Communist state.

Nasser and Egypt were on a roll. Everything was progressing according to plan. Until June 1967. That was when a cocky, successful leader decided to kick United Nations forces out of Egypt and close the Straits of Tiran, shutting off Israel's access to the Red Sea port. The result was the Six Days' War.

Israel attacked in a preemptive war and disabled the entire Egyptian Air Force while it was still on the ground. It was a humiliating defeat. Nasser was embarrassed at home and lost face around the world. He offered to resign, but his offer was rejected by the people of Egypt. They rallied around their president and showed their support. Nasser endeavored to upgrade his military so that this lesson of humiliation and defeat would never be repeated.

Three years later on September 28, 1970, before the task he had set for himself was completed, Gamal Abdel Nasser, first president of the Republic of Egypt, an activist, a revolutionary, a despotic ruler, died of a heart attack.

4

IDI AMIN
Africa's Native Son

Born: Circa 1924
Died: 2003
Ruled: 1971–1979

Idi Amin is dead.

The Butcher of Africa died of hypertension and kidney failure—a rather simple and unceremonious death for a man who thrived on blood and lust, on pomp and grandeur. He had declared himself Uganda's president for life, but he only reigned from 1971–1979. At the time of his death in 2003, Amin was living on handouts in Saudi Arabia. During his reign, The Lord of All Beasts of the Earth and Fishes of the Sea had beheaded, butchered, and castrated over five hundred thousand of his own countrymen.

Amin was a brutal personality. At one point he was killing so furiously and quickly that there was no way to dispose of the corpses. In a stroke of genius (a trait that often characterized the rise and fall of one of the greatest demons known to modern history), Amin fed the bodies to crocodiles—animals akin to him in that they, too, are always hungry for the taste of human blood. This time, however, Amin even outpaced the crocodiles. The unconsumed bodies piled up, blocking the intake ducts of the hydroelectric system in the Ugandan city of Jinja.

During his formative years, from 1933 until 1938, Amin was nurtured and raised by his mother's family. He lived the life of a shepherd, rearing and raising goats. Even as a boy, Amin made a name for himself. Though he had yet to attain the confidence to call himself "the True Prince of Africa," he was content to be known as the boy who memorized the Koran.

His devotion to the Koran began while Amin was living in the home of Sheik Ahmed Hussein, the local Muslim leader and teacher. Amin excelled at Koranic recitation and memorization, and as a teenager, he was rewarded with honors.

Looking at his later life and military and dictatorial career, it is truly ironic that the first time he tried to enter the army, Idi Amin was rejected. He was underage. In what turned out to be a life-changing opportunity, Amin landed a job as the hat-and-coat person in the grand Imperial Hotel where he met and impressed a British army officer. The officer offered to bring the now slightly older Amin into the army.

Idi Amin's dream of being a soldier began in the laundry room of the Magamaga barracks in Jinja. And in the kitchen. Finally, in 1947, he received a transfer and began real military service as a proud member of the British Colonial Army in the Twenty-first King's African Rifle Corp at Gigli. From there his unit was relocated to Somalia at Belet Uen to combat the Shifta animal raiders, and then to Fort Hall to begin training for the Scottish Military Band.

His military career demonstrates just how unique Idi Amin was. In two quick years, from 1952–1953, Amin rose from a Ugandan army corporal stationed in Mau Mau to the rank of sergeant. In Mau Mau, this soldier began mobile foot patrols in the forests occupied by locals. He was commended for his initiative and rewarded.

Official military reports from 1952–1956 cite descriptions of soldier Idi Amin Dada. The reports can best be described as a combination of comedy and prophecy. One report states that he was "a splendid and reliable and a cheerful and energetic man." Another superior describes him as "an incredible person who certainly is not mad—very shrewd, very cunning, and a born leader." And then there is this descriptive evaluation: "a splendid and good rugby player, but virtually bone from the neck up and needs things explained in words of one letter."

Amin thrived during the period he was at war with the Mau Mau. Because of his stellar performance, he was promoted to a new rank: *efandi*, which is the equivalent of a warrant officer and was the highest rank a black African was permitted to achieve in the British army of the 1950s. While fighting in Mau Mau, the man who later decided to call himself "Big Daddy," fathered a son and a daughter by Kikuyu women. These were the first of his thirty-three children by five wives.

He went from Mau Mau back to Jinja in 1954, and there he had his first brush with true royalty when he received another distinction: he was selected best in the parade for Queen Elizabeth. And then, the bright star of soldier Amin began to slowly dim. In 1957, he led a move to increase salaries for soldiers. The request was denied. A short while later, he failed both the written and oral sections of the intellectual tests required for promotion in the military. He was transferred from the field to the King's African Rifle Corps band. The next year, he retook and once again failed the exams.

Finally, he passed an exam. It was the year 1959, and not surprisingly, he passed the practical part of the field-exercises exam. At last Amin was permitted to receive a promotion. He soon found himself in Karamoja. Amin was sent there after the British army suffered an embarrassing defeat by the Turkana, and after British officer Ronald Cedric Weeding was killed by the Turkana in Karamoja. Amin did so well over there (an army spokesman described his role as "having restored the prestige of the forces of law and order in the region of Karamoja") that Sir Fredrick Crawford commissioned him lieutenant in July of 1961. The Turkana were led by Sir Edward Mutesa, and Amin was responsible for negotiating a political compromise, convincing Mutesa that the army would not rise up against the government in a coup.

Uganda won independence from Great Britain in 1962. Amin was forty years old.

Up until 1962, Ugandans serving in the British army in Uganda were separated from native British soldiers and treated as second-class soldiers. They were fighting in a white army doing the bidding of a colonial power in Africa. After independence, many British officers remained in Uganda serving as advisers to the emerging Ugandan army. The British influence continued to be felt in the army of Uganda for a long time.

From the very outset, Uganda's independence worked in Amin's favor. Just shortly before independence was granted, soldier Amin led two convoys of the King's African Rifle Corps to Turkana in order to put down unrest. Tribesmen were stealing cattle and spilling into northern Uganda. Amin succeeded in his mission, but he did it in the most brutal fashion. He threatened to cut off the penis of every man in Turkana if the resistance did not stop. Amin was good to his word. The resistance was put down. The massacre was bloody. Investigations into the actions by the British in Kenya showed evidence of the victims being beaten, tortured, and some even buried alive.

Because independence was so very close—only weeks or months away—authorities chose not to reprimand Amin. The Butcher of Africa felt no remorse. He had no reason to. He was not about to be court-martialed for his barbaric, overzealous behavior. His star shined brightly once again; his career in the military continued unhampered by his personal rules of conduct and decency.

There are signs of Amin's determination to organize and gain military strength within the Ugandan army as early as 1964. He attempted to institute a salary increase; it was blocked. He created a military mutiny; it worked. He was appointed deputy commander of the army, and Amin got his salary increase. He was even promoted to major. And then he received the greatest of all rewards: Idi Amin—the man who would later call himself "the Conqueror of the British Empire"—was now in command of the First Battalion of the Ugandan army.

In 1965, Commander Amin and his rebel army were sent to support Congo nationalists and to resist the government that was being supported by foreign influences. While there, Amin invested in the

Trans Nile bus company. His business venture was enormously successful; his rebels were defeated by Congo mercenaries.

Back at home, Amin supported Prime Minister Obote, who was being pressured to leave office. On February 22, 1966, Amin resisted a coup to oust Obote. With Amin's help, the coup leader was executed and Obote was given absolute power. His next step was to try to convince Mutesa and his general, Shaban Opolot, not to fight Obote. The mediator managed to insinuate himself into the deal and received a promotion, first to colonel and then to army commander, replacing Shaban Opolot.

A financial scandal involving the prime minister, coupled with opposition from the kingdom of Buganda, resulted in another promotion for Amin. Obote suspended the Ugandan constitution and created a new constitution that entirely eliminated the Kingdom of Buganda. Amin was placed in charge of the army. In February of 1967, the man who never graduated from high school, and who failed the written and oral sections of the promotion exam for sergeant, started English classes in the adult education program at Makerere University. It was from there that he eventually received a doctoral degree. In 1968, as reward for his loyalty during the republican monarchist crisis, Amin was promoted to major general. That same year, as head of the army, he was involved in the Israeli-sponsored support for the rebellion in southern Sudan.

The following year, 1969, Amin was challenged over his leadership of the army. The Uganda People Congress was moving to become more Socialist. Amin lost control of several units. In order to redeem himself, the man who had led massacres, executed opposition leaders, and brutalized those who opposed him chose to take courses in socialism.

While Amin demanded complete and total loyalty from others, loyalty to others meant little to him. After being publicly accused by Brigadier General Okoya of cowardice in the throes of an attempted assassination of Obote (a man who had helped propel his military career), Amin assassinated Okoya for daring to besmirch his reputation. When the true gunmen were found, it was revealed that Amin had, indeed, been involved in the unsuccessful attempt on the life of the prime minister. Almost simultaneously, he was discovered to have personally appropriated forty million shillings from the military operations fund.

Obote took action. In 1970, the prime minister had Amin removed as head of the Ugandan army. In 1971, he called for the preparation of prosecution against Amin, who ran to Kampala to avoid arrest and prosecution. Luck was with him. Soldiers at the border misinterpreted messages from a signaler and, rather than detaining him, the fugitive walked freely into Kampala. And then promptly attempted to take over power.

This was the year that Idi Amin Dada Oumee clawed his way from soldier to ruler. He moved quickly. When Prime Minister Milton Obote left Uganda to attend a Commonwealth Summit meeting in Singapore, Amin recruited the help of Rwandan rebels and seized the opportunity to grab power. The coup was bloody, but Amin triumphed. It was not enough. Just as Captain Charles Arube —foreign minister and decorated soldier—was about to volunteer to become president of Uganda, Amin appeared and accepted or rather stole the position in his place. Arube was later assassinated.

On January 21, 1971, Amin proclaimed himself president of Uganda. The coup was reportedly backed by Israel and welcomed by Britain.

The prime minister officially assumed the role of president. He behaved as he saw fit. He freed many political prisoners. He disbanded the secret police. He disbanded security units. He promised to hold elections. He created murder squads to hunt down supporters of Obote. Many Ugandans ran for their lives, fleeing to Sudan.

At the time Amin took charge, he was considered to be a good and trusted friend of the West. Great Britain, Israel, and even the United States had played large roles in his fortune and career. The self-proclaimed "True Son of Africa" ascended the ranks of Ugandan society. They had high hopes for this colorful leader; this avid sportsman, champion swimmer, and holder of a national light-heavyweight boxing title from 1951 to 1960. They placed their trust in the man who had failed the reading exam for officers in the King's African Rifle Corps and yet proceeded to get a doctorate and the rank of brigadier general.

The West had hoped that a friendly, pro-Western dictatorship in the heart of Africa would be an enormous strategic asset that could help it economically and politically. The West thought it had found a way to check the Russian influence from taking over the region.

The absolute dictator of Uganda proved them wrong.

He became more radical and even more extreme. He turned his back on them all. He revised his plans, changing the caretaker period of his dictatorship from eighteen months to five years, claiming that he needed the time to put his country's politics in order. And then he proceeded to create order Amin-style.

On August 1, 1972, he declared an economic war. Amin decided that Asians, even Asians holding British passports, were sabotaging the economy of Uganda. He expelled them from his country, giving them ninety days to leave or face imprisonment, or worse. Asians were permitted to take only what they could carry with them, excluding money. The remaining possessions were distributed among Amin's high-placed friends and favorite people.

He began to "eliminate" anyone at all connected to Obote or to the British. And then Amin took it a step further, expropriating British property and expelling British businesses and leadership. Great Britain and Israel responded by suspending arms deals and all diplomatic relations between their countries and Uganda.

Amin looked around. He needed to find a new arms ally. He turned to Libya and promised Muammar Ghadaffi he would turn his country into an Islamic state in exchange for weapons. He ran to the Soviet Union and pledged to be a front against the West. He placed his support behind the Palestinian movement.

And he turned his attention inward.

Amin further expanded the size of his army and then went on a murderous rampage. As many as a half-million civilians were killed under the pretense of protecting his leadership. Among the dead were Uganda's chief justice, supreme court judges, bureaucrats, diplomats, educators, academics, clergy, doctors, bankers, tribal leaders, business leaders, journalists, and even important foreigners.

The funds that were necessary to support the expanded army were reallocated from civilian causes. Army courts were elevated above civilian courts. Parliament was dissolved, and all government ministers were informed that they would be subject to military discipline.

Amin's paranoia knew no bounds. He perceived his enemies to be everywhere and almost everybody. His security squad during this period reached a high of eighteen thousand. His presidential guard doubled as a death squad. In August of 1974, Amin said that an economic war was more difficult than a military war and declared punishment by death to anyone who dared—or whom he perceived to dare—sabotage his economic war.

His ego knew no bounds. He offered himself as mediator with Northern Ireland. He advocated that Scotland separate from the Commonwealth. He declared that all African countries should break from South Africa. He became the chair of the Organization of African Unity (OAU) in 1975, and immediately tried to rid Africa of Western influences. He offered himself as the first volunteer in the war to destroy Israel. He awarded himself the Victoria Cross, an honor bestowed only by the queen of England. He expressed his conviction that he, not the queen, was the true monarch of England and the Commonwealth. His sense of history was warped; his sense of self was dramatically overstated.

He was a master of the absurd. Amin had a penchant for cartoons and a light-hearted, childish public image. It was that childish impression that often masked the inner, brutal, horrific depths of this man's soul. One day, he commanded all the white residents in the capital city of Kampala to gather together. He then commanded them to carry their black leader on a throne and publicly declare their oath and allegiance to him. The world called it a media stunt. It was, but it was also emblematic of his world view.

Despite his efforts at waging an economic war, the economy of Uganda worsened and more and more people disappeared.

June 27, 1976, was a pivotal day in the life of Idi Amin. Air France Airbus A-300B flight 139 took off from Athens, was hijacked, and landed in Entebbe, Uganda. Amin took center stage and declared himself in charge of negotiations. For the first time the world clearly understood that the leader of Uganda was a crazy tyrant without grounding and with no realistic understanding of the greater world. Amin, more than the hijackers, kept the world hostage.

The situation dragged on. Non-Jewish passengers were quickly removed from the hanger that had become a home and a prison cell for the Jewish passengers. The situation was finally resolved when Israel executed a superspectacular and daring rescue mission. The mission lasted fifty-eight minutes; there were only two fatalities. The first casualty was Israeli mission commander Yoni Netanyahu, killed during the operation. Yoni has become a national hero and a part of Israel's—and the Jewish people's—culture of heroism. The second fatality was a seventy-five-year-old Jewish woman with both Israeli and British passports who had been taken from the hangar in order to receive medical treatment. Witnesses saw her being dragged away. Almost without a doubt, she was ordered killed by Amin who was made to feel embarrassed and look foolish by the stunning success of the Israelis. Following the raid and rescue, two hundred senior Ugandan officers and officials, and one Jewish grandmother, were executed.

His grip was weakening. To help lessen the economic pain, Amin allowed imports to enter Uganda untaxed. As soon as goods were offloaded from ships and planes, they were delivered directly to the army. He started selling coffee on a cash basis, and the cash was paid directly to him.

Advanced, accelerated paranoia set in. An attempted coup was discovered in 1977. Amin executed all those who were involved. He became wary and distrustful of the loyalty of all those around him. He murdered complete army units that he believed to be disloyal. He began an offensive on the Tanzanian border and then refused to provide air or artillery support for his units, effectively sealing their fate. They were massacred.

In 1979, a series of small battles erupted between Uganda and Tanzania. The battle plan orchestrated by Uganda's president for life was to use the fighting as a way to divert attention from the many other growing problems in Uganda. The plan backfired. Ugandan army exiles joined with Tanzanian troops in an all-out, full-scale invasion.

Amin's regime was toppled. No coup, no attempted assassination, no theatrics. Big Daddy was ousted from power by neighboring Tanzania. In April, he fled to Libya. He had already evacuated his five wives and thirty-three children to the protective custody and good graces of his compatriot, Muammar Ghadaffi.

Amin's legacy to the people of Uganda was an inflation rate of over 200 percent and a national debt that topped $340 million. The two hundred forty-pound barbarian—the man who dressed himself up in white costumes and field-marshal uniforms, who adorned his chest with hundreds of medals, who put his personal agenda above his people's needs—was gone. He left behind the corpses of 300,000–500,000 of his own countrymen, killed by his own hands. Life in Libya was comfortable, even if not extravagant, for Amin. He was given a stipend of $1,400 dollars a month, cars, servants, and cooks. Together with four of his wives, he lived as a guest of Muammar Ghadaffi until 1981, when the two had a falling out. Amin headed for Saudi Arabia. Gone was any pretense of luxury. He lived a poor life, surviving on handouts doled out by the Saudi government. Amin, accompanied by an armed group of followers, attempted a return to Uganda in 1988. The attempt failed.

Life ended for Idi Amin Dada Oumee in Saudi Arabia. He died on Saturday, August 16, 2003, at 8:20 a.m. In an interview he gave in 1999 from Saudi Arabia for a Ugandan newspaper, Amin spoke of himself saying that he liked to play the accordion, to fish, to swim, and to recite the Koran. His one-time mentor and ally, former Ugandan president Milton Obote, called Amin "the greatest brute an African mother has ever brought to life."

Legend has it that after decapitating his perceived enemies— and even his friends—Amin would keep their bodies in freezers. On special occasions he would take the bodiless heads out of cold storage and speak to them. The conversations were, of course, one-sided but that was how Amin preferred them.

At festive meals he would invite the family members of the men he had killed. The table would be set with place settings for those guests still breathing and those who had taken their last breaths at his behest. Amin thought nothing odd of having family sit and eat at a table surrounded by the decapitated heads of those whom they had loved.

Idi Amin Dada Oumee drank the blood and ate the flesh of his enemies.

5

ANWAR SADAT
Dictator Who Made Peace

Born: 1918
Died: 1981
Ruled: 1970–1981

He was born on December 25, but the date of Mohammed Anwar al-Sadat's birth made no impression on the Arab-Muslim world. October 6 is the date that matters.

On October 6, 1981, the third president of Egypt, the most powerful country in the Middle East, was assassinated. A host of local and foreign dignitaries had gathered in downtown Cairo for a parade in honor of Sadat. They were commemorating Egypt's success in the October 1973 war against Israel. It was a major military parade. Mirage jets flew overhead. The Egyptian military strode by the reviewing stand. There were trucks; there were tanks. And in the midst of it all, in a well-conceived plan, a lieutenant in the Egyptian army strode front and center toward the reviewing stand and offered a salute to the president.

Field Marshall Anwar Sadat rose to return the salute. Khalid Islambouli, a Muslim extremist, ran toward the president shouting, "Death to the pharaoh," and a truck rolled by spewing grenades and bullets. Islambouli, jumped back onto the truck as it sped away. The president took a shot to the head.

Present and unharmed on the review stand was Egyptian foreign minister Boutros Boutros Ghali, later to become the secretary general of the United Nations. Sadat's vice president and successor, Hosni Mubarak, was wounded in his hand. James Tully, Ireland's minister of defense, and four United States defense observers were unharmed. Seven people were killed, including the Cuban ambassador to Egypt and a Greek Orthodox priest. Hundreds of radical Islamists, including Ayman al-Zawahiri, were indicted during the assassin's trial.

While Ronald Reagan, Gerald Ford, Jimmy Carter, and Richard Nixon all attended the funeral, there was almost no official Arab representation. At the time of his death, Sadat had fallen out of favor with the Arab world.

Sadat was one of thirteen children. He was born and raised in a small, poor village called Mit Abu al-Kum al-Minufiyah, located about thirty miles from Cairo. His father was an Egyptian merchant; his mother was Sudanese. Small in stature and dark-skinned, physically he looked more Sudanese than Egyptian. But emotionally and psychologically, he was a true son of Egypt. In 1938, he graduated the Royal Military Academy in Cairo and joined the Signal Corps. More significantly, he also joined a group of officers trying to rid Egypt of Britain and all colonial interests. During World War II, Sadat was arrested by the British not once, but twice, for contacting the Germans.

In 1952, the future president participated in a coup that ousted King Farouk I and cemented his relationship with another future Egyptian president: Gamal Abdel Nasser. Sadat was put in a position of responsibility; it was he who announced to the people of Egypt that the king was overthrown. He controlled all Egyptian media. And a few years later, when Nasser took over as president, Sadat became his vice president. On September 28, 1970, Sadat had another announcement for the people of Egypt: Nasser had died of a heart attack. In October, Anwar Sadat was named president of Egypt.

And he began clearing house, ridding the country of all political rivals, of all potential opponents. The Sadat-owned media called it "the corrective revolution." The president was solidifying his power and control over every aspect of Egyptian bureaucracy and government. Rather than following in the footsteps of his mentor, he eradicated them. Nasser had been a strong believer in the power of the Soviets to help the Egyptian military and economy. Sadat rejected the Soviet role. He was frustrated because the Soviets had not been more forthcoming in aid and assistance to Egypt in their attacks against Israel. He felt the collective pain and humiliation Egyptians were suffering because of their embarrassing defeat to Israel. He sent twenty thousand Soviet military advisers stationed in Egypt home. All of them.

Within a year, Egypt and Syria were at war with Israel. Sadat chose Yom Kippur, the holiest day of the Jewish year, to launch a simultaneous attack hoping to cripple—perhaps even destroy—Israel. In the first few days of the 1973 war, the Egyptians were triumphant. They recaptured a portion of the Sinai desert that had been lost in the 1967 war with Israel. It was downhill from there. In the end, the Egyptians suffered a humiliating defeat. Israel stopped just short of surrounding the capital city Cairo.

For a few moments, a few hours, a few days, Egyptians saw themselves as mighty, modern-day warriors. And they felt good. Despite the subsequent severe beating the Egyptian army took, Sadat—the master manipulator—was able to keep the good feeling going. Egypt's president transformed a humiliating military defeat into victory. Victory monuments to the October War, as it is called in Arabic, still stand today. President Sadat was able to invigorate his people, to motivate them, to rekindle national spirit and awaken Egyptian pride.

Egypt and Syria had caught the Israelis off guard. Israeli prime minister Golda Meir had received intelligence reports about an impending attack, but she pooh-poohed them. After boundaries and borders were determined in the ceasefire agreements following the war, Sadat was able to point to the ten-mile strip of Sinai desert that had returned to Egyptian control. That was his victory. The fact that Cairo was easily within reach of the Israeli army did not alter his perception of the war. What mattered was that the embarrassing defeat that clung to Egypt in the aftermath of the 1967 war—when the entire Egyptian Air Force was neutralized while still on the ground—was dissipated. What made Egypt's victory even sweeter was the knowledge that the army of Israel was no longer invincible.

Sadat was the only Arab leader to wrestle land from Israel in a war. That made him proud. That gave him stature in the Arab world. That gave him power. That gave him the political strength and personal courage to stand before the Egyptian parliament and speak about the possibility of signing a peace treaty with Israel. He called it the "peace factor." When the people of Egypt heard those words come from the lips of their leader, they were aghast. When Menachem Begin, the Israeli prime minister, heard those same words, he invited the Egyptian president to Jerusalem to deliver a speech in Israel's parliament. Sadat accepted.

Anwar Sadat was a pragmatist, not an idealist. He knew that his country was teetering on the economic brink. According to his calculation, signing a peace treaty with Israel was the best way for Egypt to climb out of an economic quagmire. Sadat's initial suggestion for a peace plan failed, but in 1978, Sadat and Menachem Begin met with United States president Jimmy Carter. The former enemies shook hands, posed for photos, and signed the Camp David Peace Accords, named for the presidential retreat located in the rustic mountains of Maryland where the historic meeting took place. A more formal treaty was signed on March 26, 1979. Sadat was the first nonbiblical Arab leader to enter into a peace treaty with Israel. Anwar Sadat made history. He restored both pride and prosperity to the people of Egypt.

Economically, Egypt was on the rebound. Once again the Soviets provided the Egyptians with monetary aid. The Americans pitched in more than Sadat had ever hoped for. Egypt became the second largest aid recipient from the United States—second only to Israel. U.S. military aid was similarly bountiful, but it just wasn't enough. The Western world recognized the greatness of the simple handshake between two world leaders. The 1978 Nobel Peace Prize was shared by Sadat and Begin, two men who had reshaped the Middle East.

The Arab world, however, was not rejoicing. In 1979, the Arab League not only moved their headquarters out of Cairo, but it also suspended Egypt's membership. The negotiated peace with Israel placed Sadat in a very critical position in the Arab world. No other Arab leader agreed with his actions. Inside Egypt, the economy was still faltering and tensions were high. Around the Arab world criticism was sharp.

In a dictatorship, you can control the press and you can scare the people, but the people will still secretly organize. Sadat knew the name and the face of his enemy; he knew the Muslim brotherhood wanted him ousted. He knew they rejected any leadership that was not Muslim and that they were particularly disturbed by his peace initiative with Israel. His response was to clamp down hard. Enemies disappeared. Opponents were killed. And on October 6 Sadat went to a parade to celebrate his victory over Israel.

The two factors that most precipitated the assassination of Egyptian president Anwar Sadat were his oppressive handling of all alternative political and religious ideals and his launching of the peace treaty. Sadat was guaranteeing a future for the people of Egypt, but the people of Egypt had no way of knowing that. Had he not held the Islamists in check, Egypt today would mirror Iran. Had he not made peace with Israel, the Egyptian economy would mirror the Palestinian economy.

Anwar Sadat was a dictator. He was also a visionary. He is remembered more kindly in world history than he is in Egyptian history.

6

SIAD BARRE
"Only the Gun Can Make Him Go"

Born: 1919
Died: 1995
Ruled: 1969–1991

Like so many other dictators, Siad Barre was not to the manor born. He was uneducated. He was a shepherd and an orphan who hoped for a better life. So he joined the police.

At the time, Somalia was an Italian colony, and local military recruits were needed to enforce Italian policy and police the locals. Seeing a better opportunity for himself, Barre left the police force and joined the army. He rose steadily through the ranks. In 1960, when Somalia gained independence from Italy, Barre held the title of vice commander of the army. Not bad for a kid who started out barefoot and hungry.

During his years in the military, Barre went to the USSR for training. He was impressed and became an adherent and firm believer in the Soviet style of Marxist government. In a military coup following the 1969 assassination of Somalia's President Abdrirashi Ali Shermake, Barre stepped in and took over the position. In title, Barre was now the president of Somalia; in practice, he was the dictator of Somalia.

Siad Barre ruled from 1969 to 1991. He ruled until he was ousted by an insurgency. His tenure as ruler had as many ups and downs and curves and dives as a roller coaster. First he was a great admirer of the Soviets, but then, after they chose not to support his efforts to occupy and annex Ogaden in Northern Ethiopia, he snubbed them. He booted out all Soviets and ran to the West, principally the United States, for support.

Somalia is situated on the Red Sea. It was a country that great powers were willing to bid over—gain the friendship of Somalia and you gained access both by land and by sea to Africa and the Middle East. During the Cold War the United States adopted Barre and began pouring support into his country. U.S. aid to Somalia continued through 1989 and reached about $100 million per year.

Economically, Somalia was fine. Foreign policy was serving Barre well. He was resourceful and therefore successful. He was powerful. In October of 1977, when a Red Army faction hijacked a Lufthansa plane bound for Mogadishu, Somalia, the West German chancellor Helmut Schmidt and the Somalian president successfully negotiated for the release of the hostages.

Internationally, Barre was a hero. Domestically, he was brutal. He met every insurgency with a counterinsurgency.

In Africa in general, and in Somalia in particular, political support is a factor of the clans and families, tribes and communities with which you have allegiances. Barre began his political career with many allegiances, but his support began to slowly dwindle in the outer areas, especially in Somaliland. Maybe not so ironically, Somaliland is the region in which he was born.

An attack against his dictatorship by rival factions that lasted from 1988 to 1990 resulted in Barre's clamping down on and dislocating hundreds of thousands of Somalian people from their homes. At least sixty thousand civilians were killed.

The international community—especially Africa Watch, which is an extension of Human Rights Watch—started applying enormous international pressure to oust Barre. That pressure, along with the long insurgency, led him to leave Mogadishu, the capital of Somalia.

Barre's son-in-law controlled a part of southern Somalia, and the former president first sought refuge there. He tried to reassert his dictatorship but was repulsed. He tried again to reassert his dictatorship, and again, he was repulsed. He left for Nairobi, but was there only two weeks; Nairobi did not want Siad Barre.

Barre lived out the few remaining years of his life in Nigeria, the only country that would have him. In death, he was allowed to return to the country he had ruled. Permission was granted to allow the remains of Mohamed Siad Barre, president of Somalia, to be buried in his hometown in his homeland, Somalia.

7

BEN ALI
Benign Muslim Dictator

Born: 1936
Died: Still living
Ruled: 1987–present

Ben Ali is the absolute dictator of Tunisia. He is often called on by both Middle Eastern and Western countries to mediate disputes. Now in his declining years, he rules as a benevolent dictator. In his earlier years, he was only vicious and authoritarian.

Zine al-Abidine Ben Ali assumed power as president of Tunisia on November 7, 1987. Only a month before, in early October, he received the appointment to be prime minister of Tunisia. How did he change the face of Tunisian politics so quickly? He declared the former president incompetent and senile, and he even had an affidavit signed by seven doctors to prove it. He played around with the constitution and had himself appointed the new president of Tunisia. The coup he masterminded was underhanded, brutal, and brilliant.

Playing around with the constitution is something Ben Ali enjoys doing. He often rearranges matters to suit his personal needs and desires. When the constitution only provided for a president to be in place for three consecutive terms, it was no problem for Ben Ali. He had the constitution amended so that there are no limits of tenure. And when the constitution stated that a president could serve only until seventy years of age, that wasn't a problem either. When you are middle aged, seventy seems old and far away, but now that Ben Ali himself is climbing up in years, he amended the constitution once again, upping the age to seventy-five.

And who's going to stop him?

In each of the several Tunisian elections in which Ben Ali has been on the ballot, he successfully received over 99 percent of the vote. It is hard to imagine that there is any significant distinction between the 99.27 percent of the vote he received in his first election in 1989, the 99.9 percent he received in 1994, and the 99.44 percent he received in 1999, but when you're a dictator every point matters. As his fist has loosened, as his reign has gotten a little less fierce, a little more benevolent, he has dropped in strength. Ben Ali had his lowest numbers ever in the October 2004 election for president of Tunisia. During that election, he only received 94.5 percent of the vote.

Ben Ali was born in Tunisia, received his military training in France, and received more training in the United States. He steadily made his way up through the military ranks and then joined the security forces. Like many power-hungry, strong-willed, and egotistical men in the military, he maneuvered his way into the world of power and politics—and eventually, diplomacy. He was military attaché in Morocco, and then in 1979, Ben Ali received two appointments: he became a general and the ambassador of Tunisia in Poland. From there he went on to become director of national security, secretary of state of national security, minister of national security, interior minister, and minister of state for internal affairs. It was his ties with the security establishment that helped Ben Ali mount his coup and cement his position as prime minister.

In the beginning, he ruled in moderation and tried to accommodate all the disparate forces in his kingdom, the country of Tunisia. The Islamists in Tunisia are members of the Nadha Party. The radical Islamic movement was becoming too strong, too much of a threat, and they needed to be brought under control. Ben Ali was familiar with the threat posed by radical Islam and had already dealt with the problem as head of national security. From 1990 through 1992, he clamped down hard. He arrested thousands. Others were forced into exile. Many were killed.

Now, Ben Ali is coasting along internally. Now that he has dealt with the Islamic radicals, he can attend to other issues. He is concentrating on the infrastructure of Tunisia. He is building—housing projects, airports, highways, and byways. The economy is rising, but unemployment is not going away.

He is the lead story and star of the country's news every day. His activities, his declarations, his wants and wishes are what the news in Tunisia covers. He is married and is the father of six children by two wives. Ben Ali has heirs and spares. His second and present wife is a hairdresser.

On an international level, Ben Ali has taken Tunisia to a level of "trusted broker." Tunisia is seen as not having an axe to grind, not needing to strike out or get even with any other country. This has been both an asset and a liability. During the first Gulf War of 1990–1991, Ben Ali did not come out against Saddam Hussein after Iraq invaded Kuwait. He did say that the allied response was unfair. In a sense, he defended Iraq. He tried to remain neutral, and in the end, he offended both sides.

Both Kuwait and the United States withdrew their support for Ben Ali and Tunisia. Since then things have improved on the international front. Ben Ali may have learned his lesson. We'll see. If the president has his way, the constitution will be amended again and Ben Ali will remain in place and in power as president of Tunisia for life.

In Tunisia there is only one leader and only one way to vote. Just ask any of the locals.

8

AL-BASHIR
The Demon of Darfur

Born: 1944
Died: Still living
Ruled: 1989–present

He is known simply as al-Bashir. He is the dictator of Sudan and one of the most notorious leaders in the world today.

He has authorized his militias to murder, maim, and rape. Insurgents are beaten and starved. He has suspended a constitution, disbanded a national assembly, and stripped his predecessor of power. He harbors terrorists but denies it. He promises democratic elections but discourages them. He rules with an iron fist and destroys anyone who dares to challenge his leadership. He is Omar Hasan Ahmad al-Bashir, president of Sudan. Field marshall is a title that suits him better. He is a dangerous man; he is a thug.

Two of the worst massacres in modern history have taken place in Sudan. It is not that they happened under his watch; it is that they happened under his orders.

For al-Bashir, like for many other dictators, life began to take shape once he entered the military. The young man from the small village of Hosh Bonnaga joined the Sudanese army, studied military strategy at a military academy in Cairo, and became a paratrooper. In 1973, during the Yom Kippur War, al-Bashir fought as a soldier with the Egyptian army against Israel. He returned to Sudan with a wealth of experience and was put in charge of the forces responsible for putting down the People's Liberation Army in southern Sudan. He rose through the ranks, and by 1980 he was a well-placed general.

General al-Bashir organized a successful military coup in 1989 in which he overthrew the democratically elected prime minister and personally assumed the role of leader. He banned political parties, eliminated the free press, abolished the parliament, and took for himself the positions of prime minister, chief of state, head of the armed forces, minister of defense, and chairman of the newly formed Revolutionary Command Council for National Salvation. He was the man—the only man—in charge.

He initiated a program that would turn Sudan into a fundamentalist Islamic state. Al-Bashir instituted a public-order police and imposed Sharia law throughout northern Sudan. The law was brutal; enforcement was reminiscent of fourteenth- and fifteenth-century legal systems where thieves lost their hands and transgressors were publicly stoned. Al-Bashir was pleased. He was named president of Sudan. The Revolutionary Command Council ceased to exist and a new constitution and parliament were put in place.

In 1999, National Islamic Front leader Hassan al-Turabi—speaker of Sudan's National Assembly and a man with whom al-Bashir had allied himself—dared to threaten the power of al-Bashir. Al-Turabi wanted to remove al-Bashir from power, put real power in the hands of the National Assembly, and reinstate the position of prime minister. He failed. Al-Turabi was arrested, the cabinet was purged of all al-Turabi supporters and reformers, and a state of national emergency was called. Rather than gaining power, the National Assembly was suspended.

When new elections were held, al-Bashir was handed an overwhelming victory. But the country was divided. Civil war raged between northern and southern Sudan for nineteen years. The war ended only in 2004 when al-Bashir promised to allow the southern section of the country—the other side, in al-Bashir's eyes—autonomy for six years. We'll see what happens come 2010.

Sudan is one of the largest oil-producing countries in the region. The winds of civil war were fueled by al–Bashir, who supported the north against the south and funded them with the profits of his oil sales. Under the knowing and watchful eye of the dictator al-Bashir, northern soldiers perpetrated gruesome horrors against the people of southern Sudan. There was mass destruction, mass murder, and mass rape. There was no medical treatment. Millions of people were homeless and displaced.

Immense pressure from the international community was heaped on al-Bashir to compromise with the south. Finally, in 2003 and 2004, agreements were signed that split oil revenues between northern and southern Sudan and allowed southerners to participate in a referendum for independence.

Just as one human atrocity was ending, another was beginning. Northern and southern Sudan were now quiet and—at least supposedly—at peace. It was time for al-Bashir to turn his attention to the west—to the province of Darfur where rebels had risen up to oppose the government. Rather than send in the army to keep peace, al-Bashir chose to throw his support (albeit secretly) behind the *Janjaweed*—Islamic militias who were combating the rebels. The Janjaweed are killers and pillagers; they are believers in ethnic cleansing.

According to most sources, it is clear that a genocide is taking place in Darfur, perpetrated by the Janjaweed. And that genocide is being sponsored by Omar Hasan Ahmad al-Bashir, the leader of Sudan.

Al-Bashir is not letting international observers or aid workers into Darfur to see what has really happened. He is not letting humanitarian aid into the region. But the international pressure continues. A cease-fire is in place but is being ignored. The mass murder continues. The famine continues. The uncontrollable disease continues. Millions of Sudanese have already died; millions are homeless; millions have fled the country. Millions.

Al-Bashir is claiming that he has put down the rebels and that there is no more military action in the region. He is lying. The rebels continue to be paid and continue to perpetrate their barbarous acts. The barbarian does not care.

Al-Bahsir is a complicated character. He cannot be trusted. He is wily. He has harbored and supported terrorists for years. Osama bin Laden lived in Sudan for five years, leaving in 1996 after being banned from the country. The banks of Sudan are easy conduits for laundering monies and moving them into Europe or other countries across the globe. The Sudanese leader insists that he offered to hand bin Laden over to the Clinton administration; the United States denies the story. Whether he made the offer or not makes no difference. Al-Bashir would never have handed bin Laden to the West—of that we can all be sure. But to make the point that they did not trust him in 1998, the United States bombed a factory in Tunisia claiming that the factory produced chemical weapons for bin Ladin. We now know there were no weapons in the factory, but the point was certainly made.

Interestingly, it was al-Bashir who spoke out clearly against al-Qaeda after the terrorist attacks of 9/11. And it was al-Bashir who pressured Saddam Hussein to allow UN weapons inspectors to return to Iraq in 2002. But that does not mean he has changed his ways or his ideology. It only means that he is becoming a better player at the game of international diplomacy.

Al-Bashir of Sudan is by far one of the most ruthless dictators alive and ruling today. He struts around—medals emblazoned across his chest—and thumbs his nose at us all.

MOHAMMAD REZA PAHLAVI
Brutal Oppressor, Political Ally

Born: 1919
Died: 1980
Ruled: 1941–1979

Shah of Iran is quite an impressive title. But titles can be deceiving. Known to the world simply as the shah, the Middle East ruler who reigned over Iran from 1941 until 1979 was anything but impressive. And the Pahlavi dynasty? Not impressive at all.

Mohammad Reza Pahlavi was the eldest son of Reza Shah Pahlavi and Reza Shah's second wife, Tadj ol-Molouk. The father was the first shah of the Pahlavi dynasty; his son was the second—and last.

The father took over and assumed his royal role as the result of a coup. The second shah, born into royalty, witnessed the dissolution of his dynasty. This heir to the throne—a man who could have ruled with absolute power and authority—was actually spineless. Had he been stronger of spirit, he would have been able to successfully fend off the Muslim revolution that ousted him and his family from their position and from their home.

The shah was a study in contradictions. He was shah because of his father, yet he was a party to his father's abdication. Reza Shah, the father, pledged neutrality during World War II. After the war, it appeared as if he were a Nazi sympathizer and that Iran might actually become a member of the Axis powers. Great Britain and the Soviet Union could not let that happen. The British gave Reza Shah a choice: either give up the throne or suffer a coup and be ousted.

Reza Shah resigned. On September 16, 1941, Pahlavi assumed the throne as the new shah of Iran.

A government was established. Life in Iran moved along at its natural pace. If you were loyal to the shah, you lived your life simply and safely. If you dared oppose the shah, you were mercilessly punished. Financially, Iran thrived. Iran had oil—lots of oil that greased its wheels of fortune. The Persian Corridor, the first major cooperative effort between Iran and the West, was established. The British and the Americans were able to channel aid to the Soviet Union via Iran.

And then in 1953, Iran decided to nationalize its oil. Call it national pride; call it arrogance. The decision was a major blow to the British economy because the Anglo-Iranian Oil Company was a significant player in England's economy. It was the main producer of oil in Iran, and now it was being closed out. In response, Britain slapped Iran with an embargo. The conflict continued until the United States and England orchestrated a coup. The coup was not to oust the shah—he was a pawn in this whole matter. It was to oust the Iranian prime minister, Dr. Mohammed Mossadegh—the mastermind behind the decision.

The entire success of the coup depended on the shah. He needed to have the guts and the gumption to sign the papers and fire the prime minister. Interestingly, the plan for the coup was designed by Kermit Roosevelt Jr., the grandson of President Teddy Roosevelt and a senior-level CIA person.

One of the most vicious acts perpetrated by Pahlavi during his reign as shah was the creation of SAVAK (the National Organization for Information and Security). This was the shah's personal secret police. It was the Iranian version of the KGB, only far worse. It was diabolical, notorious, and brutal.

SAVAK was created in 1957. Both the American CIA and the Israelis played parts in its structure and creation. SAVAK had total, unfettered power. It spied on everyone, including politicians and friends of the shah. It even assassinated its own leaders. The first head of SAVAK was assassinated by SAVAK. The phone of the head of SAVAK in the United States was bugged by SAVAK.

SAVAK employed fifteen thousand people full time. No one knows how many informants were attached to the secret organization.

During the 1960s and '70s, there was remarkable growth and economic development in Iran. While for other countries that sounds like good news, it did not bode well for the shah's Iran. Why? Because the growth was coupled with Western influences that included very close relationships between Iran and the United States, and Iran and Israel. These relationships and the success that followed were what laid the foundation for the rise of radical

Muslims in Iran, resulting in the eventual overthrow of the shah.

Economic growth and the shah's support of women's rights were nails in his royal coffin. On January 16, 1979, the shah and his wife left Iran at the request of Iran's prime minister. They hoped that one day things would calm down and they would return home to a calmer situation. They wandered from country to country—first to Egypt, later to Morocco, the Bahamas, and even Mexico.

Two life-defining crises occurred during the shah's absence from Iran. Iranian prime minister Shapour Bakhtiar dissolved SAVAK and freed all the political prisoners SAVAK had rounded up, interrogated, and tortured. Then he invited the long-ago-exiled Ayatollah Khomeini to return to Iran.

The shah became ill—very ill—stricken with lymphoma. In October of 1979, after much debate, U.S. president Jimmy Carter allowed the shah to come to the United States for medical treatment. That was it. Muslim militants in Iran had had enough. In response to the humanitarian move by the U.S. president, Muslim militants took hostages, setting off one of the biggest crises in the Middle East.

The shah left the United States in December. Restless, homeless, and unwanted, he went to Panama and then settled in Egypt, the country that became his final resting place.

At sixty years of age, on July 27, 1980, Pahlavi died. He is buried in one of the most famous mosques in Islam, the al-Rifa'i mosque in Cairo. His coffin lies buried next to another deposed monarch, King Farouk of Egypt.

The shah of Iran was married three times. His first wife was not only royalty (Princess Fawzia of Egypt, daughter of King Faud and sister to King Farouk), she was also famed for her beauty. The couple had one child—a daughter, which made for an inappropriate heir. They divorced. Fawzia returned to Egypt only to be exiled after her brother Farouk was deposed.

The shah's second wife was a major step down in status. Soraya Esfandiary Bakhtiari was not royalty but was the daughter of a member of the Iranian intelligentsia: the ambassador to Germany. Her mother was German. The shah and his second wife had no children. The two divorced, after which Soraya became an actress. She eventually became the companion to Italian film director Franco Indovina.

The third and final wife of the second and final shah of Iran was the daughter of a captain in the Iranian army. Her name was Fara Diba. Together they had four children: Reza, Farahnaz, Ali, and Leila. Mohammad Reza Pahlavi, the shah of Iran, finally had a crown prince. But he no longer had a dynasty.

10

SEYYED RUHOLLAH KHOMEINI
The Extreme Extremist

Born: 1900
Died: 1989
Ruled: 1979–1989

T*ime* magazine named him "Man of the Year" in 1979. He is Ayatollah Seyyed Ruhollah Khomeini. Ayatollah, because he was chosen to be the supreme religious leader of the Islamic faith in Iran. Seyyed Ruhollah, because that was the name given him by his parents. Khomeini, because he was born in the town of Khomein and according to tradition, when a cleric reaches the position of ayatollah he assumes the name of his home town.

Ayatollah Seyyed Ruhollah Khomeini. Friends and family called him Ruhollah. Iranians addressed him as Imam. The world knew him as "The Ayatollah." Without exception, he was the most famous religious leader in Iran.

He was charismatic, had vast religious knowledge, and enjoyed recognized standing. He had reached the level of a "source of emulation" in Islamic-religious learning. He was a leader whose style was unforgiving but effective. He developed an entire political theory: a theocracy that was unique to Shiite Islam. And he successfully created a revolution that ousted Mohammad Reza Pahlavi, the last shah of Iran, placing himself in control. He was great.

Seyyed Ruhollah came from a very religious family. He was born in 1900 in Khomein, which is about two hundred miles south of Teheran. His father was murdered when he was only five months old. His mother and an aunt were the essential adult images in his life until they both died when he was fifteen years old. But a tragic life was saved because Ruhollah's family had *sayyed*, or status. According to Shiite tradition, a family had status if they could trace their lineage as far back as the prophet Mohammed.

Ruhollah studied under some of the greatest scholars in Islamic tradition. He became a teacher of the Sharia (Islamic jurisprudence), of Irfan (Islamic mysticism), and of philosophy. He was only in his twenties when he reached the pinnacle of Islamic religious life and authority: the high position of ayatollah.

If he had lived in the West, the ayatollah would have been labeled a rebel. He publicly denounced the shah of Iran and the shah's government, resulting in his imprisonment. He denounced the United States and was deported from Iran. He was sent into forced exile—first in Turkey, then in Iraq where he was permitted to live because it is the site of many Shiite holy places. That lasted until 1978, when Saddam Hussein personally chased him out.

France was the ayatollah's next home, and it was where he hung his galabeya. From there he began—in earnest—his campaign to overthrow the shah. It was also there that the ayatollah wrote his greatest work: *The Guardianship of Islamic Jurists*. The book extols the importance of Islamic law and society. It sets forth the author's view that the leader of an Islamic state must be a *faqih*—a religious legal authority—and that Islamic leaders cannot and should not be secular.

The impact Ayatollah Khomeini had even from his place of exile was enormous. His strength and charisma shone through. His influence was totally underestimated by the shah, by the shah's allies, and by the United States. An entire revolution was run from France—a revolution that caused the shah to flee his own country and brought back the ayatollah as supreme leader.

The shah left Iran on January 16, 1979, and the ayatollah returned on February 1. He came out of exile and was received in a style that was greater than the reception given a king. Millions upon millions of Iranians came out to welcome Ayatollah Khomeini home—some estimates put the number as high as seven million. Though emotions ran high among the people, the ayatollah was perfectly composed.

On the plane returning him from exile, a reporter asked the man who had deposed a shah, "What do you feel?" The Ayatollah's response: "Nothing." Millions of people were waiting, pouring out their love; the world was holding its collective breath, not knowing what to expect next from this man. And he felt nothing.

Immediately, Ayatollah Khomeini assumed the position of supreme leader. Within weeks he had proposed a referendum in which the Islamic Republic would be the new form of government in Iran. All people over the age of sixteen were eligible to vote—male and female. And so it came to be that 98 percent of the

Islamic electorate voted in favor of replacing the monarchy with an Islamic republic.

Ten months after the ayatollah returned from exile, the United States Embassy in Tehran was surrounded. Sixty-three hostages were taken by students—members of the revolutionary movement. Three more U.S. hostages were taken from the Iranian Foreign Ministry. Thirteen of the hostages, mostly blacks and women, were soon released; the remainder were held hostage for 444 days. The media dubbed it the Iranian hostage crisis. The ABC program *Nightline* was launched during the crisis, and the days were counted down.

Then U.S. president Jimmy Carter lost an election. Carter had ordered a commando raid to save the hostages, but it was a botched attempt. The helicopters failed—desert sand lodged in the engines, and the machines dropped. The entire event was seen as a fiasco, and republican Ronald Reagan easily defeated Carter in the next election. Iranians viewed the failure differently: they saw it as nothing short of divine intervention.

So the Iranians gave Ronald Reagan a present. As Reagan left the podium after swearing his oath of office, he was handed a note. The hostages were freed. It was clear that the Iranians believed Reagan would not handle the hostage situation the same way Carter had.

Now the ayatollah directed his venom against Iraq. He saw a country with a majority Shiite population being controlled by a Sunni minority. In the ayatollah's book, that was wrong. He began to harangue his adherents across the border, trying to organize them from afar in the same way he had ousted the shah of Iran, successfully pulling the strings from France. But there was a difference. Saddam Hussein was no shah.

Iraq immediately attacked Iran. The war raged for eight years, from 1980 until 1988. The Iranians became victims of chemical warfare at the hands of the Iraqis, losing more than a half-million people. The Islamic army was not prepared for such a vicious attack. The Iranian air force was nonexistent, and the entire military class, fearful of execution for having served under the shah, had run away from Iran when the ayatollah returned. In contrast, the Iraqi army and air force were highly trained and well organized. The Iraqis would regularly bomb small villages, almost crop dusting the landscape with poison to murder the Iranians.

Iran, in the person of Ayatollah Khomeini, wanted to create a united Shiite Islamic republic. The ayatollah knew that many of the holy sites for Shiites were in Iraq—after all, that is one of the reasons he went to Iraq upon being exiled. And he knew that the Iraqi Shiites were potentially oppressed victims of a whimsical Saddam Hussein.

Meanwhile, back at home the ayatollah laid out an obligatory dress code. By law, women had to cover their bodies and their hair. For men there were to be no short pants and no short-sleeved shirts. Media was restricted, as was freedom of speech. No one, according to the new law, could disagree with Islamic law as set down and interpreted by the Ayatollah. Refusal to obey was met with execution.

Some unforeseen changes took place because of these oppressive policies. Women started receiving a better education and going out to work. Yes, they ventured out in modest dress, and yes, they were limited in the positions they were allowed to hold. But women's employment increased by significant numbers. Now, more Iranian women than men hold degrees of higher education, and women are a major part of the workforce.

The ayatollah made other promises yet to be realized. And with his death in 1989, the chances of those promises ever being fulfilled is extremely slight. In a speech delivered in Teheran's central cemetery, he promised the citizens of Iran free heating, electricity, and telephones. He made a promise of free oil. He also promised that no Iranian would remain homeless. One promise he did fulfill was allowing transgender Iranians to get medical care and then have the ability to alter their birth certificates to reflect their changed sex.

One of the greatest attacks against the ayatollah came from outside Iran. It came in the guise of a book entitled *The Satanic Verses*, written by Salman Rushdie. In the book, Rushdie called to task the Islamic Republic, labeling it an oppressive and irresponsible power interested in self-aggrandizement rather than religious fulfillment. The ayatollah labeled the book blasphemy and issued a fatwah, or death sentence.

Rushdie took this death threat very seriously and went into hiding. The fatwa permitted any Muslim to kill Rushdie because he had blasphemed the Koran, the prophet Mohammed, and Islam. *The Satanic Verses* was an enormous, best-selling success.

On June 3, 1989, the ayatollah died. Millions of supporters at home and around the Muslim world participated in his funeral. Actually, Ayatollah Khomeini had two funerals.

The first time around, he was laid out in a wooden coffin, open for all to see. The throngs of supporters came in a stampede and mobbed the casket. They so wanted to see and touch the ayatollah—and tear off a bit of his shroud—that the casket toppled and his body nearly fell to the ground. Thousands of Iranians were injured during the melee. For his second funeral the ayatollah was encased in a steel coffin, and security was brought in. The masses were kept at bay, able only to pay their respects at his burial site.

The ayatollah is dead but his legacy continues.

11

HAFEZ ASSAD
Stable, Predictable, Brutal

Born: October 6, 1930
Died: June 10, 2000
Ruled: 1971–2000

His title was president, but he ruled as a dictator.

Hafez Assad became president of Syria after leading a successful coup against his mentor, and he was not going to let that happen to him. Anyone who stood in the way of President Hafez Assad, the autocratic ruler of the police-state Syria, was eliminated. As the queen of hearts in *Through the Looking Glass* proclaimed, "Off with their heads!"

One common characteristic of world-class tyrants, dictators, and despots is their predictability. Get in their way and you are killed. Do as they say and you are rewarded—or better yet, left alone. Assad was many things: he was a trained air force pilot, a determined master planner, and a cool head in the hotheaded Arab world. Most of all, he was predictable both in international affairs and in his handling of internal challenges. Assad always had a reason for his behavior. He always calculated his moves and never overstepped his power or overplayed his hand.

Hafez Assad did not fit in and so had to fight to retain his position and his standing. He was an Alawite—a break off of Shiia Islam—from a small community in Syria. The majority of the Syrian people are Sunnis who view the Alawites as heretics. The only way that Assad the Alawite could maintain control over Syria was through tyranny and strong-arm tactics. The only people he really trusted were his family, until one day even that trust proved to be misplaced.

Assad's brother attempted to wrest control away from the president by leading a coup. The coup was put down, leaving Assad crazed and fighting mad because of the betrayal by one of the few people he actually trusted. In response, he eliminated his brother and established fifteen intelligence agencies. The agencies competed against each other, and after culling through all the information, Assad would make his decisions. Any attempt to overthrow Assad, including attempts by siblings, was met with cruelty and strength.

In the end, history reflects that during his rule, Assad was the leader of the most stable country in the Middle East. This was a real accomplishment in the world of upheaval and coups and conflict that emblemizes the Middle East. During the thirty years of Assad's rule, the Middle East saw trendemous growth and movement toward the West. With the fall of the Soviet Union, Middle East leaders broke from their Communist patron and opened up to the West. But not Assad. His rule remained constant.

Assad's stability is credited to his ruthlessness. Take the Syrian city of Hama, for example. Should you ever visit Syria, don't bother looking for it. Hama no longer exists. Assad had the village and all its people decimated.

A local group of Syrians from Hama attempted an insurrection against Assad. The locals were members of the Muslim Brotherhood—an Islamic movement bent on ousting Assad. Not only did Assad put down the insurgency, but he put under the village. In one day, the entire population of Hama—men, women, boys, and girls—were obliterated along with the buildings they lived in, prayed in, went to school in, and shopped in.

The process of destruction began before dawn. The people of Hama were awakened by the roar of bombs being dropped by the Syrian air force on the roads surrounding the village. All escape routes were cut off and destroyed. Then came the artillery. Tanks that had stealthily been pulled into position during the course of the night began hammering away at the village. Soldiers of the Syrian army made their way, house by house, killing every living being in Hama and looting whatever possessions they took a liking to. For good measure, the village was gassed. In less than twenty-four hours, Hama was no more.

The point was made. It reverberated throughout Syria and into the far reaches of the Middle East. Do not cross President Hafez Assad. Official reports put the death total at twenty thousand. Given the sheer vastness of the destroyed area and the numbers of missing persons, humanitarian organizations put the death count much higher.

That was Assad. Ruthless. Relentless.

Assad planned his own succession of leadership. He spent years grooming a favorite son for the position. The son, reckless and ruthless like his father, was killed as he sped out of control in a car accident. Assad, suffering from poor health at the time, was forced to settle for second best. He chose his son Bashar, who showed no interest in carrying on his father's tradition and who had, instead, opted for a career in medicine as an ophthalmologist. Bashar had no choice but to obey and took over the presidency after the death of his father.

Assad graduated from the Syrian Military Academy, eventually becoming a general in the Syrian army. He received his fighter-pilot training in the Soviet Union. That Soviet education and the contacts Assad made during his time there were the most important and formative components of his early career. The future president forged essential alliances and links with the USSR. He cultivated a cadre of top Soviets who would later become Assad's biggest sugar daddies as they all grew in power and politics.

Back home in Syria in 1963, when the Ba'ath Party took over the country, Assad became an air force commander. In 1966, he participated in the Ba'athist coup that successfully overthrew the government, resulting in Assad's term as Syrian minister of defense. Assad's own coup in 1970—the one he orchestrated and during which he ousted his own political mentor, Salah al-Jadid—was the coup that allowed him to take over the presidency.

Assad was a masterful planner and tactician. He believed in a greater Syria, defying borders and boundaries. An avowed enemy of Israel, the vast majority of his political career was dedicated to fighting the Jewish nation. He tried to redeem the Golan Heights that

Israel took from Syria in the 1967 Six Days' War, which took place during Assad's tenure as defense minister and commander in chief of the Syrian air force. He was relentless in asserting that every inch, every rock, every blade of grass was to be returned to its rightful owner, despite Israel's obvious strategic strength. Assad actively supported Palestinian terrorists in their actions against Israel.

At one point, Egypt was united with Syria as one nation under a concept called Pan Arabism. The union was short-lived and unsuccessful. The reality was that Assad had serious conflict with everyone, especially those with whom he was in closeest proximity: King Hussein of Jordan, Saddam Hussein of Iraq, and both Anwar Sadat and Hoshi Mubarak of Egypt. Neighbors on all sides of Syria were engaged in quarrels and power plays with the Syrian despot.

Lebanon was of particular interest for Assad as it was always seen as a province of Syria. Even today, there is no ambassador from Syria to Beirut. For Assad, Lebanon was simply an extension of his land—a place to exploit for its natural resources and its creative and cultural strengths. It was just another piece of land under his jurisdiction and rule.

Assad was a tireless worker. Eighteen- to twenty-hour days were his norm. His marathon meetings were as famous as his powerful bladder. No one was ever permitted to leave a meeting with Assad— even to relieve himself—until the president declared the meeting over. And no one ever knew when the meeting would start.

Forcing guests to wait for hours on end before being invited in to scheduled meetings was a game Assad loved to play. He loved to hold people hostage—literally and figuratively. Especially members of the Western, non-Arab world, like Warren Christopher, U.S. president Bill Clinton's first secretary of state.

On one now famous occasion, Christopher—a dapperly dressed, soft-spoken diplomat—was kept waiting for hours until Assad declared himself ready for their meeting. Why would the senior representative of the most powerful nation in the world allow himself to be so shabbily treated? Because Christopher understood the importance of the meeting and knew that the only way to have any time with the Syrian dictator was to play by his maniacal, demeaning rules. And so Warren Christopher waited.

Henry Kissinger was the first U.S. secretary of state to meet with Syria's president in twenty years. He described the Assad method of diplomacy this way: "His tactic was to open with a statement of the most extreme position to test what the traffic would bear. He might then allow himself to be driven back to the attainable, fighting a dogged rear-guard action that made clear that the concessions could be exacted only at a heavy price and that discourage excessive expectations."

Hafez Assad exacted a heavy price from all around him.

12

ALI KHAMENEI
Supreme Leader Jr.

Born: 1939
Died: Still living
Ruled: 1989–present

This ayatollah is not "The Ayatollah." That would be Ayatollah Khomeini, founder of the Iranian revolution. This ayatollah is Ayatollah Ali Khamenei—different spelling, different person, different rank and religious standing. Khomeini and Khamenei were friends, however, and after Khomeini's death, Khamenei was chosen to be Iran's ruling ayatollah. How did it happen that a cleric of comparatively low status made it into the position of supreme religious leader? The other clerics wanted it that way. They needed someone they could control—a puppet, a figurehead. At the time, Khamenei went along with the plan. But he eventually grew into the position and now rules as a true ayatollah.

Khamenei entered religious life early and became a teacher of religious studies. In 1981, after the assassination of Iran's second president and revolution supporter Muhammad Ali Rajai, and at the behest of the clerics, Khamenei was the first cleric to hold the position of president of Iran. Ayatollah Khomeini was against the move; he felt that clerics should stay out of mainstream politics. But after internal discussion and debate, he changed his thinking.

Khamenei was in position, and an election was called pitting him against three other candidates. With almost seventeen million people eligible to vote in Iran, Khamenei received over sixteen million votes. It was a farce. The opposition—all three of them combined—garnered fewer than five-hundred thousand votes. In 1985, Khamenei was reelected. And then in 1989, when Ayatollah Khomeini died, Khamenei was appointed to rule.

Under the constitution of the Islamic Republic of Iran, the supreme leader can overrule any court and any leader. He can overrule any government official, including the president, any media director, and any law passed by the parliament. But in order to attain the position of supreme leader under the constitution, the cleric must have attained a high religious ranking—a ranking higher than the position held by Khamenei. So the constitution was amended.

Khomeini's religious status was "a source of emulation." Khamenei was nowhere close to that religious level. In Iran, when religion meets politics, religion wins every time. It was easy to change the constitution to meet the demands of people who make the decisions. Tapping a mid-level cleric to become the supreme leader of Iran is classic.

Even though Khamenei already had the position of president, his power was minimal because of his lower religious ranking. In Iran, the strings are pulled by the clerics. The religious body that plucked

Ali Khamenei out of relative religious obscurity was not ready to have a potentially independent person in the position of supreme leader. Once again, in a move similar to the one that made Khamenei president, Iran's religious leadership made Khamenei its puppet leader. They wanted someone whom they could prop up to fill the post so that they could call all the moves and script all the directives, reserving for themselves ultimate religious control.

But even with the backing of Iran's religious establishment, the new supreme leader was not universally beloved. He suffered some serious blows to his credibility during his early years in the position, but because he was backed by the powers, nothing mattered. Religious leadership censored the press, controlled public opinion, and called the shots in elections.

In June of 1991, Khamenei was nearly assassinated during a press conference. A tape recorder wired as a bomb was positioned close to the ayatollah and exploded. Khamenei was lucky. He did not lose his life—just his right hand.

Afterward, he began to assert himself. When Iran's President Muhamad Ahmadinejad ruled that women could attend soccer games, Ayatollah Khamenei overruled and nullified the president's ruling. Not that Ahmadinejad had suddenly embraced liberal values of equality. Even in Ahmadinejad's ruling, women and men would have been separated at the games. But the ayatollah ruled no, and no it was.

Today, Khomeini would be proud of Khamenei. It is not simply that Khamenei is anti-Western and extreme. He has zero tolerance for anyone who is not as extreme as he is.

Ayatollah Khamenei regularly arrests other clerics—even more highly ranked clerics—whom he finds offensive or disrespectful. In 1997, he arrested Ayatollah Hossein Ali Montazeri. Montazeri, a respected scholar, dared to call Khamenei religiously and legally incompetent. Montazeri was not the only one who criticized the supreme leader, but very few others made their statements publicly. After his arrest, Montazeri's school was closed and he was publicly humiliated.

Khamenei is known for his radical anti-United States policy and anti-Israel attitudes. He arrests Iranians whom he thinks might be embracing the trappings of Western culture and calls for the destruction of Israel.

Khamenei regularly arrests editors and television producers. His objective is to intimidate the media. He wants the media to be run the correct way—that is, his way. He says he wants to protect the media and insists that the Iranian media not be controlled by "enemies of Islam." In 1999, he even appeared on television to explain his stand and to hammer home the point that all media in Iran, print and electronic, must adhere to Islamic values.

And yet, as extreme and as radical as he is, and as extreme and radical as he demands Iran to be, there are some inconsistencies in Ayatollah Khamenei's practices. He has not come out against the Internet in Iran. As a result, many Iranians run to the Internet to get information about what really happens in the world and are exposed—with sanction—to all that the ayatollah finds loathsome and deviant.

Reliable sources report that Ayatollah Ali Khamenei has issued a *fatwa* (a religious ruling) forbidding the development of nuclear science. According to sources, the fatwa forbade the production, stockpiling, and use of nuclear weapons. On several occasions, secular Iranian leadership has referred to this ruling in response to Western concerns about Iranian nuclear threats and stability. But nobody can find the fatwa in writing.

13

FAHD IBN ABDUL AZIZ AL-SA'OUD
Gambler, Playboy, Monarch

Born: 1923
Died: 2005
Ruled: 1982–2005

Imagine dropping more than $6 million in one night at a casino in Monte Carlo. According to rumor, that was the life of Fahd ibn Abdul Aziz al-Sa'oud—gambler, playboy, jet setter, and prince. Fahd was the son of King Abd al-Aziz al-Sa'oud, the founder of Saudi Arabia—a country that flows with black gold.

There are stories about women and parties, about an almost uncontrollable attraction to expensive whiskey and good liquor, and about countless indiscretions on the part of Fahd. The fast-living royal was in line to rule the birthplace of the prophet Mohammad, where gambling and drinking are sins strictly forbidden by law.

That was the life. At least until 1982, when Fahd the party animal turned Fahd the king, the ultimate ruler of Saudi Arabia.

When the appointed time came, Fahd set aside his youthful passions, reinvented himself, and assumed leadership of the country his father had founded. With the position came power and responsibility. King Fahd proudly wore the mantle of ruler along with a *mishlah*—a tan robe made of 100 percent spun gold. According to tradition, the king of Saudi Arabia always wears a flowing white gown covered with a mishlah.

It sounds odd to talk about the tradition of such a young country. How much tradition could there be when Fahd was the son of Saudi Arabia's founding ruler? Prince Fahd was the oldest of the seven sons born to His Majesty King Abd al-Aziz al-Sa'oud and his favorite wife, Hassa bint Ahmadi al-Sudayri. The boys were close friends and political allies; they became known as the Sudayri seven. In total, the first king of Saudi Arabia had thirty-seven sons. In the Saudi Kingdom, girls don't count, so the number of daughters born to the first king has never been officially recorded. Fahd became the fifth king to rule.

Like his brothers, Fahd was educated at home in a school created by the family for the family. Fahd was placed in many leadership positions over the years. At the beginning, he was just being tested. He passed with flying colors, handling each of his governmental and royal positions efficiently and effectively. He was minister of education and interior minister. He was named crown prince and was appointed deputy prime minister.

As a young boy, Fahd was there to see his father sign the Treaty of Jedda, officially creating the Kingdom of Saudi Arabia. In 1945, he paid his first state visit to the United States for the opening session of the United Nations General Assembly. Years later, in 1953, he attended the coronation of Elizabeth II of England. He was an official leader of the delegation to the Arab League in 1959. Without knowing it, Fahd was being groomed for the position of ultimate power in the House of Saud.

The story reads like a mythological tale.

After the death of the founding king in 1932, Prince Abdul Aziz ascended to the throne. Aziz reigned until 1953, when the crown was passed to Saud. Faisal reigned from 1964 to 1975, when he was assassinated by his own deranged nephew. Khalid, half brother of Fahd, took over the kingdom and appointed the loyal Fahd crown prince and deputy prime minister.

Khalid was a nonpolitical person and not a very effective leader. It was as if the crown was foisted upon him; he was not interested in ruling. Real power belonged to Fahd, and it came with the blessings of the ruling monarch. The transition of power after the death of Khalid on June 13, 1982, was an easy one. Fahd was already first deputy prime minister, and through birthright he was next in the line of succession. Fahd was in the perfect position, both politically and hierarchically, to assume the throne after Khalid.

The scepter was formally passed from the hand of the man who held it to the hand of the man who had been pointing it all along. Fahd began making changes in the monarchy, including the terminology of kingship. Four years after assuming the role of monarch, Fahd made the decision to eliminate the title "His Majesty." It was too Western. "His Majesty" was replaced with the new titles "Custodian of the Two Holy Mosques" or "Servant of the Two Holy Sites." It was a reference to the two Muslim holy sites—Mecca and Medina—both located in Saudi Arabia.

King Fahd, custodian of the two holy mosques, was creating a situation for his country, himself, and his successors that would lead to great tension. The man who loved good liquor and fine casinos had turned and embraced Arabic and Islamic foundations. He reached out, accepted compromise, and appeased radical Islamic elements within his kingdom. At the same time, he was developing productive economic relationships with Western oil companies and Western countries like the United States, England, France, and Germany. Fahd tried, but you can't have it both ways.

Radical elements from within Saudi society reached out to destroy a monarchy that had included them. Fahd had chosen to embrace Wahabi Islam in order to gain popular support and to give himself standing within the masses of Islamic culture. He made concessions to religious radicals and officially endorsed the Wahabi educational system. But Fahd's efforts backfired.

To this day, the Wahabi educational system teaches against the interests of the royal family. It prefers *Sharia*, or religious law, to the laws of the monarchy. It advocates that the royal family has no place at all in rule making or, for that matter, in society.

It is Wahabi Islam that empowers terror in Saudi Arabia and around the world. It was the perfect breeding ground for Osama bin Laden and the entire al-Qaeda movement. Irrational as it seems, Saudi Arabia has been a significant target of homegrown Wahabi terror. The once-promising crown prince was making bad choices as king. Following a series of terrorist attacks from within the kingdom directed at Saudi rulers, a crackdown policy went into effect. In May 2003, Fahd flip-flopped; he introduced a program against extremist teaching.

Why did he allow it in the first place? What had possessed Fahd to embrace Islam? It all began in 1979, even before he ascended the throne. Fahd was inclined toward Western-style thinking. But in 1979, he was witness to the ousting of the shah from Iran by Ayatollah Khomeini. From the relative safety of his home in Saudi Arabia, Fahd watched as the ayatollah and his Islamic Revolution ousted a secular, pro-Western, Muslim monarch. He envisioned himself in that position and learned a lesson for the future.

That same year in his country's city of Mecca, radical Muslims took over the holiest place in all of Islam: the mosque. The radicals shouted for the ousting of the royal family on religious grounds and demanded a monarchy with true Islamic leadership. Fahd was determined not to let his family be eliminated by Islam—certainly not during his reign.

He decided that he would be the world's leading Islamic leader. He would not allow Iran and the Shiites to become leaders of Islam for the world. And so he invited Islam into his country, even if not into his heart. It was a political, not a religious, move. He then poured hundreds of millions of dollars into Muslim holy sites in Saudi Arabia and expanded his country's ability to accommodate more and more pilgrims to the holy sites. He established a religious police that would publicly enforce Islamic law. That police force would humiliate and arrest any woman who did not comport herself properly or dress properly or cover her face properly. Fahd the womanizer did this. He transformed Saudi Arabia into a very traditional Islamic society.

King Fahd died on August 1, 2005. He wasn't ousted. He didn't abdicate. He had a stroke that left him incapacitated for many years. He was married at least three times and had at least six sons and some daughters. (We don't know how many daughters, as they have no role in the House of Saud.) He was an eccentric—a night owl who would frequently call his government together for meetings that began at midnight. He slept during the day. He was a micromanager. He needed to approve every detail of every project and so created an enormous backlog of paperwork requiring his approval. He was a benevolent dictator.

Crown Prince Abdulah took the reins of power during the final years of Fahd's illness.

14

YASSER ARAFAT
Master Manipulator

Born: 1929
Died: 2004
Ruled: 1993–2004

Yasser Arafat is his nom de guerre. His real name was Muhammad Abd al-Rau-al Qadwah al-Husayni. His friends called him Abu Amar. He was a larger-than-life symbol for the Palestinian people. He was their liberator, their leader, their warrior, their father figure.

Arafat was a career terrorist, and for most of his career he never slept in the same bed twice. He was afraid of being killed in his sleep. He had good reason to be afraid. In the beginning, he feared the Israelis; he was afraid they would succeed in capturing or killing him. Toward the end it was some of his own Palestinians he was frightened of.

He was the master of political double speak. In English, Arafat would appease the United States, the West, and Israel with talk of the "beace of the brave." (There is no "p" sound in Arabic.) Then in Arabic he would turn to Muslim and non-Western countries, calling for *jihad*—a Muslim holy war.

To understand Arafat, you have to understand the meaning of symbolism. Symbols informed Arafat's character and his dress. The two were intertwined. He always wore a military uniform and carried a holstered pistol. Even when visiting the United Nations, the center of international peace, Yasser Arafat brandished his weapon. It was his persona. He was a warrior—a general. His followers got the message; the West did not.

The *kafiyah* sitting atop Arafat's (bald) head was legendary. He was never seen without the black-and-white checkered scarf, and it was always styled just so. In general, Arafat had a rather slovenly, unkempt appearance; but in actuality he was perfectly, symbolically put together.

The kafiyah design was actually Bedouin in origin, but Arafat borrowed it and then owned it. The cloth became a symbol of Palestinian nationalism. It adorned his head in such a way that it took the shape of Palestine as Arafat conceived it be. The tweak, the point, and the peak were the outlines of a map of the future Palestine. The tail draped down Arafat's back in a long triangle representing the Negev desert. The top was the hills of Judea and Samaria, including Jerusalem.

His salt-and-pepper beard looked ungroomed, but that was because he had some hairless spots on his face. His beard was actually always perfectly trimmed. He had a staff of full-time barbers whose responsibility was to make certain his beard and kafiyah were always properly arranged. The beard was symbolic of a leader who had no time to shave; a visionary who had no time for minutia or for trivial pursuits like grooming.

His clothes were always fatigues. Even at state dinners, Arafat wore fatigues. That decision, too, was symbolic. During the famous signing of the Oslo Agreements on the north lawn of the White House in September of 1993, a huge dispute emerged between President Clinton and Arafat—and thus between the United States and the Palestinians. Arafat refused to take off his holster and weapon. He said they were part of who he was and what he represented. The United States was adamant. It was, after all, the signing of a peace treaty, and there was nothing less appropriate than a gun at a peace treaty.

Arafat duped the United States and the West. During the Clinton administration, he was the foreign leader who logged the most visits to the White House. The United States and the West still did not get the message that Arafat was telegraphing out. The Arab world understood what he was doing. Even those who despised Arafat for his duplicity and corruption snickered as he played the West for suckers.

And suckers they were. After Arafat's death, the big question was not who would be his rightful successor, but where is the money? Where were the billions—yes, billions—of dollars the world gave Arafat and the Palestinians? (After an initial promise by the United States to give monetary aid to the Palestinians, Arafat arrived in Washington with empty suitcases—real suitcases—expecting to fill them up and bring them back home.)

Billions of dollars were unaccounted for. Arafat, the devoted Palestinian leader, had successfully socked them away. Even though he was the uncontested winner in an election, he was in the most classic of ways a demagogue and a dictator. Palestinian streets remained unpaved. Sewage plants were never built. In his eyes, the billions of dollars of international aid given to the Palestinians was given to him personally. He was the embodiment of the Palestinian people. The money was his. For years Arafat would dole out cash in envelopes. He had little pieces of paper with scribbled numbers on them. Even when terrorists would make an appeal for $100 to carry out an operation, he would famously scratch out their request with his red pen, write "25," and initial it. He promised money to the families of terrorist martyrs, but he never paid out. Arafat never made good on his end of the deal.

The birth of Yasser Arafat, savior of the Palestinian people, is clouded with confusion. Intentionally. Arafat claimed to have been born and raised in Jerusalem, once again adding to the symbolism and creating mystique. Other sources record his birth and childhood in Egypt and then have him transplanted to Jerusalem with extended family.

According to all sources Arafat was born in 1928, the fifth child of a very successful merchant. After his mother died when he was only four years old, he spent significant periods of time living with his uncle in Jerusalem. But he always returned to Egypt, where he received his basic education. He studied engineering in Cairo.

At the time of the Nakba (Israel's 1948 declaration of indepence), Arafat was nineteen years old and had not yet entered the military. Neither did he participate as a soldier in the 1956 Arab war with Israel.

In Jerusalem, Arafat was heavily influenced by Haj Amin

al-Husseini, the grand mufti of Jerusalem and scion of a family that controlled Jerusalem for centuries, even in the present day. During World War II, the mufti was a guest of Adolf Hitler in Berlin. It is said that Hitler took a liking to Arafat, preferring him to another young Jerusalem man who was also showing leadership potential. That man—Arafat's contender—was George Habash, who later founded a break-off of Arafat's political and terrorist movement, the Palestine Liberation Organization (PLO). Habash formed the Popular Front for the Liberation of Palestine (PFLP).

Yasser Arafat is known as the father of modern terrorism. He co-founded the movement for the national liberation of Palestine, or Fatah, in the late 1950s. In the beginning, the movement unsuccessfully attempted to hit soft targets within Israel: the national water carrier and the trains. But they improved. Soon Fatah started attacking small Israeli villages.

In 1969, Arafat became the chairman of the PLO, the umbrella organization for all Palestinian national activity that had centralized in Jordan in the 1960s. He always preferred the title chairman to president. The PLO became the world's most notorious airline hijacker. On February 21, 1970, and under the umbrella of the PLO, the PFLP hijacked Swissair flight 330 on its way to Tel Aviv. Forty-seven passengers and the airline crew were murdered.

On September 6, 1970, the PLO embarked on a quadruple hijacking—shades of the 9/11 al-Qaeda attack. One hijacking failed thanks to air marshals aboard an El Al flight. One plane was hijacked to Cairo. The passengers were let go, and the plane was blown up.

The last two, a TWA flight and a Swissair flight, were taken to Jordan and landed in the desert. The 310 passengers and crew were divided into groups: Israelis, Americans, Swiss, and West Germans. Everyone else was let go.

On September 13, 1970, King Hussein of Jordan had seen enough and began an attack on all PLO facilities. Within two weeks, Arafat and the entire PLO were packed up and on their way to Lebanon. Over two thousand PLO members were killed in the fighting with the Jordanians, and the hostages were released. This period in PLO history is known as Black September.

Two years later, on September 5, 1972, Arafat's PLO conducted another major attack. It was the Munich Olympics, and the target was the team of Israeli athletes participating in the games. The group that carried out the attack was called Black September. Eleven Israeli athletes were murdered at an event dedicated to harmony, world peace, and unity. The games went on.

In 1973, Arafat's Black September kidnapped the U.S. ambassador to Sudan and the Belgian charge d'affaires. They demanded the release of several Palestinian prisoners: Sirhan Sirhan, the Palestinian assassin of Robert Kennedy; one Palestinian woman imprisoned in Israel; and others imprisoned in Jordan. Nobody took them seriously. So the PLO executed the American and the Belgian diplomats.

From Lebanon, Arafat sought to continue his reign of terror and attacks against Israeli and worldwide Western targets. On November 13, 1974, the PLO was granted observer status in the United Nations. Gun-toting Arafat was the PLO representative to the assembly. The only people who stood up to him were the guards at the UN, demanding that he check his weapon before entering the revered assembly hall.

Arafat had created his own little fiefdom—a PLO ministate in Lebanon. And in 1982, Israel invaded southern Lebanon to clean them out. In exchange for a cease-fire, Arafat was expelled from Lebanon. He moved to Tunisia to set up shop in Tunis, eventually returning to the Palestinian territories. He established his government right outside Jerusalem in Ramallah, a stone's throw away from the Temple Mount and the holiest of all Muslim sites—the al-Aqsa Mosque. Arafat was a survivor, a cat with nine lives.

Terrorism and nationalism aside, Arafat made several mistakes that angered the international community and diminished his place in world politics. And it's likely he knew just what those mistakes were. In 1985, his terrorists attacked the Achille Lauro cruise ship. They chose a sixty-nine-year-old Jewish man from New York who sat in a wheelchair, shot him, and dumped him overboard. Another mistake was Palestinian participation in the cheering squad for Saddam Hussein during the first Gulf War. Images of Palestinians cheering as scuds fell on Tel Aviv hurt Arafat. He had miscalculated. But Arafat was like Teflon—nothing stuck. Arafat redefined himself as the ultimate man of peace. In September of 1993, Arafat, Bill Clinton, and Yitzhak Rabin signed the Olso Accords on the lawn of the White House. The Palestinian Authority was created. And in 1994, Yasser Arafat—the man responsible for the planning, implementation, and funding of terrorist attacks that left hundreds dead and thousands wounded around the world, and specifically against Israel—was awarded the Nobel Peace Prize.

He had fooled the world again. Two years later, Arafat gave a speech in Stockholm, Sweden—the very place that confers the Nobel Prize. Speaking in Arabic, the Palestinian leader said, "We plan to eliminate the state of Israel and establish a purely Palestinian state. We will make life unbearable for Jews by psychological warfare and population explosion. . . . We Palestinians will take over everything, including Jerusalem."

Arafat easily reconciled his actions with his words. He would frequently refer to the Khudaibiya treaty that the Muslim prophet Mohammed made—and then broke—with the Qoresh. The lesson Arafat took to heart was that it was perfectly moral to enter into a ten-year agreement with your enemy, knowing that you would be breaking that agreement in order to regroup, regain strength, and then go out and conquer.

After 9/11, it became more difficult for Arafat to deliver his double messages. The United States was finally listening to both Arabic and English pronouncements. U.S. leaders wanted world leaders to be consistent in their messages and to fight terror. Arafat couldn't do it. He could not change his ways.

He was a master at saying the right thing, but he could not change his ultimate goals. He was bent on perpetrating terrorist attacks, specifically against Israel, regardless of what was said between him and the United States. Congress refused to hand over any more Palestinian aid. President George W. Bush finally cut him off, refusing any form of communication with the now old and ailing Arafat. The final straw for the United States was a terrorist attack in the Jerusalem neighborhood named French Hill. Publicly, Arafat condemned the attack. But the Bush administration was shown incontrovertible proof that Arafat had actually paid for the attack.

After several more horrific terror strikes against Israel, with the terrorists given sanction to hide out in the presidential compound in Ramallah, Israel decided to encase Arafat in his compound until he gave up the terrorists. Arafat remained in his compound until he was airlifted to France for medical treatment and died.

Very few people in the world have been able to transform society and put their cause on the map through evil and terror. Arafat did just that.

Arafat was not buried in Jerusalem. He was not buried on the Temple Mount. He did not live long enough to fulfill his dream of gazing out onto the Temple Mount from the parliament building he was constructing in East Jerusalem. Yasser Arafat's office had a floor to ceiling window with a panoramic vista of Jerusalem from almost every room, including his private latrine.

15

MUAMMAR GHADAFFI
Eccentric Tyrant

Born: 1942
Died: Still living
Ruled: 1969–present

Outside of the self-given title colonel, the man who willfully and independently rules Libya, the man who is undeniably one of the greatest powers in the Arab world, has no other official title.

Colonel Muammar Ghadaffi often conducts official business from tents. It is from there that he also conducts formal sessions with other world leaders. On a visit to Belgium, he traveled with two planes: one for him and his female bodyguards (he insists on only female bodyguards), and the other for his white stretch limo and tent.

Ghadaffi pitched that tent in front of the grandiose castle designated as his guest residence, and from there he conducted all his business. He entertained diplomats and heads of state in a tent in the midst of the cold winter weather of Belgium.

Under the leadership of Colonel Ghadaffi, Libya has been a true foe of the West. However in the recent past, Ghadaffi seems to be performing a turnaround. But is it just a performance? How trusted can a former terror-supporting dictator be in a post-9/11, post-Saddam world?

For Libya's Ghadaffi, it's all personal. The characterization of Ghadaffi as an anti-Western leader is an oversimplification of the man and his vision. There is nothing more important to Ghadaffi than self-preservation. He is constantly maneuvering in order to further entrench himself in power and solidify his future. He will do whatever it takes to maintain his position and ensure that the mantel of leadership is passed to his selected delegate. Ghadaffi wants his name and face on sculptures, buildings, and billboards so that his presence will be felt for generations to come.

Ghadaffi was born a peasant and raised in a Bedouin tribe of nomads who lived in the Libyan countryside. His early years were uneventful. Young Muammar had what is referred to as a traditional primary education; he was taught both Islamic and Western subjects with only a slight emphasis on the Islamic courses. The seeds of his future, and the future of the fledgling Libyan monarchy, were planted during Ghadaffi's high school years.

At the behest of the United Nations, the Libyan National Assembly met in 1950 and elected Emir Idris king of the emerging new country. On December 24, 1951, King Idris I declared the establishment of the United Kingdom of Libya.

Initially, Libya welcomed help given it by the United States and Great Britain to develop the new nation. Among the many improvements implemented by the great powers was Libya's new naval base.

The naval base was constructed in Libya for reasons that were both altruistic and practical, both for Libyan use and because the location served as a perfect place to monitor the USSR's advances in the region. With the assistance of private British investment money, British Petroleum (BP) discovered oil on Libya's soil in 1958. Voila. Overnight, a poor country was transformed into one of the wealthiest countries in the region.

At the same time, Ghadaffi was attending the Sebha Prep School in Fezzan. It was in prep school that he was introduced to and became part of a clique that would eventually compose the inner core of the military revolutionists who would, in the not-too-distant future, take over Libya. Precisely because of his early activities, Ghadaffi was expelled from Sebha. He still managed to get accepted to law school, and immediately after graduating in 1963, he enlisted in the military academy at Benghazi.

In the military, Ghadaffi and his buddies secretly created a group that actively plotted the overthrow of the Libyan monarchy. Unaware of his intentions, the army sent him to England for a year after graduation to continue his military training. Ghadaffi studied at the famous Royal Military Academy at Sandhurst. In 1966, he returned to Libya and began his career in the signal corp.

In a bloodless coup on September 1, 1969, Ghadaffi and his fellow officers ousted King Idris I. At the time of the coup, Idris I was in Turkey receiving medical treatment. The reins of power had been placed in the hands of Sayyid, the king's nephew. Coup leaders knew Sayyid would quickly crumble under their pressure. The king was easily deposed and the monarchy fell.

It was not automatically assumed that Ghadaffi would attain the position of Libya's new leader. Following the success of the coup came a short power struggle between Ghadaffi and his group of young officers and the older officers and political leaders. In January of 1970, Captain Muammar Ghadaffi was officially ensconced as the leader of Libya and the commander of all of the Libyan armed forces. He gave himself a ceremonial promotion to colonel, a title he has chosen to keep.

With Ghadaffi's take over came the expulsion of all U.S. and British military and civilian personnel. A few days later, on September 14, he took control of 51 percent of the banks.

Ghadaffi's next step was to try to merge the interest and powers of the Arab world under one umbrella—his. He determined that one of his greatest objectives—and by extension the Arab world's greatest objective—would be to sponsor terror worldwide. He also chose to put special emphasis on aiding Palestinian terror against Israel.

That same year, on December 26, a confederation deal was signed between Libya, Egypt, and Sudan. Later, on August 2, 1972, an official merger was declared with Egypt. Seventeen months after that, Libya merged with Tunisia, but that deal lasted only a few hours.

Terrorism was not the only weapon in Ghadaffi's arsenal. Perhaps his best-brandished weapon against the West was oil. Libya has been one of the most powerful forces in the Organization of Petroleum Exporting Countries (OPEC) for years. It was Libya that demanded and convinced the group to put great limits on production. Driving up the prices of oil and natural gas was a tool that Ghadaffi used specifically to antagonize the West. It was Ghadaffi's influence in

OPEC that led to drastic gas shortages that virtually incapacitated the United States in 1973.

But not all Arab nations bought into Ghadaffi's plan. In OPEC, there has historically been tremendous tension between Saudi Arabia and Libya or, better put, between the Saudi royal family and Muammar Ghadaffi. The conflict is over the use of oil production as a fulcrum to achieve greater Arab goals in the conflict against the West. The 1973 OPEC oil embargo on the United States, for example, was part of Ghadaffi's plan to shift support away from Israel and toward the Palestinians and the Arabs. Though the tension has subsided slightly, Ghadaffi did put a hit out on Saudi Arabia's crown prince.

Libyan disdain for all things Western flourished even though that disdain brought with it terrible economic hardship. Such was the case when Libya was being embargoed by the United Nations and other Western democracies—an embargo begun in direct response to Ghadaffi's obvious and public sponsorship of world terror.

This decades-long support of terror has been particularly focused on the training and financial support of Palestinian terror. As a result, the United States declared Libya a state sponsor of terrorism on December 29, 1979, and began an embargo against the nation in March of 1982.

In 1986, Libya was linked to the terrorist bombing of a club in West Berlin. One U.S. soldier was killed and many were wounded. At that point, then president Ronald Reagan gave the okay to assassinate Ghadaffi, because the Libyan leader was in direct contradiction to stated American foreign policy. On April 17, 1986, the United States bombed Tripoli.

There are many large-scale terrorist operations not only sponsored but carried out by Libya, including the bombing of Pan Am flight 103 over Lockerbie, Scotland, on Christmas Eve 1988. In April of 1992, even harsher sanctions were imposed after Libya refused to turn over two suspects involved in the airliner bombing. That terror attack killed 259 people in the jetliner, plus another eleven who were on the ground.

Libya is also responsible for the 1989 bombing of a French airliner flying over West Africa in which 196 people were killed.

Ghadaffi apparently had a change of heart concerning the use of terror in 1994. Since then, Libyan sponsorship for international terror has decreased, largely due to the international sanctions imposed on the country. Those sanctions hit Libya in the pocket, severely limiting its economic growth. Libyan oil sales around the world were restricted, and anyone doing business with the West was prohibited from buying anything Libyan, even through a third party.

Finally, on February 13, 1999, Ghadaffi agreed to extradite the two suspects accused of the 1988 Pan Am disaster. On April 5, the two were handed over to the United States, finally suspending U.S. sanctions against Libya. On September 12, 2003, the United Nations voted to suspend all sanctions against Libya after Ghadaffi accepted a deal to pay the families of the 270 victims of the Pan Am terror attack.

In another turnabout, Ghadaffi called for the Pan Arab expulsion of all Palestinians in September of 1995. His call was the result of ongoing Palestinian-Israeli negotiations aimed at determining a final resolution of their conflict. Ghadaffi felt betrayed by the Palestinians, accusing them of having abandoned their true goal by negotiating with Israel. He said that in turn, the entire Arab world should abandon the Palestinians.

Libya was definitely one of the biggest and proudest sponsors of terror the world has known. It looks like things may be changing, but you never know. The public change in Ghadaffi's attitude seemed to come about with the U.S. invasion of Iraq and the capture of Saddam Hussein. One telling note is that Libya footed part of the bill for the democratic defense of Iraq's Saddam Hussein. Indeed, Ghadaffi's daughter Aicha even joined Saddam's defense team.

There are two possible explanations for Ghadaffi's apparent change of heart. Perhaps he witnessed what happened to Saddam and assumed that he was next on the list. Maybe he saw the light and decided to redeem himself rather than face similar embarrassment in front of his fellow Arab brethren. Or perhaps a light came on in his head and he realized there was a vacancy in the position of dominant Arab leader in the Middle East.

So now Ghadaffi is making nice. He has voluntarily offered to give up his own weapons of mass destruction and has visited Washington for diplomatic talks.

Even before the U.S. invasion of Iraq, Ghadaffi had a manipulative relationship with the West. He wants to be a player in the world but sees—and fears—the risks of exposing his society to Western influences and culture.

Almost everyone in Libya is Sunni Muslim. Less than 1 percent of the population is Kharji. There are also about fifty thousand (which doesn't even merit a percentage point) Roman Catholics, almost all of them in Tripoli. Catholics are still there as a remnant of the original Italian colonizers. The country has about 20 percent non-Libyans and in some areas, especially in Tripoli, that number is up to 50 percent non-Libyans.

There has been a tremendous Berber influence in Libya, and many among the population are a mix of black African and Berber. The Berbers are the original inhabitants of North Africa. Roman colonization of Africa was the first real blow to the Berber identity; the next was the Arab conquest, which almost wiped out Berber culture and language.

Ghadaffi has outlawed Islamic fundamentalist groups in Libya. The groups that do exist, organize and operate in a clandestine manner. Powerful security forces actively search out and arrest fundamentalist leaders found in Libya.

There is no chance for democratic change in Libya short of a coup or an invasion. Since Ghadaffi seized power in 1969, the leadership in Libya has been stable. Ghadaffi rules. There have been a number of attempts on his life, including several by the United States, but by and large his system is in place and is there to stay.

The line of succession is firmly in place, and it is almost a certainty that one of Ghadaffi's sons—al Saadi, a soccer player, or Saif Islam, a British-educated PhD student—will take over the mantel of leadership at the designated time.

However, there is certainly a movement afoot for the current and future governments to liberalize and open their society. It all depends on Ghadaffi's self-interest as leader. It is a trade-off: if he liberalizes his society, he must cede some of his power to the masses or to others in power; if it is worth the risk, he will do it— even though it scares him.

Surprisingly, there are national elections in Libya. But not for Ghadaffi; he does not run for office. The elections are held to choose committees for the General People's Congress, which then elects a prime minister.

Ghadaffi created a new form of government in Libya that has not been seen or experienced anywhere else in the world. He called it a *jamahiriya*. It is a modification of the Arabic word *jumhuriya*, which means "republic." Translated, Ghadaffi's jamahiriya means "the people's state." It is an unusual blend of socialism in Islam, out of place in the world in which they live, and very foreign sounding even in Arabic

Not to be outdone by any rival ruler, Ghadaffi has created his own, singularly personal theory of politics and life. In a direct rip off of Mao Tse-Tung's *Little Red Book* Ghadaffi wrote and distributed his *Green Book*. For Mao, red was the symbol of Communism. In Ghadaffi's version, the color green was chosen because for the Muslim and Arab worlds it symbolizes the fertile crescent, Islam.

At times, he refers to himself as "First Citizen." He is often called "Father of His People"—a title he enjoys. Most often, however, the despot Ghadaffi is called "Leader of the Revolution."

No doubt about it. This Libyan leader runs a true dictatorship under the guise of a pure Socialist state.

Ghadaffi is a leader who likes to shake things up, which makes it hard to know what he really has up his sleeve. He is unpredictable, and his actions are often spontaneous. His reactions seem to come from the gut with little care for repercussions or world opinion.

Since the fall of Iraq and the capture of Saddam Hussein, Colonel Ghadaffi has displayed some uncharacteristic moves. He has met with U.S. officials and offered to allow them in to monitor Libyan weapons of mass destruction. In a word, the man who openly sponsored terror against the West opened up—at least on the surface—to the largest power in the West. Power move? Ploy? Fear of the same fate met by Saddam? Desire to take over the Arab world with U.S. approval? We'll see what his next moves are.

16

BASHAR ASSAD
Myopic Eye Doctor

Born: 1965
Died: Still living
Ruled: 2000–present

It all began in 1970 when Hafez Assad seized power in Syria and was named president. His son would be groomed to eventually assume the legacy of power.

It was a perfect fit. The son grew up to be full of personality, the consummate sportsman, the artful playboy, and a menacing thug. With a little more cunning, he was someone who could easily carry on in his father's large and dictatorial footsteps. Cunning was his father's trademark; it was a trait that made him simultaneously dangerous and successful.

Everything was going according to plan until one day in 1994 Basil—the son who would be king—crashed his car while driving 150 miles per hour and died. The Syrians blamed the Israeli Mossad for the death of the beloved Basil, but in reality it was bravado and machismo that killed Syria's heir.

And that left Bashar.

Bashar Assad was second best. It was never intended for this shy, retiring son who had remained aloof from his father's regime to inherit the mantle of leadership. He stood six feet five inches tall, was rather ungainly, and always looked uncomfortable during public appearances. Rather than pursue political and military power, Bashar opted to study medicine and become an ophthalmologist.

Unwilling to relinquish power to his brother, and instead of handing over the reins of authority to other members of his ruling Ba'ath party, Hafez chose to groom Bashar for leadership. In ill health, the father knew he had to work quickly. He never dreamed he would have as little time as he did.

Returning to Damascus from London where he was pursuing a postdoc after the death of his brother, Bashar had little time to hone his skills in martial law. He became an army doctor and then gained the rank of colonel in the Syrian army. It was his only military experience, but as his father knew, it was important for the future president to have at least a cursory military credential. Hafez Assad died in June of 2000. Bashar was hardly ready for a position of Syrian leadership.

Despite their hesitations, the old-guard members of the Ba'ath Party fought for the younger Assad. They pushed through his election to the presidency rather than risk losing ultimate political power to rival factions within the government. He was made head of the Ba'ath Party and of the armed forces. Bashar Assad was confirmed by popular referendum on July 10, 2000.

If he is looking down at his son today, Hafez must be smiling. It was a rocky start—and the going is still very tough—but Bashar has taken his father's legacy to heart, and Syria remains a dictatorship.

His first days, however, were far from this father's dream. When Bashar Assad came to power, no one thought he could handle it. The Syria he inherited was one of the poorest countries in the Middle East. It had a staggering balance of trade and extremely high unemployment. Lebanon was a major part of the economy of Syria. He had no link to the regime and no friends. The Americans thought he would soften Syria's stand on Israel. The French thought he would ease his control over Lebanon. Saudi Arabia thought they could buy him off.

Bashar initially displayed a liberal, liberated approach to ruling. He legalized mobile phones. He legalized the Internet. He arrested a former chief of intelligence on charges of corruption. It looked as if the West might finally have an ally.

One of Bashar's first public comments concerned the Internet: he wanted everyone in Syria to be using a computer online. It was a crazy comment and proved just how little Bashar understood about the country he was governing and how far removed his leadership was from the people of Syria. Before using the Internet, you need phones. And with the Internet comes freedom. The people of Syria had neither. They still have neither. The concept of the Internet is completely contrary to the governance of his father, of his own advisors, and—now—of President Assad. The plan died. Reforms stopped. The new ruler learned his lesson quickly.

Syria is a poor country divided by ethnicity and religion. Even though the majority of Syrians—seventeen million citizens—are Sunni, the country is ruled by the minority Alawites. On January 3, 2001, the Syrian newspaper *Al-Sharq al-Awsat* published a wedding announcement: Bashar Assad had chosen for his wife a London-born Syrian, who was the daughter of a distinguished Sunni family. It was an astute political move.

The new Mrs. Assad (Asma al-Akhras, or Emma to her friends) grew up in West London and graduated from London's Kings College with a degree in computer sciences. After graduation, the bride worked for Deutsche Bank and JP Morgan. She speaks Arabic, English, French, and Spanish. Bashar married a Western woman with Muslim roots and then kept her in seclusion for three months.

When Asma al-Akhras al-Assad made her first public appearance, she was unveiled and wearing a skirt that ended above her knee. The occasion was a meeting with the president of Bulgaria. In contrast to her mother-in-law who was rarely seen publicly, Asma has joined her husband on trips abroad and stood by his side when the pope paid a visit to Damascus.

It did not take long before Bashar became a feared tyrant. Bashar and his government were behind the February 14, 2005, assassination of Lebanese prime minister Rafik Hariri in a car-bombing that also killed twenty-two other Lebanese. Killing the Lebanese prime minister protected Bashar's regime. Syrian control was on the wane in Lebanon as the popularity of Americans, Saudis, and French grew. Something had to be done, and assassination was the answer.

Bashar had kept most of the tyranny of leadership at arm's length. The reality is that he tapped his brother-in-law, Assef Shawqat, to act as his own long arm of justice. Shawqat, deputy chief of military intelligence, is responsible for purging the entire old guard and security establishment. With Bashar's blessing. They are jointly responsible for the elimination of economic reforms in Syria.

Bashar has become even more conservative in his attitude toward the West than his father had been, and more antagonistic toward Israel. All high hopes for the younger, enlightened Assad have disappeared.

Bashar Assad is a known supporter and sponsor of terror.

After 9/11, the Syrian ruler showed his strength. He began to share intelligence with the United States. The two countries even created a liaison for sharing counterterror information. But after the U.S. invasion of Iraq, it became clear that Bashar was providing support for the forces that were fighting the United States. He may even have hidden Ba'athist fighters and materials, including weapons of mass destruction.

Relations between Syria and the United States are strained. The U.S. Congress has passed an essential piece of legislation titled the Syria Accountability Act, which stipulates that Syria must fight terror or lose its benefits from the United States. One of the most important factors in all decisions made by Bashar is the opinion of his sister, Dr. Bushra Assad—a pharmacist by training and the wife of trusted aide General Assef Shawqat. Bushra is called the brain of Syrian politics and had a very active and influential role in her father's decisions. If there is any line connecting the dots between father and son, it is Bushra, the daughter and sister.

Bashar is a study in complexity and ambiguity. He speaks English and French like a native. He is still very enamored of Western technology and culture, but none of that makes him any less a tyrant. Bashar has been developing strong ties with Iran. Ahmadinejad, the tyrannical leader of Iran, has become a close friend of Bashar.

As far as Bashar is concerned, he is in the perfect position. He is a true ally of the Arab world but he can, at will, open channels with the Western world. He represents Arab honor and defies the West. He is extending his hand to Iran because the countries are united in their perception as pariahs.

On a Tuesday in December 2001, President and Mrs. Assad announced the birth of their first child—a son. The baby was born in England where his maternal grandparents reside. He is named after his paternal grandfather: Hafez. Syrian tradition continues.

17

SADDAM HUSSEIN
Dean of the Demons

Born: 1937
Died: 2006
Ruled: 1979–2003

According to a wise old folk expression, a person lives up to his or her given name. The name Saddam is Arabic for "one who confronts."

He is Saddam Hussein, also appropriately known as the "Butcher of Baghdad." He is the most recognized Arab leader of the twentieth century, and arguably the most recognized Arab leader of the entire modern era. And by now, we have all seen him in his underwear.

In the Arab and Muslim world, Saddam Hussein was both hated and loved. He was hated as a ruthless tyrant, a demon, and a dictator. He was hated because he was a mass murderer. He was loved because he was the one who stood up to the West: he showed no fear of the United States, and he refused to accept or acknowledge the existence of Israel.

To this day, the "Arab street" loves Saddam Hussein. The "Arab street" is a concept in the Arab world that most closely resembles the Latin concept of vox populi, or the voice of the people. It is the notion that one can take the pulse of a society by listening to the voices of people on the street. For the Arab world, it is a very important concept.

He was hated, he was loved, and—for good reason—Saddam Hussein was feared.

Hesitant to broach the subject for fear of the consequences, a British journalist once shyly, and with great trepidation, asked the ruler of Iraq if it was true that he tortured, killed, imprisoned, and eliminated his opponents. The response was bone chilling: "Of course. What do you expect if they oppose the regime?"

Saddam Hussein was a megalomaniac of the highest order. There are few leaders in modern world history who have achieved his level of self-love and self-delusion. Everything Saddam did was to better secure his hold on Iraq. Everything.

The life of Saddam Hussein began rather simply and sadly. The man who would rule Iraq as ultimate dictator for nearly a quarter-century—who was able to intimidate the world until he was ousted from power by United States and Coalition forces—was born on April 27, 1937. His father died when Saddam was very young, and his mother remarried. At age ten, Saddam left the small town of Tikrit and his abusive stepfather to seek refuge with his uncle in Bahgdad. The uncle, Kharaillah Tulfah, was one of the leaders of a Nazi-backed coup to oust the monarchy.

Saddam's uncle put him in school and made certain the boy graduated. But it was Saddam's uncle who taught him his most valuable lessons. In word and in deed, Kharaillah Tulfah taught his young nephew and protégé never to show weakness and never to back down from an enemy, regardless of how formidable the enemy may appear.

Under the influence of his uncle, Saddam joined the Ba'ath Party, a political party that embraced pan-Arabism, Arab socialism, and Arab nationalism. The Ba'ath Party, Saddam Hussein's earliest political affiliation and party of choice, was modeled after the Nazi party.

In 1958, he joined a movement to overthrow the monarchy in Iraq. The movement succeeded in ousting King Faisal II, but Saddam was displeased with the new government. As a result, he participated in a CIA-backed plot to assassinate the new prime minister. Saddam was shot in the leg during the assassination attempt. He fled back to Tikrit, and with the aid of the CIA and Egypt, he was secretly taken to Syria and then to Lebanon. In Lebanon, Saddam Hussein joined in CIA training sessions.

Saddam made his way to Cairo where he studied law at Cairo University. Law was a good choice for Hussein. He spent years in and out of prisons and more than once chose to defend himself. The future ruler of Iraq returned in 1963 to his home country, where the Ba'ath party was in control. But it was short-lived. Iraq was a country in chaos; there were coups and corruption. Murder and mayhem ruled, even before Saddam Hussein ascended his throne. He just exacerbated an already bad situation, taking it to unforeseen and unimaginable heights.

Hussein remained in jail until his party returned to power in July of 1968. He then decimated everyone who stood in his way to becoming the president of Iraq. It was a bloody road filled, literally, with heads and torsos. On July 16, 1979, Saddam Hussein was elected president of Iraq.

The country of Iraq is divided into three large groups. The majority of the population is Shiite, followed by the Sunnis—a significant minority, but a minority nonetheless. The smallest of the groups is the Kurds. Saddam is a Sunni. The majority was not rightfully his, so he beat his opponents into submission through intimidation. He unleashed poison gas on the Kurds to weaken them significantly enough so that their fighting force would be seriously reduced. He murdered hundreds of thousands of his own citizens. According to the doctrine of Hussein, the only way to keep Iraq from splitting off into little provinces is to rule with an iron fist. It was fear that kept the population of Iraq in line.

Everywhere Iraqis turned, there was Saddam. Ancient Middle Eastern rulers built temples in their own honor and erected statues of themselves. Saddam built the statues, and then he erected billboards—big, life-sized billboards of Saddam Hussein, despot, dictator, demon. The only people Hussein felt he could trust at all were his family members and the members of his clan. The clan was an extended family of people who came from his village of Tikrit. They were his greatest powerbase and strength. They were his allies—most of the time.

Sometimes, even his clan violated the sacred trust of Saddam Hussein. He married a cousin, and together they had several children. The children married and the family grew. On one occasion, two of Saddam's sons-in-law—members of the inner circle and destined for high-powered positions—crossed the border into Jordan to seek refuge. They defected, requesting asylum. Jordan granted their request. But then there was a turnaround; Iraqi diplomats were dispatched to bring the renegade sons-in-law back home.

The men were put in a vehicle and brought back to the Jordanian-Iraqi border. They got out of the car on the Jordanian side and crossed the border to vehicles waiting to return them to Saddam. That was the last time they were ever seen.

The future of Saddam's Iraq was placed in the hands of his sons: Uday and Qusaay. Uday was the older brother, and was badly injured in an assassination attempt. The assassins were dispatched by his father. Yes, Saddam even intended to kill his son.

Remember, this is the Iraq of Saddam Hussein. The concept is almost medieval: a father, a powerful and mighty leader, so threatened by his son that he would place the order to have him killed. In the end, after the botched attempt on his son's life, Saddam and Uday became closer. Uday was vicious, more brutal than even his father. He took pleasure in gratuitous violence. He enjoyed instilling pain, inflicting torture, murdering, and raping. Hussein's evil was predicated upon political purpose. Uday's brutality was predicated upon his own sheer enjoyment.

After the invasion of Iraq by the United States and Coalition forces, Saddam went into hiding. He was discovered in a spider hole on December 14, 2003. But was it the real Saddam?

As mighty and masterful and crafty as Saddam Hussein was, he was also extremely paranoid. He had doubles. He altered the faces of Iraqi men to look like him. They dressed like him and moved like him. He sent these men out into public. Had there been an attempt against his life, he rationalized, someone else would die. He would be safe, hiding in a bunker within a bunker within a palace.

Saddam Hussein was tried and convicted for perpetrating a mass murder that took place in 1982, a mass murder that left 148 Shiite Muslims in the northern town of Dujail dead. The Butcher of Baghdad was tried for just one incident, convicted for just one case of mass murder. In truth, Saddam Hussein was guilty of tens of thousands of mass murders, but one gruesome example was enough.

On December 30, 2006, at 6:00 a.m. in a place called Camp Justice—formerly known as Banzai, the seat of his Military Intelligence Unit,—Saddam Hussein was executed. It was at Banzai that many Iraqis were tortured and then hung by decree from Saddam.

Even in death the Iraqi leader insisted on calling the shots, on doing things his own way. As he was being prepared for execution Saddam Hussein refused to cover his face by donning the black hood. He was not afraid. He would die as a hero. He would die as a leader. Only minutes away from death, Saddam Hussein still saw himself as a proud fighter. And that is why he preferred to be executed not on a gallows but by a firing squad—a choice he was denied.

The hanging was a farce. In an unfortunate flip-flop of moral destiny, it was Saddam Hussein who maintained his dignity while his executioners sunk to emotional lows by looking their charge in the face and shouting out, "Go to hell."

The moment was recorded on a cell phone camera. Almost immediately the execution of Saddam Hussein was posted on the

Internet. Way before there was an official version of the death, local Iraqis and citizens of the world heard the trap door open and listened for the snap of Saddam Hussein's neck.

The world is a better place.

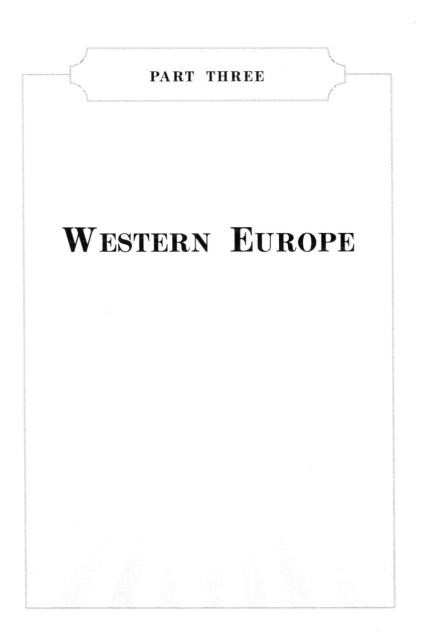

PART THREE

WESTERN EUROPE

The continent of Europe gets it name from Europa, the character in Greek mythology. Europa was the daughter of Phoenix, king of Phoenicia. She was stunningly beautiful, and the god Zeus was captivated by her. Disguised as a white bull, Zeus carried Europa across the sea to Crete. She became the mother of Europe. She was, in essence, Europe's first queen.

The Greeks laid the foundation for European civilization. The Romans expanded civilization by taking it across borders, integrating new cultures, and incorporating new ideas. The Romans brought Christianity to Europe. They brought it from the Holy Land where Queen Helena, the mother of Roman Emperor Constantine, became a Christian. The Roman Empire fell in the fifth century, but Europe survived and rose anew. The Vatican became the new Rome.

For the next thousand years, there was a breakdown of classic tradition, revived only in the fifteenth century by the Renaissance. The sixteenth century saw the birth of the Protestant Reformation, which gave rise to new ideas and new forms of religious expression. The groundwork was laid so that the Enlightenment could flourish in the seventeenth century.

The Enlightenment was a movement that embraced the concept of the citizen. Everyone was equal and everyone had rights—natural rights bestowed by the Creator. And the Enlightenment gave rise to emancipation. Greece and Rome were replaced by France and Germany. Constitutions were written, and laws were passed protecting the freedom of the people. It was that emancipation that ended the right of kings. After the French Revolution, the free people of Europe no longer needed the rule of monarchs.

For centuries the concept of leader in Europe meant a religious leader. The pope was the real leader. Kings were warriors; they were there to protect the religious doctrine and faith. Many of the formal names of the kings of England included "Defender of the Faith," "Protector of Christianity," or even "Liberator of Jerusalem."

Freedom was on the fast track in Western Europe. With freedom came industrialization, and with industrialization came anxiety followed by economic instability. The response was to step back into history; Western European nations handed over their freedoms of their own accord to thugs and dictators.

1

ALEXANDER THE GREAT
The Classic Dictator

Born: 356 BCE
Died: 323 BCE
Ruled: 334–323 BCE

Alexander was the greatest thug of all time. The greatest warrior of all time. The greatest dictator of all time. Alexander the Great conquered the world. He did not do it alone. At his side in every battle was Bucephalus—a huge beast of a horse.

Alexander was the son of another great warrior, Philip of Macedonia. One day—as the story goes—Alexander watched as his father and his strong men tried and failed to tame a beautiful but wild horse. Alexander was mesmerized. All of ten or eleven years old, Alexander asked for a turn with the black stallion. He approached the animal, whispered in its ear, mounted, and rode away.

The rest is history—or legend. Alexander was flesh and blood, but his spirit, courage, bravery, and mastery of the military soared so high above everyone else that he took on mythological proportions. Even his mother attached supernatural qualities to her son. His true father, she said, was not Philip but the god Zeus.

Gordium was the name of a town in Galatia. In the town square stood a wagon tethered to a post with a knotted rope. The rope was so knotted and gnarled that it had never been successfully untied. The knotted rope on the wagon in Gordium became legend. Whoever shall untie this knot shall conquer Asia, went the legend.

As it so happened, Alexander was in the area on the way to meet his general, Parmenio. Always up for a good challenge, he took the rope in his hands. He twisted and turned. He consulted with advisors. And then Alexander unsheathed his sword and sliced the rope in two. *Luein* has a double meaning in Greek: one is "untie"; the other is "resolve." Alexander resolved the problem. Today, "to cut the Gordian knot" is a way of saying a problem is solved. Naturally, Alexander went on to conquer Asia.

Alexander was taught to think by the great philosopher Aristotle. He was taught to fight by his father the great military tactician Philip of Macedonia. Philip bequeathed to his son Greece, great wealth, and a military legacy. Philip left his son a military strategy so effective that it is still being used today: Philip taught Alexander to arrange his army to form a phalanx.

Alexander would study a battlefield and devise a plan for how to best defeat his army. He would arrange his men in phalanx formation. The men in Alexander's armies were exclusively Macedonian; it was an insurance policy on loyalty. His unit consisted of 256 men arranged so that there would be sixteen men on each side. The members of the phalanx would carry a special spear called a *sarissa*.

Alexander's spears were only about thirteen feet long, making them easy to wield in tight situations. The hasta, or conventional spear, that was used by Alexander's enemies was at least three feet longer and much more unwieldy in battle.

Most often the phalanx was a square, but it would alter shape depending on the needs of each battle. It could be formed into a line, wedge, triangle, or even a circle. The army would get directions from Alexander, who would communicate with his men by transmitting his battle commands through the waving of flags and the sounding of trumpets. And as he led them, he was often the first into battle.

Alexander fought using battering rams, siege towers, bridges, and catapults. There were horsemen for each battle—heavy cavalry and light cavalry—and javelin throwers. When the battle was over, the men were sent home to Greece to relax, to be with their wives, to enjoy the spoils of war, and to spread the word of Alexander the Invincible.

Alexander never lost a battle, but he was wounded many times. His head, neck, thigh, leg, and shoulder were all injured. Even his lung was pierced with an arrow in India. Alexander was a survivor. He did not set out to conquer the world. He set out on a journey to see the world, accompanied with artists, historians, and botanists. Then he enveloped the world. He came, he conquered, and he instituted democracy. It was not democracy as we know it, but a form of government and economic life that revolutionized each society and the world.

Leading by example, Alexander knew his soldiers' names and praised them for acts of heroism. His troops were motivated and confident. Alexander risked his life but never showed fear. He knew that war was as much a psychological game as it was a military game. And that is why Alexander the Greek chose for his wife a Persian woman.

The world was a big place—even bigger than Alexander ever imagined it to be. His empire grew: he conquered regions, states, and other empires far away from Greece. Alexander knew he had to consolidate his power base.

Traditionally, Greek leaders maintained a sense of distance from their conquests, keeping Greece pure and free from potential contamination. Alexander thought that unwise. He proved that he was a leader unlike any other. He was a leader bent on staying— not just raping and reaping the benefits of his conquest.

Love was not part of the equation in his choice of a wife. Alexander married a woman from Persia in order to integrate his own Greek tradition with Persian tradition. He encouraged his men to do the same. In Macedonia, he dressed like a Macedonian. In Persia, Alexander dressed like a Persian.

Alexander the Great did not die in war. He died of fatigue, alcoholism, and the residual effects of his wounds. He died of a high fever while on a boating trip in Babylonia. He died like any ordinary man.

2

JULIUS CAESAR
Loved by the Masses, Hated by Friends

Born: 100 BCE
Died: 44 BCE
Reign: 49–44 BCE

J ulius Caesar has the honor of being one of the greatest leaders of all time. And the assassination of Julius Caesar, dictator perpetuus, is probably the most famous murder in history.

March 15 is referred to as the Ides (or middle days) of March, and it is always remembered with a warning. "Beware the Ides of March," said the oracle. One never knows what will happen on that day. Julius Caesar certainly had no clue it was the day he would meet his death.

Caesar was killed by the people who were closest to him—the people one would have expected to support and protect him. The plotters of his death were all patricians, family, and supposed friends. They were leaders and senators, his protégé and adopted son, the famous Marcus Brutus.

Brutus began the conspiracy and orchestrated the assassination. A group of senators invited Caesar to the Forum in order to present him with a petition. But the petition was a hoax. Caesar was brought there only to be killed. One true friend and supporter, Mark Antony, tried unsuccessfully to warn Caesar of his impending doom.

It was bloody and gory. So gruesome was his murder that Caesar was blinded by the amount of blood that came gushing into his eyes. But before going blind, the emperor Caesar saw his attackers. His response is immortalized in *Julius Caesar*, the great Shakespearean play: "*Et tu Brute*?" Caesar asked. You, too, Brutus? You too; the man I cherished like a son?

Julius Caesar was a great warrior, statesman, and politician. He ruled over Rome and transformed it from a republic into an empire.

According to tradition, Julius Caesar was born by caesarean section. Maybe. Until that time the operation was performed exclusively on dead mothers—women who died during labor or for some other reason—in order to save the child. But Caesar's mother was alive long into his life. Folklore has it that the operation was named after the child. We don't know for sure, but we do know that the name Caesar comes from the words *caesus sum*, "to cut."

Caesar was born to aristocracy. His parents were citizens, not slaves, but they were of modest means. In upper-class Rome, there were those who had money and those who did not. This family did not. Then Caesar's aunt Julia married a general in the Roman army—a man named Gauis Marius who, through connections and experience, created a small fortune. With time, Marius became one of the richest men in all of Rome, and the wealth trickled down to the rest of the family.

Much of what we know about Julius Caesar comes from the writings of a series of ancient historians and from his own writings.

According to Plutarch's history, we know that Caesar was educated on the island of Rhodes where he had the same teacher as the great orator Cicero: Apollonius Molon. As he crossed the Aegean Sea on the trip back to Rome, Caesar was kidnapped by a band of pirates from Cilicia. The ransom was twenty gold talents. Caesar was incensed—not that they had successfully kidnapped him but that they asked such a paltry sum for his release. He was, in his own estimation, worth much more—at least fifty talents. Caesar ranted and raved that he would make his captors pay for their mistake. When they ignored him, he continually reminded them of his vow of vengeance. Eventually, the ransom was paid and Caesar was freed. He put together a fleet, easily captured the pirates, and delivered them to local authorities. The governor put them in prison. Caesar was incensed, and he made good on his word.

Caesar went to the prison where his pirate captors were held. He took them out of the prison and publicly killed each one, leaving them hanging for all to see.

You either loved Julius Caesar, or you hated him. For most of his public life the masses adored him. His peers, however, rejected him. They taunted Caesar and plotted against him, but Caesar was a man who set his goals early in life. He forged ahead. He had the skill, determination, and ruthlessness to combine military strength with political insight. With that he captured the world. His military strength allowed him to impose the Roman influence on all areas he conquered and occupied. His political insight taught him to entice those same communities with Roman culture and politics. In outlying areas, Caesar's subjects actually yearned to be more Roman than Rome.

The first real political position Caesar attained was Pontifex Maximus. The election was a tough race against several of the most powerful personalities in Rome. But Caesar emerged victorious. Next, he was elected praetor of Outer Iberia, a position that allowed him to conquer and envelope even more lands for Rome. His soldiers loved him; they revered him. In 60 BCE, Julius Caesar became a member of the Centuriate Assembly as a senior consul of the Roman Republic. Later he was appointed proconsular governor of Transalpine Gaul and Illyria.

Caesar was expanding his power base, forging political alliances, making friends, and making enemies. For the most part—with notable exceptions—Caesar's friends were like family, and family members were friends. According to Plutarch, Caesar conquered eight hundred cities and three hundred tribes. A million men were sold into slavery, and three million died in battle. Suffice it to say that there were a lot of people who died and many, many slaves were sold.

Then Julius Caesar, the man portrayed in art with a garland crowning his head, achieved his crowning glory in battle. He started the Gallic Wars, during which he conquered Gaul (today's France), and Romanized its people. It is the great victory of Gaul that has spawned the historic parallels between Alexander the Great and Julius Caesar. Gaul would never again have a revolution until the fall of Rome in 476 AD.

Even with this great victory, Caesar remained unpopular among his peers.

Led by Pompey, the Roman senate in 50 BCE demanded that

Caesar return from Gaul to Rome and send his army home. The senate said Caesar's term as proconsul was over, that he had no authority to command an army and no permission to renew his position in absentia. Caesar refused. He suspected that he would be arrested as soon as he returned and knew that with no official political position and with no army as backup, he would have neither power nor immunity.

Pompey had once been Caesar's ally. He was the husband of Caesar's daughter, Julia, who had died in while giving birth. He had also been Caesar's student and was treated like a son. Now he was Caesar's adversary. Pompey publicly condemned Caesar and called him treasonous.

On January 10, 49 BCE, Caesar crossed the Rubicon—the official Italian border—on his way to Rome. That crossing has given rise to another famous expression: the crossing of the Rubicon. Caesar traveled with only one army legion, the Thirteenth Legion, but no one knew that. He proclaimed, "*Alea iacta est.*" Today historians differ on the meaning of those words. Some claim Caesar was saying, "The die is cast." Others read, "Let the dice fly high." The first interpretation would mean that his destiny was already set; the second would mean that his future was up to the chance of rolling dice. Either way, it was a powerful pronouncement.

Caesar pursued Pompey and Pompey's armies. With his victory, Caesar was appointed dictator. Then he resumed his hunt of Pompey, who had fled to Egypt. An officer of King Ptolemy the XIII, the pharaoh of Egypt, brought Caesar Pompey's head. When Caesar saw the decapitated head, he cried. It was probably because of that specific act—the bringing of the head—that Caesar sided with

Cleopatra against her brother Ptolemy in their struggle for power and civil war.

Caesar had three wives and many mistresses. He had one legitimate daughter, Julia. As public as the relationship between Caesar and Cleopatra was, it was not considered adulterous according to Roman law. Adultery, like marriage, could only take place between two Roman citizens. And since Cleopatra was queen of Egypt, it was considered to be nothing more than a long, glitzy affair. They had a child together—Ptolemy XV Caesar, known as Caesarion. Caesar and Cleopatra moved to Rome. From there, Caesar darted quickly from conquest to conquest, from the Middle East to Africa to parts in between and then back home again. His conquest and subsequent annihilation of King Pharnaces II of Pontus was so quick, even for Caesar, that he described the event with the words *veni, vidi, vici* (I came, I saw, I conquered).

Despite the disdain his peers had for him, Caesar was without any real enemies upon his return home. Quite the opposite, actually. There were games in Caesar's honor, and he was awarded the gown of triumph—the purple robe of kingship in ancient Rome.

Julius Caesar, who had served as dictator for ten terms, had bestowed upon himself the title of dictator for life. Statues were erected in his honor. Coins were struck with his likeness. He was granted the title liberator, meaning he brought Roman civilization to the world. He was invincible.

He tried to reform Rome by instituting new laws, including one that said if a citizen killed a noncitizen or anyone of a lower class, the property of the citizen would be forfeited. He tried to institute proper taxing and management of farms and industry.

Julius Caesar was declared king (*rex* in Latin), but he rejected the title. His response was, "I am the Republic," by which he meant that he was not simply the leader of a place or society; rather, he represented the entire system that was in place. It was clear to everyone but his jealous rivals—his fellow leaders—that only Julius Caesar, son of Gaius Julius Caesar the Elder and Aurelia Cotta, could really keep everything together in Rome.

And yes, he was bald. The great Julius Caesar, ruler of the Roman Empire, sported one of the most famous comb-overs in history.

3

HENRY VIII
A Very Fat Ruler

Born: 1491
Died: 1547
Ruled: 1509–1547

Henry VIII was the master of many titles. He began life as a monarch with the title Henry the Eighth, by the Grace of God, King of England, France and Lord of Ireland.

As reward for attacking Martin Luther and defending the church, Pope Leo X attached another title: Henry the Eighth, by the Grace of God, King of England and France, Defender of the Faith and Lord of Ireland. Pope Paul III tried to remove "Defender of the Faith" after Henry broke with Rome, but an act of parliament ensured the title remained.

The king himself changed the title to Henry the Eighth, by the Grace of God, King of England and France, Defender of the Faith, Lord of Ireland and of the Church of England in Earth Supreme Head.

In an effort not to offend the Irish, who believed that the pope, not the king, was their Lord, "Lord of Ireland" was changed to "King of Ireland."

Finally, the king of England settled on the title Henry the Eighth, by the Grace of God, King of England, France, and Ireland, Defender of the Faith and of the Church of England and also of Ireland in Earth Supreme Head.

On top of all that, he was the first monarch in England to make use of the title majesty.

Majestic titles aside, Henry VIII was the ultimate thug. He intimidated, beat, and beheaded. He was a drunk, a gambler, a cheat, and a womanizer. He had affairs with relatives. He stooped to the lowest levels to get his way. He was gluttonous. At the time of his death he was grossly, obscenely obese.

Henry was a dangerous egotist. Combined with his enormous arrogance was an insecurity of the highest order. The insecurity led to paranoia; the paranoia led to tyrannical and totally unpredictable behavior. Henry even claimed that one of his wives was having an affair with her brother and that they were plotting to assassinate him.

His reign was often determined by whim. There were two forces that motivated Henry: unbridled and unconventional sexual urges, and the desire to produce a son as heir to the throne. Everything about Henry—all his moves, his decisions, his conquests—was done to assuage his ego and guarantee his personal satisfaction.

The young man who was groomed for the throne was not the same man who grew old on the throne. Henry was a descendant of the Tudor dynasty; his father was Henry VII and his mother was Elizabeth of York. As a young man he was praised as a gifted thinker. He was a gambler and played a good game of dice, but he was also an exceptional sportsman, excelling in jousting. He loved music, and as king, he actually penned a somewhat famous musical score called "Pastyme With Good Company"—also known as "The Kynges Ballade."

Henry was a thinker and a writer. He excelled in argumentation and made a name for himself early on as defender of Rome and the Church. This was to prove ironic in his later years when he broke from Rome. In Henry's 1521 treatise against Martin Luther, the king of England argued that the Lutheran reformation was heretical and the antithesis of established religious norms.

Henry used his head and his hands. While most kings commissioned buildings, Henry actually got down and dirty and built the buildings with his own hands. Some of those buildings still stand for us to marvel at today—impressive structures like King's College Chapel in Cambridge and Westminster Abbey in London.

But most of all, Henry VIII is known for his wives. With six wives in all, it gets a bit complicated. Even Henry had a hard time keeping them straight. Among his wives, there were two women named Anne, three women named Catherine, and one woman named Jane. Henry also had a lover named Jane who just happened to be the sister of the first Anne, who was the second wife of Henry.

Some background is essential. Henry was only the second Tudor king. For those who remember their Shakespearean plays, Henry's father killed Richard the Third—the last of the protestant dynasty. Henry was not the eldest son in the family. His brother Arthur was the heir apparent, and his father, Henry VII, was intent on signing a treaty with Spain. The best way to ensure that treaties were not broken was to sign in blood; marriages were arranged between the son of one signatory and the daughter of the other. With the marriage of Arthur and Catherine of Aragon—daughter of Ferdinand II of Spain—Henry VII made his alliance.

Catherine and Arthur were married at the tender age of fifteen. Alas, their union was never consummated; Arthur fell ill and died. All grief aside, the two fathers needed to make a match in order to take advantage of their treaty and attack France. But to arrange a marriage, they now needed the approval of the pope. Rather than saying that Arthur and Catherine's marriage had never been consummated, the monarchs chose to tell the pope that the marriage had been annulled. A papal dispensation in the form of a Papal Bull was granted.

But Henry VII soon became discouraged with the idea of his second son marrying Catherine. The ruling monarch was no longer interested in an alliance with Spain, and the prince announced that the marriage had been arranged without his consent. The merger was called off by canceling the engagement. Henry VII died soon afterward, making his son King Henry VIII.

Ferdinand II still had hopes of controlling England. Despite the hesitations of the pope, the marriage between Henry and Catherine eventually took place. Henry VIII now had both a throne and a wife. He was eighteen years old.

The king was tall and striking. And he quickly became obsessed with the idea of siring a son. Henry was a student of history who believed England had not fared well under female leadership. He was also a student of science and knew that child mortality was very common in England.

Catherine suffered a miscarriage almost immediately after the wedding. The next year a boy was born, but the joy was short lived —he died while still in infancy. Other miscarriages, stillbirths, and infant deaths followed. And then, finally, Princess Mary was born.

In the midst of all this midwifery mayhem, England and Spain were feuding. Politics influenced personalities: there was talk of divorce, and there was reconciliation. Henry tired of his wife but enjoyed his mistresses, Mary Boleyn and Elizabeth Blount. Then one day Henry decided he would no longer wait for Catherine to provide him a son.

Divorcing Catherine was not easily accomplished. The king wanted the original decision permitting the marriage to be rescinded. The only man who could make that decree was Pope Clement, who was in the pocket of Emperor Charles V— Catherine's uncle. Charles V was not about to let Henry be freed from the marriage. Henry and the pope were in conflict, eventually resulting in Henry's excommunication from the Church.

The only way out of the marriage now was for Henry to establish his own church. He became head of the Church of England, and in his church divorce was permitted. Poor Catherine. Not only was she divorced, she lost her title. And little Mary—no longer heir—was declared illegitimate.

Henry decided to marry again, and for his wife he chose the sister of his mistress: Anne Boleyn. It was the same story. Failed pregnancies and then—finally—his daughter Elizabeth was born. Henry was no longer paying attention to his wife; it was Jane Seymour who now captured his fancy. Anne was arrested on Henry's trumped-up charges of witchcraft. The king also accused his queen of treason and of having numerous adulterous relation-ships, including one with her own brother. Anne and her brother were sentenced to death. The pair would either be burned at the stake or beheaded; it was the king's choice, and so off with their heads. Several days later, Henry married Jane.

Like her half-sister Mary, Elizabeth was declared illegitimate. The line of succession now belonged to progeny produced by Jane. Queen Jane died two weeks after the birth of her son, Prince Edward. The entire court mourned with the king.

Henry was skeptical about the heir to his throne, Prince Edward, Duke of Cornwall; the prince was not a healthy boy. The King needed insurance, and he needed an ally against the Church. He found both in the person of Anne of Cleves, sister of the protestant Duke of Cleves. But Henry had only ever seen a portrait of this Anne. It was a doctored portrait and an arranged marriage.

When the king laid eyes upon his future wife, he was appalled. Nevertheless, the marriage took place because, for Henry, it was politically expedient. Yet that marriage, too, was annulled. Anne said the two never consummated their union. She said her hus-band entered her room every night, kissed her on the forehead, and left. Needless to say, this marriage produced no heir. The man who had arranged the marriage, the Earl of Essex, was beheaded.

The very same day that the Earl of Essex was beheaded, Henry took for his wife a young woman named Catherine Howard—the first cousin of Anne Boleyn. This Catherine committed two griev-ous sins: she had an affair, and she hired a former lover to be a member of her court. She was condemned by parliament and sen-tenced to die. The king, who ultimately granted Royal Assent to the sentencing, was given special permission to abstain from the court hearing because it would have been too painful for him. The marriage was annulled, and Catherine was executed. She was eighteen years old at the time of her death.

It was time for another wife. The lucky lady was a widow named Catherine Parr, who worked hard to keep the marriage and the monarchy going. She persuaded the king to reconcile with his daughters, and, although they remained legally illegitimate, the two were back in the line of succession as heirs to the throne. Interestingly, the Tudor monarch who ultimately made the most significant impact on England was not a son, but a daughter: Elizabeth.

Henry VIII chose for his royal motto the *Coeur Loyal*, or true heart. The motto adorned all of the king's royal clothing and was depicted by the word *loyal* (or *loyall*, as it is spelled in Old English) embroidered in the center of a heart.

4

LOUIS XIV
A Monarch's Monarch

Born: 1638
Died: 1715
Ruled: 1643–1715

As tradition dictates, Louis became king of France when his father died. The crown was passed from the head of the thirteenth to the head of the fourteenth in 1643. But the crown was a little too large for the new king. He was barely five years old.

The kingdom belonged to Louis, but only when he came of age. Until then, France was to be governed by one of the great cardinals of the day—Cardinal Mazarin. Like Cardinal Richelieu before him, Mazarin was no ordinary man of the cloth. He was a master leader and a keen manipulator. He was a strategist who understood perfectly not only the games of church politics but also the games of national and international politics. He understood the dynamics of war. And better than anyone else, Mazarin—like Richelieu—understood the pope.

These were all issues far beyond the scope of even the most purebred and precocious wonder child.

Marazin led the country of France until his death when Louis, at long last, was deemed ready to rule one of the greatest powers in the world. And rule he did. The year was 1661. The king was twenty-three years old. The reign of Louis XIV lasted for seventy-two years; he personally ruled for fifty-four of those years. Louis XIV wore the crown longer than any other monarch in all of European history. The great French philosopher Descartes dubbed the seventeenth century the "century of Louis XIV."

Louis XIV was a dictator of the highest order. Motivated by his ego and by vanity, he ruled France with an iron fist. He was also motivated by an obsessive need to be viewed by history in a particularly flattering light—a rather odd concern for a truly despotic leader, but Louis was no ordinary ruler.

Ego dictated most of King Louis' decisions. He chose to go to war because he felt war was a good way to make a mark in history. With an ego that size, Louis naturally assumed France would emerge victorious and that the spoils would be his. Wars with Spain, Austria, and England were where his legacy was to lie.

Louis was dedicated to dominating the seas; he believed waterways would give France the advantage. Ultimately, the king's thinking was correct, but the problem with his analysis at the time was that the great conflicts of France were not across the ocean or even the Mediterranean. France's biggest conflicts were local—Denmark, Sweden, Poland. It was in the regional arena that the real and most significant future would rest.

The impact that Louis XIV, the Sun King, had on the culture of

France is unparalleled. His influence reverberates even today. The king seized upon his own areas of interest and brought them to the world. Louis chose the symbol of the sun—as portrayed with the great Apollo, god of peace and the arts—to be his own emblem.

He was undaunted and determined. His birth long-awaited by his parents, Louis was heralded by France as a gift from God. He was an absolute ruler in part because he was so absolutely confident that the rule was his.

And yet, despite his confidence in his personal right to rule, it was during King Louis' reign that serious questions about the role of the king in European society were raised. The questions centered on the divine right of kings. Was the king the emissary of God? Was he God's intermediary? Was the position of king truly a gift of God, and would a challenge against a king not be a challenge against God?

Louis' greatest contribution to the world—greater but less documented and less popular than the impact that he had on culture and the arts—is the impact he had on religious thought.

In its understanding of the divine right of kings, the kingship took upon itself many roles. The king was the undisputed political and military ruler. He was also chief judge and executioner. Perhaps most significant in the undertanding of divine right, the king assumed the responsibility of chief priest. He was head of all church matters both financial and theological.

Louis XIV took his role as chief priest seriously. He authored an extremely harsh treatise against religious leaders who swayed from his personal understanding of Catholicism. In the world of religion according to King Louis XIV of France, there was no religious office higher than that of king—not even pope.

Seventeenth-century France was a religious country. Louis' strong belief in his own religious powers probably explains why he had fewer religious advisers and appointees in his government than did his predecessors. He appointed religious leaders, but not as government leaders. Most of his religious appointments were at the level of bishops. Because the bishops were in contact with the people, they were the power for the people at the grass-roots level in every major district in the French empire.

The argument as to the role of king and his ultimate responsibility continued to emerge despite every effort by Louis XIV to squelch dissent. His reign produced some of the most important political discussions and writings in history on the dilemma of the divine right of kings.

Does the king make the people, or do the people make the king? That was the debate. If the people make the king, there is no divine right. Therefore, the king is but a political appointee whose role and responsibility is to and for his people. His successes can be judged by the services he provides for the people.

However, if the king makes the people, then nothing the king does is wrong and he has no accountability. The only redress of grievance is by God or the sword. The king could be either defeated in battle or assassinated—both of which would be seen as God's will and punishment.

Not surprisingly, Louis XIV had a problematic relationship with Rome—the seat of religious power. On the one hand, because he was in charge of his own kingdom and head of his own church, he would not submit to Roman authority. On the other hand, he understood the place Rome had in tradition and religious leadership throughout the centuries. He knew the role that popes had played in wars and European governances. Stability and marriages, peace treaties and property deals were influenced by Rome. Alienating Rome would have been unwise, to say the least, and Louis XIV was not unwise.

Tensions were constant between France and the pope. The French ambassador to the Holy See was even excommunicated because of the activities of King Louis. The conflict between the king and the pope was about power and money—nothing else. And yet, the same king and pope united in battle against those who dared to practice forms of Christianity different from theirs—principally the Protestants, Jansenists, and Quietists.

Protestants bore the brunt of the persecution.

Under the dictate of King Louis XIV, Protestants were not permitted to hold any official position in government at any level. They were more heavily taxed than Catholics. They were considered heretics and were fined for refusal to convert. Numerous laws were passed in order to force Protestants to become Catholics. In that way, he was perfectly in sync with Rome.

It is the fierce persecution of non-Catholics pursued by Louis XIV that includes him as one of the most significant thugs and despots in all of history.

Louis possessed a sense of self that allowed him to bend his own rules for his own purposes. He was a womanizer; he collected women the way he collected art. He loved to look at them, to possess them, to caress them. And he had many children with them. Unlike most monarchs before and after him, Louis XIV took pride in his illegitimate children. And he took care of them. They were educated, presented to society, and married off to royalty so that they could one day legitimately wear the royal titles. But they could not inherit their father's crown.

The heir to the throne of Louis XIV died during his father's lifetime. Louis' chosen successor—Louis XV, the son of the Duke of Burgundy—was five years old when the crown was placed on his little head. History repeats.

5

MAXIMILIEN ROBESPIERRE
Off With Their Heads in the Name of Liberté

Born: 1758
Died: 1794
Ruled: 1793–1794

Terror. The word was introduced into our political vocabulary by Maximilien Robespierre—one of the ringleaders and masterminds of the infamous Reign of Terror.

Maximilien Francois Marie Isidore de Robespierre was one of the most important personalities in the French revolution. Maximilien Francois Marie Isidore de Robespierre was at once many different types of people.

He was an honest gentleman above reproach. And it was precisely those positive attributes that turned him into one of the most ruthless men in history. Robespierre needed to be perfect, and he wanted others to be perfect like him. Monarchy and nobility were imperfect. They needed to be eradicated from France.

He was heavily influenced by Rousseau's philosophy of enlightenment, which espoused the theory that a society could be uplifted and vastly improved when it was freed from the bonds of non-democratic leadership.

Rousseau believed a contract should be established between leadership and the people. He called it the "social contract." An authoritarian government of any name, was the antithesis of the social contract, he believed, even if the monarchy was benevolent.

Robespierre was convinced that it was essential for France to move beyond the oppressive monarchy and the revolution. It was his mission. He coined the phrase "Reign of Terror" to describe the period in history following the French Revolution. During that time, supporters of the Republic of France carried out vicious and violent acts of brutality against all who supported the monarchy. Robespierre himself was at the helm of the Reign of Terror.

Robespierre originally entered politics with the intention of shaping the New French Republic. He hoped to liberate society from the ugly and unjust monarchy. All vestiges of the old monarchy needed to be eliminated—all the old cronies, supporters, and sympathizers.

On July 27, 1793, Robespierre became an official ruler of France with his election to the Committee of Public Safety; he became one of the twelve men who ruled France. He had reached his peak of power and politics. The Committee of Public Safety was responsible for the beheading of tens of thousands of French citizens. Anyone with any affiliation to the monarchy was beheaded. Simply believing the monarchy had a role in French society earned a death sentence. Beheadings were so common that they became a form of entertainment in town squares. Refreshments would be sold as the curious and strong of stomach gathered to witness the behead-ings of royalists.

The most common method of beheading was the guillotine. It was quick and easy. One at a time, necks still attached to living, breathing bodies would be placed in the mount and a blade would drop. The severed head would fall into a basket; the blade would be lifted, and the guillotine readied for the next neck. The basket would fill up with heads until there was no room and it needed emptying.

The Reign of Terror was instituted by the Committee of Public Safety in order to liberate France. It made sense to Robespierre, who believed it was a rational extension of his search for perfection. He explained the policy of terror simply and clearly: "Terror is only jus-tice that is prompt, severe, and inflexible. Terror without virtue is disastrous; virtue without terror is impossible (or powerless)."

For Robespierre, terror was a form of government. The object of terror was to create a lifestyle that forced everyone to tow the line. Terror was justice. Terror was unbending.

In 1781, the young Robespierre had become a lawyer. A brilliant student with a promising career ahead of him, he was appointed a criminal judge. But Robespierre resigned his judgeship. Ironically, he couldn't bring himself to pronounce a death sentence. Robespierre's passion for abolishing monarchies could be seen as early as the debates surrounding the fate of King Louis XVI. He argued fervently for the public execution of the monarch. In his eyes, the concept of a king was antithetical to all forms of government. Monarchies had to be permanently done away with. Only when a monarchy was completely decimated would society be free of any future claims to the throne. It would not be enough for Louis XVI to simply step down. His very life was a blight on the future of the Republic and a source of empowerment for the Republic's enemies. And so the king was executed.

The popularity and political power of Robespierre grew quickly. He was without opposition and became the acknowledged dictator of the committee. His laws were passed immediately. And just as quickly the tables were turned. Allies became enemies as Robespierre's power grew, making him a potential threat. He was called a tyrant and was arrested.

Freed by his followers, Robespierre escaped and was taken to the Hotel de Ville in Paris. His brother, Augustin, and several colleagues—his only supporters from the committee—were with him. When the new committee leadership learned Robespierre and others had gained their freedom, another arrest was ordered.

The second arrest was different. His brother, Augustin, jumped from a window. One of Robespierre's associates, Lebas, shot himself. Another, a man—Couthon—was found in a stairwell with broken arms and legs. And Robspierre was shot in the jaw.

According to some historians, Robespierre was shot by a young police officer named Merda. But most historians conclude that he was injured in a botched attempted suicide. They theorize that he fired at his own head and missed, nearly removing his jaw. The next day the father of all terror was brought out to the guillotine and executed. He died the same way he had killed so many others. Almost. The executioner placed Robespierre in the guillotine face up instead of face down. Adding insult to his already dishonoring death, Robespierre's head and body were buried in a common grave in a collective burial site.

6

LEOPOLD II
King of Exploitation

Born: 1835
Died: 1909
Ruled: 1865–1909

Leopold II was a monster in Western clothing.

The cultured king of Belgium gave a direct order that resulted in the murder of between five million and fifteen million people in Africa's Congo.

For some mysterious reason, history is forgetting the evil acts of this despotic devil. The Royal Museum for Central Africa—an official building commissioned and built by Leopold in the capital city of Brussels—makes no mention of the atrocity. The Belgians are whitewashing their history.

Leopold II became king of Belgium on December 10, 1865, and ruled for forty-four years until his death in 1909. He was married to the daughter of the Archduke of Austria. He cheated on her, fathering illegitimate children. But he is neither judged nor condemned for that indiscretion. He had sons with his mistress—a prostitute he married in a religious ceremony five days before he died. The marriage is invalid under Belgian law, but he is neither judged nor condemned for that indiscretion.

Those were indiscretions. What he did in the Congo was an abomination.

At the time Leopold owned the country, it was called the Congo Free State. Only later was the country's name changed to the Belgian Congo, then Zaire, now—mercifully—the Democratic Republic of Congo.

Leopold II ruled his monarchy in much the same way other monarchs ruled theirs. He entered into conflict and controversy over his vision for the future of Belgium. Leopold had visions of an empire and wanted Belgium to acquire colonies. He tried to push through his argument with claims that the natural resources of colonized nations would boost the Belgian economy, catapulting the country into the circle of world leadership.

The parliament and other politicians did not agree. So Leopold went about getting a colony on his own.

As a private citizen, he set about acquiring a colony for business and profit. To that end, he organized a holding company called the International African Society and set it up as a philanthropic and scientific organization. In 1879, he hired one of the great explorers of his time, Henry Morton Stanley, to venture forth and find him a colony in the African Congo.

During the Berlin Conference of 1884, it was decided that Leopold would control the area he and Stanley had staked out. Since Leopold had acquired the colony as a businessman and not under the auspices of his crown, conferees essentially made a private citizen king of the Congo.

Leopold set up mines and industry for diamonds, rubber, and ivory. The locals were enslaved and brutally mistreated. They were murdered for the smallest infraction or for no reason at all. Even Franz Joseph, the emperor of Austria-Hungary, called Leopold a "thoroughly bad man," and as the saying goes, it takes one to know one.

After visiting a small village in the Congo, a missionary wrote the following note to Leopold's head office in the Congo:

> I have just returned from a journey inland to the village of Insongo Mboyo. The abject misery and utter abandon is positively indescribable. I was so moved, Your Excellency, by the people's stories that I took the liberty of promising them that in future you will only kill them for crimes they commit.

In 1908, the Belgian parliament forced its king to hand over his private property, putting the Congo Free State into the care of Belgium.

Historians have used the word *genocide* to describe Leopold's action and behavior, drawing parallels between the Belgian king and Hitler. King Leopold ranks among the greatest murderers of the modern era.

Leopold was booed by his own people at his own funeral. And yet, for some warped reason, a twenty-foot-tall statue of Leopold was erected in the Congo. Hours later the statue was removed. The minister who erected the edifice said it was important to see the good and the bad of Leopold, and the statue was put in place once again. This time when the statue disappeared, it disappeared for good.

Official Belgiam history refers to Leopold as the "King Builder." He built the train station in Antwerp, the national museum in Brussels, and other great nineteenth-century edifices. Sadly, the Belgians do not remember him for what he did best: enslave, exploit, and murder innocent Africans to gain personal profit.

The builder was a barbarian.

7

IOANNIS METAXAS
The Man Who Evicted Mussolini

Born: 1871
Died: 1941
Ruled: 1936–1941

Metaxas was the dictator who ruled Greece from 1936–1941. Officially his position was prime minister, but like so many other dictators, he suspended the checks and balances of the democratic system and took total control. This Greek dictator modeled his style of leadership after Italian Fascist dictator Mussolini.

To this day Greeks are emotional when talking about the reign of Metaxas. Was he good for Greece or bad? Was his tenure constructive or negative? Undeniably, Ioannis Metaxas returned stability to Greece and gave its citizens a gift: he restored their pride in their country. He put Greece back on the international stage. Metaxas was a hero.

How did he do it? He did it by modernizing the army and forcing the Italians out of Greece. He also did it at the expense of democracy;

Metaxas suspended the constitution. Bottom line, Metaxas was a benevolent dictator. A military man through and through, soldiering was much more than his career and means of political advancement; it was his life. Soldiering was the prism through which Ioannis Metaxas viewed the world. His understanding of military might gave Metaxas an edge over every other Greek leader.

Born in Greece but schooled in Germany, he returned to help modernize the Greek army as a member of the Greek General Staff. After the Balkan wars of 1912–1913, Metaxas was promoted to the rank of general and appointed chief of the General Staff. In contemporary terms, he was chief of staff of the army.

Throughout his early career, even when it was an unpopular and unwise position to take, Metaxas supported the monarchy. In his mind, the alternative to a monarchy was unacceptable. That unwavering support cost him dearly. Because they rejected the idea of having Greece enter the fray in World War I, both the king and the army chief of staff were sent into exile.

After the war, both returned to Greece. The monarchy was officially put aside in 1922. At that point, Metaxas made his leap into politics. Until then, he had played the perfect role of loyal and obedient soldier, following the policies of political leaders. Now the time had come for Metaxas to enter politics. In 1923, he founded the Freethinkers' Party. Even in politics, Metaxas was involved in the military.

Metaxas was appointed minister of war in the mid-1930s. The Greek government was in deep crisis, and he was asked to break the deadlock. His selection as interim prime minister was Metaxas's big break. The country was in crisis: industry was a mess, and the people were polarized. Metaxas saw an opportunity and seized it. He declared a state of emergency and took over the country. Democracy and most of the constitution was suspended. The dictator was in place.

He outlawed all political parties. He outlawed strikes. He arrested political activists. He was especially forceful against the Communists for fear that they were the best organized and possibly the most dangerous opposition to his rule. He censured all media and shut down agencies that did not tow the line.

Metaxas initiated some of the most important social reforms since the time of Alexander—reforms that would have pleased even the most die-hard Communists. He instituted a mandatory eight-hour work day. He demanded safe working conditions. He established Greek social security. Metaxas artificially increased prices on agriculture to improve the lives of farmers. His government assumed the debts of the farmers so they could continue to grow and produce for the nation. He also modernized and improved the army. He was the perfect image of the benevolent dictator.

The Greek leader hoped that the British would help insulate and protect his country from the constant pressure he was getting from Italy and Mussolini—his original role model. As with World War I, Metaxas wanted to stay out of World War II. But Italy was pushing hard to occupy some important strategic sites within Greece to further its own military goals.

Mussolini demanded, in the form of a formal request, to enter Greece. The answer from Metaxas: "Then we shall have war." That response has gone down in Greek history and lore. Greece entered the war against the Axis powers and fought against Italy.

Metaxas and the Greeks, because they were well prepared and well trained, repelled the Italians and made great strides in defense and counter attacks. Greece remained intact. The army created the Metaxas Line—a defense line dedicated to protecting Greece from foreign influence and soldiers.

Ioannis Metaxas died mid-war on January 29, 1941. It was a sad farewell for a military hero. He looked just like every other Greek grandfather. Until you looked into his eyes.

8

ADOLF HITLER
The Short, Great Dictator

Born: 1889
Died: 1945
Ruled: 1933–1945

Some people can't bring themselves to say the name of Adolf Hitler without spitting three times. Hitler, *puh, puh, puh*. They are warding off the evil spirit.

Adolf Hitler, the German leader, was responsible for bringing the entire world to war. He almost brought the world to the brink of disaster.

In the beginning, it looked as if Hitler and his Nazi Germany were going to win World War II. And if Germany had won, the world would be a very different place today. Winners make the rules. Winners determine morality. Winners determine what is right and what is wrong. Hitler's Fascist dictatorship was built on the principles of extreme nationalism. All power rested in one office: his. He had an agenda—a series of thought-out plans and goals.

Goal number one was to conquer the world. Goal number two was to rid the world of one of its biggest problems: the Jews.

It is not just happenstance that Hitler's extermination of the Jews was called the "Final Solution." The world had a problem (the "Jewish problem") and Hitler had the solution (the "final solution"). Eliminating the Jews would make a better world. Simple deportation was not enough.

Hitler attempted to murder all the Jews. It was not just a holocaust; it was The Holocaust. In the end, he successfully murdered eleven million people, six million of which were Jews.

The Holocaust, Hitler's special brand of genocide, was different from any other genocide in history. Until Hitler if you wanted to kill an enemy you used whatever killing tools were available. Not Hitler. Special machines were created just to kill the Jews: gas chambers to exterminate lives and crematoria to dispose of bodies. They were built for maximum product output; the product was death. Output was timed—how many Jews could be killed and disposed of in a week, a day, an hour?

Disposing of the bodies was crucial, prompting the construction of crematoria. It wasn't that Hitler wanted to hide his crimes against humanity—he couldn't have cared less. But dead bodies build up, and that buildup limited the number of Jews the Nazis could murder. It was all about efficiency. The faster the Nazis could dispose of the bodies, the more they could kill.

Few people actually lived in the death camps for any length of time. Jews just got off the train, stripped naked, and walked into the gas chambers. Then their bodies were burned. Shoes, jewelry, eyeglasses, suitcases—anything on their persons—were all left behind. Gold teeth were removed from the dead bodies.

Treblinka. Belzec. Sobibor. Chelmno. Majdanek. All names of death factories. In addition to death camps, the Nazis maintained concentration camps—also known as labor or prison camps. Auschwitz-Birkenau did double duty as both a labor camp and a death camp.

Hitler was Austrian and not German. But he felt German. That's important. The concept of a greater Germany was palpable long before the two world wars. He was born on April 20, 1889, in the border village of Braunau am Inn, Austria. His father, Alois (1837–1903), was a customs agent on the border, so the family moved often. His father was also often drunk and usually abusive. Hitler's mother Klara (1860–1907) was warm and caring and significantly younger than her husband. The couple had six children, but only Adolf and his sister Klara made it to adulthood. Child mortality was very common in nineteenth-century Austria.

Alois also had another wife and two children—Adolf's half-siblings, Alois Jr. and Angela.

Alois was born out of wedlock, so he used his mother's name, Schicklgruber. Later, Alois began using the name of his stepfather, Hiedler. Through some error in transcription, Hiedler became Hitler. No one knows who Hitler's paternal grandfather was. There were rumors that Hitler was one-quarter Jewish, but they were never substantiated. Hitler's rumored Jewish lineage was used as propaganda in electioneering pamphlets in order to discredit him. The opposition got a kick out of alleging that the leader of the anti-Semitic party had Jewish blood.

Hitler was a very good primary-school student. He excelled in history and literature. Hoping he would become a priest, his mother enrolled him in a religious school. His favorite playground game was "king of the mountain." Of course, he was always king. Once out of primary school, learning became difficult for Hitler. He had to repeat a grade. He was a serious behavioral problem (he smoked in the bathroom) and was kicked out of school. He had no skills, no qualifications. But he had self-confidence and a little bit of talent. He considered himself an artist.

He lived on the orphan's stipend given him by the state after his father's death. With the stipend, Hitler went to Vienna, where he twice applied to the Academy of Art and was twice rejected for lack of talent. So Hitler made his living painting postcards. Long before picture postcards, there were painter postcards—postcards painted by artists. Hitler probably painted thousands of cards. He also had a steady hand, which he put to use painting moldings and trim in houses. In 1907, his mother died of breast cancer and Hitler went back for the funeral. He blamed Klara's Jewish doctor for her death. In reality, the doctor tried valiantly to save her and make her comfortable. He did not even charge for Klara's care. The doctor and his patient had a warm relationship.

When World War I erupted, Hitler wanted to serve in the army, but he failed the physical—several times. Then he discovered that he could apply for the Bavarian Reserve Regiment by mail.

Hitler was a runner. Too small to be a real soldier, he could run through the trenches delivering messages from the officers to the soldiers right on the front line. He was wounded—shot in the lower rear—and received an Iron Cross, Second Class, to prove it. Seldom was that honor bestowed on an enlisted man.

In the last stages of World War I, Hitler was wounded again—this time by mustard gas. He was hospitalized, and when he woke up, the war was over. But it had not ended well for Germany. Before his injury, it looked as if Germany was winning. Not only had they lost, but a truce was declared before even a single foreign soldier occupied German soil. So how could Germany have possibly lost the war?

Germany's loss in World War I led to the most important motivational factor in Hitler's rise to power. Germany lost because of a divisive, backbiting, and destructive group from within. It was winning on the battlefront but lost on the home front. Germany was stabbed in the back. Thus was born the "stabbed-in-the-back" theory. Communists, Socialists, liberals, and of course Jews were all out to stab true Germans in the back. It was the greatest conspiracy theory. And the masses of Germans believed it.

World War I forced Germany to accept war guilt, to demilitarize their strategic valleys, to breakdown down their military caste system, and not to amass soldiers on their borders. These were severe insults to Germany. Hitler used these slights to galvanize support for the new party he joined in the interwar period. It was called the National Socialist Workers Party. In German, the acronym is NAZI.

Germany was split. There were enormously liberal and exciting cultural energies on the left and a movement that rejected liberal ideas on the right. The left embraced the Jews; the right rejected them. German Jews in the 1920s rose to great heights in cinema, music, philosophy, theatre, and science, even while racist undertones were trying to push them out. Hitler gave voice to the undertones; Hitler wanted the Jews out and only the Aryan nation in.

During the Weimar Republic—the post-World War I democratic period—there was a real clash of ideas on the future of Germany. And there was a terrible economic crisis. Hitler promised stability and a return to the greatness of the past. He promised to restore Germany's honor.

In 1932, there were two elections for the Reichstag, the German parliament. In the July election, Hitler's Nazi party gained more seats than the entire left and right combined. But the president would not have Hitler form the government, and in November there were elections again.

This time Hitler's plurality was asked to form a government, and in January of 1933 Hitler was sworn in as Germany's chancellor—the equivalent of prime minister. Yes, Hitler was voted in democratically. And yes, even Jews voted for him. One of the first things the new chancellor did was pass the Enabling Act, suspending democracy indefinitely. Hitler was elected to power democratically and then promptly disbanded the very democracy that put him in power.

He went about putting his vision for Germany into action. He applied the Nuremberg Laws, officially disenfranchising the Jews from Germany. Their rights and citizenship were taken away. Ostensibly, Hitler went to war against Poland to expand German land and property and to reunite German lands. The concept is called *lebensraum*, which means "living room or space." In August of 1939, he made a pact with Russia to sandwich Poland in an invasion. They agreed to divide Poland into thirds: one-third to Germany, one-third to Russia, and one-third a protectorate of Germany.

The Jews were rounded up and put into ghettoes. They were made to wear yellow identification stars. It was World War II. In

January of 1942, in the suburban resort of Wansee, Germany adopted the "final solution." Jews in and around Germany were to be murdered en masse using gas chambers. The protocols of the meeting actually list every country and the number of Jews in each one. When the camps were ready, the Jews were deported.

As in World War I, the tide of war changed and Hitler's Germany began to retreat. The Battle of Stalingrad in February 1943 ended with the entire German Sixth Army encircled and destroyed by Russia. It became clear that Germany would lose the war.

In July of 1944, there was a coup attempt against Hitler. The coup was organized by the highest echelon in the army that was negotiating a separate surrender, independent of Hitler, who refused to admit defeat. A bomb was planted in a briefcase under the conference table where Hitler sat. The bomb exploded, but the heavy German furniture absorbed the impact of the explosion. The conspirators were caught and executed, but the point had been made: the end was coming for Adolf Hitler.

World War II officially ended in 1945.

Hitler spent his last few days hidden in his secret bunker with his longtime mistress and new wife, Eva Braun. The Soviets arrived in Berlin and inched their way through the city. When they were just a block away, Hitler bit down on a cyanide pill and then shot himself in the head.

The bodies—his and hers—were put in a crate, doused with gas, and burned. The Soviets conducted an autopsy, including comparison of dental records.

Hitler, the little man with the little mustache and the funny salute, was dead.

9

BENITO MUSSOLINI
He Who Kept The Trains on Time

Born: 1883
Died: 1945
Ruled: 1922–1943

Truly, Mussolini was one of the great leaders of the twentieth century. He was a true dictator and a great dictator.

He called himself Il Duce and created an enormous mystique about himself. He was the man who never slept. He was the man who was never wrong. He was the man who could solve all problems. He was the man who could find the solutions whether they were political or economic problems.

Mussolini was a good-looking Italian and very popular with the ladies. He was charismatic and adept at charming a crowd. In fact, he was more comfortable in front of crowds than he was in intimate circles. He was totally in charge of the media. Literally, because of his position. Figuratively, because of his secure, imposing presence. He was a *mucho bella* media manipulator. Mussolini played Italy very well.

The Italian leader created fascism ten years before Hitler was even elected to power. It was Hitler who drew heavily on Mussolini's concepts—not the other way around. Mussolini envisioned fascism to be the total unification of power in the hands of one individual: Benito Mussolini. He crafted a philosophy of governance that perfectly suited his own personality and style of leadership.

Mussolini's given name was Benito Amilcare Andrea Mussolini. Benito, after the great Mexican-reformist president Benito Juarez. Amilcare and Andrea after two Italian Socialists: Amilcare Cipriani and Andrea Costa.

His mother, Rosa—a teacher—impressed upon her son the need to create change in society for the sake of future generations. His father, Alessandro, was a blacksmith. He also had essential lessons to bestow upon his son. They all boiled down to one thing: question authority.

Benito adored his father and did his best to please him. Alessandro joined the first Socialist International, and later Benito joined as well.

As a kid Benito Mussolini was a real troublemaker. His mother's church banned him for pinching congregants and throwing stones at people as they came through the church doors. He was sent to—and thrown out of—a reform school. His crimes were stabbing a student in the hand and throwing an inkwell at a teacher. Even with his delinquent behavior, Benito was an excellent student and received good grades. He did so well that he qualified to become a school principal.

Mussolini chose to run from the World War I draft. He ran to Switzerland, was arrested, and was sent back to Italy where he was forced into the army. He ran away to Switzerland again and was about to be deported again when Swiss Socialists came to the rescue. They found him a job as editor of a Socialist paper. It was a perfect match. While at the paper, Mussolini wrote his first book— a novel called *His Cardinal's Mistress*. The author described his work as a rant and smear against religious authority.

Mussolini returned to Italy to be near his mother who was in ill health. Once again, Mussolini found work at a newspaper. This time it was *Avanti*, which means "forward." Mussolini took the media and made it his own. In the beginning, he disseminated a Socialist message. Later, his message changed to fascism.

The word *fascism*, or *fascio* in Italian, was not coined by Mussolini. He just made it his own, fashioning it into what was to become one of the most powerful political forces in European history.

Mussolini manipulated the newspaper world and gained entrée into the Fascist world. While he was editor of *Avanti*—the largest and most important Socialist newspaper—the syndicalists broke with the Socialists. Syndicalists were a combination of extreme socialism, unionism, and anarchism. They believed that through strikes, factories would be brought under the control of the workers. The syndicat was a free association of workers. Mussolini believed in them and defended them. When asked how he could reconcile being the editor of the Socialist flagship *Avanti* and side with the syndicalists, he decided it was time to leave both socialism and his job. He was fed up with both socialism and anarchism. He tried fascism, and it stuck.

He went to work for another paper, and then finally the draft caught up with him. It turned out to be a quick diversion. Mussolini entered the army and was promptly wounded in grenade practice. He was sent home and went back to his newspaper. It wasn't until after World War I that Mussolini entered politics. Before that he just covered it. He lost his first election, but by 1921, Mussolini was elected to the Italian parliament.

He was a certified, official representative and member of the fascio. He organized bands of veterans—*squadristi*—who roamed the streets beating up Socialists, Communists, and anarchists. They claimed they were protecting the honor of Italy. They broke up strikes, often with force. And the hands-on Mussolini would be there. Industrialists were enormously grateful to the squadristi since the Fascists were against the strikes as well as anarchy. Mussolini was running on a platform of law and order. His popularity was soaring.

He organized the March of Rome to take back the government. As a result of his new fame and remarkable success, King Victor Emmanuel III asked Mussolini on October 28, 1922, to form a new government. Three days later, at only thirty-nine years old, Mussolini became the youngest prime minister in Italian history. The quick succession of events makes it appear that Emanuell handpicked Mussolini because of the success of the March. But that's not the way it happened. The king asked him to accept the premiership of Italy even before the march. The March of Rome was just a show conceived and organized by the master of media manipulation: Mussolini. Today we would call it a media event.

There were many reasons for Mussolini's success and rise to power. Mostly, it was his sheer force of character—his charisma and personality. Economic instabilities helped. There was a lack of faith in the parliament. There was no long standing history of democracy. Italians were afraid of another world war. They were disdainful of unions and socialism, especially because it hinted of Russia. The Italians were ripe for the picking. They were ready to embrace a handsome, powerful leader. They needed Benito Mussolini, and Benito Mussolini needed them. He fashioned himself into everything the Italians wanted. He won them over. Then the real Benito Mussolini emerged.

Mussolini grabbed on to issues of nationalism. He restored pride to the Italians. Nationalism became the mantel upon which everything rested. He began to attack all the Socialist organizations and programs that were in place. His motto was "Root out the evil Socialists and everything they stand for."

He began to move the power from the people back into the hands of an able government. The strength of Mussolini's Fascist model was the ability to combine totalitarianism with extreme nationalism and a fervent hatred of Communism, socialism, and unionism. For two decades Mussolini's platform was unbeatable.

Mussolini was a workhorse. He would hold as many as ten ministerial portfolios. He would be the minister of interior, of finance, of corporations, of the army, and of public works. He was a one-man show. He was a dedicated public servant. He was also the head of the National Fascist Party. And he was head of the Black Shirts.

The Black Shirts went from place to place enforcing Mussolini's laws and terrorizing those who did not tow the party line. Any resistance, especially from Communists, was met with strong violence.

Il Duce was in charge of everything in Italy. Everything. He paid special attention to the media. It was the media that got out his message; it was his personal propaganda machine. From experience, Mussolini knew the media was the way to educate and inform the masses. The more control he had, the easier it would be to manipulate the masses.

He created new agricultural programs that made Italy much more productive, increasing grain output by 50 percent. He raised money by asking people to donate their gold to the treasury. In return, donators were given metal bands that read, "Gold for the Fatherland." Similar to the popular rubber-like, charity-linked bracelets worn today, it was a brilliant tool to raise money and garner support for the nationalist cause. Almost all of his energy was spent on internal propaganda. He had to continually convince people of the importance of his mission and of their value in it.

Mussolini had a great gift of naming things. In 1936, he chose the name "Axis Powers" to refer to the Rome-Berlin Axis. He then changed the name to "Pact of Steel" in May of 1939 when they signed a treaty. Later he would refer to the same relationship as the "Pact of Blood."

During World War II, Mussolini was oriented toward North Africa. He wanted Malta, Corsica, and Tunis. He wanted Libya, Egypt, and Kenya. He wanted the Holy Land. He was greedy and overextended. Things did not go well. He declared war against France, England, the United States, and the Soviet Union. And he suffered defeat after defeat. Hitler was not helping.

On June 25, 1943, Mussolini was stripped of his power by senior military officials and sent to Gran Sasso, a mountain retreat in the Alps. Italy's King Emmanuel was ousted. There was bedlam.

Mussolini was eventually rescued by the Germans and created a puppet government called the Italian Social Republic.

As Mussolini and his entourage were about to board a plane to escape back to Switzerland on April 27, 1945, the former dictator of twentieth-century Italy was captured by Italian Communist partisans. (There is another story floating around that Mussolini and his gang were executed with the aid of a British intelligence officer, but such a story is highly unlikely.)

The next day, on April 28, 1945, Benito Mussolini, Claretts Petecci (his mistress of the moment), and sixteen fellow travelers—most of them ministers in his government—were executed.

Mussolini's special brand of humiliation for Communists had been to kill them and hang their bodies upside down on meat hooks in the piazza. Not coincidentally, Mussolini's body was hung upside down on a meat hook in the piazza.

10

FRANCISCO FRANCO
Fascist Obsessed

Born: 1892
Died: 1975
Ruled: 1939–1975

His official title was "*Por la Racia de Dios, Caudillo de Espana y de la Cruzada*" ("By the Grace of God, Leader of Spain and of the Crusade"). His given name was even longer. He was Francisco Paulino Hermenegildo Teodulo Franco y Bahamonde. He was most often referred to as Generalissimo Francisco Franco, general of the Spanish armed forces.

He was an absolute, authoritarian dictator. Franco was the leader of Spain for thirty-six years. In 1947, in an effort to keep his country together and appease the monarchist element, he proclaimed Spain a monarchy but never appointed a monarch. While he never assumed the royal title himself, he assumed the royal pomp. He wore the uniform of a captain general—a position only attained by kings. He lived in a palace. His face adorned Spanish coins. He walked under a canopy. And he added that special phrase, "By the Grace of God"—a phrase reserved for monarchs—to his title.

Generalissimo Franco had the distinction of having a candy unnamed after him. In 1931, the department store Marshall Fields started selling a brand of chocolate mints called Francos. They sold very well. In 1933, after Franco aligned himself with Hitler, the store changed the name of the candy from Francos to Frangos. The candy is still selling well today.

By all standards, Franco's life began modestly. His father was a drunkard who served in the Spanish navy; he was a paymaster. The son would do anything to please his father. He intended to join the navy and follow in his father's footsteps. But at the time Franco was ready to enlist, the naval academy was closed to recruits. He joined the army instead, and his father was not pleased. Franco entered the Infantry Academy in Toledo and graduated as a commissioned second lieutenant. It was 1910—a perfect time for those interested in a military career to advance. In 1912, the lieutenant was off to war in Morocco.

He did well. At only twenty-three years old, he was already a captain. He was badly wounded, but rather than hamper his career, the injury helped. Because he survived, the locals called him Baraka, "the blessed one." He brought them luck. Franco was promoted to major and became the youngest staff officer in Spain. In 1928, he was appointed to direct the elite Joint Military Academy at Zaragoza. He was soaring.

It was a series of fluke incidents that landed Franco, a nonpolitical personality, in the role of Spain's *jefe del estado*, their head of state.

It all began with the Spanish Civil War. As much as he did not want to get involved politically, he eventually did. Franco joined forces with the Fascist rebels and became their leader. The resistance he ran eventually forced everyone else to unconditionally surrender. The republic officially fell on March 27, 1939, and the war ended on April 1. Franco was the official and undisputed leader of Spain. Hail to Generalissimo Franco, dictator of all Spain.

The civil war left Spain in economic and social turmoil. There was no significant economy or industry. The war had torn the country apart, and the people were demoralized. Before Spain had a chance to recover, World War II began. In many ways, for the people of Spain the World War was an extension of their own internal war. Those who could continued to fight for the republic; but instead of fighting Fascists, this time they were fighting underground against the Nazis.

World War II began in September of 1939. Once again, Franco did not really want to get involved. Franco and Hitler met in 1940. Photos of the evil men of Europe standing side by side mugging for the cameras are legendary. Hitler wanted to persuade Spain to join the war on Germany's behalf. Franco set out a series of very difficult terms for Germany to accept. Terms included significant amounts of food, military supplies and equipment, and the island of Gibraltar. The major sticking point was German mining rights in Spanish mines.

Some historians believe Franco had devised the perfect ploy to keep Spain out of the war. His requests were so unreasonable that he knew Hitler would not—could not—accept them. However, what Franco had done in concession to the Germans was offer

Hitler the use of Spain's naval bases. The offer was significant. It came after the fall of France, and it brought the German fleet that much closer to Africa.

When the tide of the war changed and Hitler's end was near, Spain was once again able to claim neutrality. In his defense, it must be said that a Franco-controlled Spain proved to be one of the most significant escape routes for Jews—mostly from France— escaping Hitler's murder camps. After the war, Franco was caught between the Cold War poles. Because Franco always tried to hedge his bets, he could never quite figure out how to take advantage of either side.

It is impossible to tally the number of people murdered by Franco. His rule was marked by the severe repression of human rights. Tens of thousands of Spaniards were arrested and many more ran into exile to save their lives. They ran to South America and even to France. During the wars, he carried out thousands upon thousands of summary executions. By 1939, every single execution had to be signed and approved by Francisco Franco.

The Franco government had no fear. In 1940, they executed Lluís Companys, president of the Catalan regional government. Anyone who was loyal to the republic during the war could be targeted for assassination or arrest: Communists, anarchists, loyalists, atheists, intelligentsia. He targeted the military. He targeted the moderates, the democrats, the leftists. Everyone was accused of treason, and the punishment for treason was often the firing squad. Only the Fascists were safe. Spain was in tremendous internal turmoil. Under Franco, only one trade union was legal—the government union. All cultural activities were censored. All nationalist groups were outlawed.

Prostitution and homosexuality were criminal offenses; they were not in tandem with Spain's Catholic doctrine. All language sub-groups were outlawed. Any document not written in Spanish was null and void. Any road sign, store sign, or advertisement not printed in Spanish was torn down. All was for Spain, but Spain was not for all. In 1960, some of these laws were relaxed—a little.

Civil guards patrolled every town and city. They walked in pairs, machine guns at their sides. Their job was to make certain that there was quiet—that the rules were adhered to. They did their job well. Franco's reign of brutality and terror is best described in his very own words: "Our regime is based on bayonets and blood, not on hypocritical elections."

Franco's obsession with fascism kept him alive. Literally. Franco was dying; he may have already been dead. But he ordered his doctors to keep him alive—or to hide the fact of his death if need be—until November 20, 1975. That was the day that Jose Antonio Primo de Rivera, ideological leader of the Fascists, was executed by the republic. Franco wanted to die on the same day.

Spain is now almost Franco-free. Statues have been taken down. Street names have been changed. But some things will not go away; the legacy of Generalissimo Francisco Franco Bahamonde will always haunt Spain.

11

HENRI PHILIPPE PETAIN
Very, Very Vichy

Born: 1856
Died: 1951
Ruled: 1940–1944

During World War I, Henri Philippe Petain was a French national hero. During World War II, he was head of the Vichy government and a Nazi collaborator. He knew how to push France's emotional buttons par excellence.

His story begins simply, as many other stories begin. Petain was a soldier who rose through the ranks of the military. He reached the ranks of colonel, brigade commander, and division commander. After proving himself as a brilliant military tactician and hero, he was appointed commander in chief of the French army and awarded the rank of marshal.

Notoriety and fame came during World War I.

The Battle of Verdun is the most famous battle fought during World War I. It is also the longest. The battle began on February 21, 1916, and ended on December 19, 1916. As a battle, Verdun symbolized France's internal fortitude and their ability to hold back the Germans. Two hundred fifty-thousand men were killed in the battle, a half-million soldiers were wounded. Every French citizen knew someone who had fought at Verdun, been wounded at Verdun, or been killed at Verdun.

As commander of the French Second Army, Philippe Petain stopped the German army at Verdun. It was the battle that changed the entire tide of the war. It was the battle that made Petain a national hero.

Petain went to Morocco to join the Spanish in their attack against Abdel Kareem. They were successful. When France officially recognized the new Spanish government under Francisco Franco, Petain was named ambassador to Spain. He was the perfect liaison. Franco had served under Petain in Morocco.

With the German invasion, France was on the verge of total collapse. Petain was recalled in 1940. Fascism was on the rise. The government needed to appear strong and credible. It needed to stabilize a very precarious political and military situation. It was a public relations gambit. Bringing home "the Hero of Verdun" was a political ploy. Petain was made deputy prime minister of France under Paul Reynaud.

But Petain had his own ideas. He thought it was a better idea to pursue a truce with Germany than to maintain hostilities. On June 16, 1940, Reynaud was ousted. Petain was now the new prime minister of France.

By June 25, Germany had occupied two-thirds of France. A rump French parliament was formed. The expression *rump* in German means "without opposition." In this case, it meant that there was no political opposition or resistance to the creation of the new French parliament. Similarly, after his election in Germany, Hitler created the Rump Reichstag, a German parliament without opposition.

The constitution of the Third Republic of France was suspended. The hero of France signed away control to the Germans of large portions of his country, including the capital, Paris. The rest was left to become its own separate regime. And that is how Petain assumed the position as head of state at Vichy in what was called unoccupied France. Vichy, the new capital, was a resort town.

In diplomatic terms, *unoccupied* means "puppet state." The Germans nominally ruled that part of the country. The rest of France, with Paris as the capital, was occupied and completely controlled by Germany. In Vichy, there was an illusion of independence.

When the British invaded Vichy, Petain opened his arms. But not to the Allied power. With Petain's blessing and guidance, the German army under the command of SS Colonel Joseph Darnand was defending Vichy.

When the Allies invaded France on June 6, 1944, Petain went deep into Germany for safety. From there he went to Switzerland. But in the summer of 1945, when the French charged him with treason, he returned to his native country to stand trial.

Petain always argued that he collaborated with the Nazis for the betterment of France. There is serious debate on this matter. The French court was not swayed by his arguments and justifications. Henri Philippe Benoni Omer Joseph Petain, dictator and appendage of Hitler, was sentenced to death. Charles de Gaulle, head of the provisional government of France, reduced the sentence from death to life in prison. In solitary confinement.

PART FOUR

EASTERN EUROPE

Eastern Europe always lagged behind Western Europe on issues of freedom and enlightenment.

Traditionally, the Eastern-European model was feudal. Eastern Europeans were slower than their Western counterparts to modernize. It meant unshackling the people, and the rulers were in no rush to grant freedoms or encourage independent thought.

In Eastern Europe, there was less of a chance for social mobility—or even physical mobility—than there was on the western side of the continent. Most of the people lived spread out in rural environments. Villages were the norm rather than cities. Education for the masses was rudimentary at best. Even transportation was undeveloped. One of the major changes in the quality of life for Eastern Europeans was the train. Finally industry and culture could be brought to the people. Finally the isolation was broken.

The term *Eastern Europe* is relatively new and not very scientific. Serfdom and autocratic governments continued as a whole in one part of Europe long after they had disappeared in the other. The countries on the western side of the continent embraced change and modernity; the countries on the eastern side clung to the ways of old.

Some countries are resentful of being labeled as Eastern European. For them, the term has become pejorative. They have modernized and democratized, and they are free. They want to be recognized for who they are now—not shackled by the memory of what they once were.

In parts of Eastern Europe today, there are people who work the land in the exact way their ancestors worked the land two hundred years ago. Autocratic rule flourished in Eastern Europe. All the criteria were there. In some countries, the criteria are still there.

1

IVAN IV
Terribly Awesome

Born: 1530
Died: 1584
Ruled: 1547–1584

We call him Ivan the Terrible for very good reason. The atrocities he committed as ruler were ghastly. His lifestyle was bawdy, loud, and obnoxious. And his early years were just plain terrible.

He was a paranoid, murderous tyrant. He was also a creative genius. He used every spare moment of his awful life to glean new knowledge that would help him lead.

Ivan the Terrible actually inherited the crown and became czar of Russia at age three when his father, Vasili III, died. He did not, however, assume the throne until 1544, when he reached the ripe old age of fourteen.

After the death of Vasili, Ivan's uncle decided to wrest away the throne. The attempt was unsuccessful, resulting in the uncle's arrest, imprisonment, abandonment, and eventual starvation. The monarchy went to Ivan's mother with the intention that she, Jelena Glinsky, would run the country until Ivan IV came of age. Jelena had Ivan's other uncle killed before he, too, could make a move on the monarchy.

Jelena died at a very early age. While unproven, it is assumed that she was poisoned.

Ivan was eight at the time of his mother's death. The role of managing the land and properties of his kingdom was put in the hands of Russian aristocracy. The job of running the day-to-day operations of the country, including foreign affairs, went to the Belsky and Shuisky families.

There was much animosity between the leading families and the future leader. Ivan, who had once been a bright, curious, well-behaved boy and a voracious reader, became the center of a bloody and violent battle for control. The families resented the fact that the little runt was to be czar while they were doing the actual work of running the country. They teased and taunted Ivan. They ransacked his living quarters. And they neglected him.

Ivan had a brother who was a deaf-mute. Rather than being treated like the royalty they were, the two little orphan boys were forced to become beggars in their own castle. They relied on the good graces of their subjects for such simple necessities of life as food and clothing.

Psychological historians like to blame these incidents of early abuse for his later vicious and uncontrollable rage, as well as his unrelenting disdain for his aristocratic peers.

Young Ivan and his gang would gallivant around the city of Moscow drinking and brawling. They would indiscriminately beat up anyone who crossed their path or looked at them crossways. They knocked down old people. They raped young women. And then, to make certain there would be no complaints, Ivan would hang or murder his victims. Sometimes he would bury them alive or throw them to wild animals.

He derived tremendous pleasure from terrorizing cats and dogs. He would drop them out of the windows of the Kremlin to see what would happen. The drop could be well over a hundred feet.

When he was thirteen years old, Ivan arrested Prince Andrew Shuisky—one of his worst tormentors—and threw him into a pack of hungry wolves.

Finally in 1547, the crown was placed on the head of the king in waiting. Ivan, the czar of all Russia, began to institute serious and important changes aimed at liberalizing his society.

He standardized the churches and reformed the army. He reduced corruption. He went to war and conquered the Khanates of Kazan and Astrakhan. He started building. It was a wonderful way to employ artisans. More importantly, it was a way of insuring his own architectural legacy.

Ivan created victory monuments celebrating his own military successes. The great cathedral in Moscow, St. Basils, was built in honor of his military victories. The cathedral was so beautiful in Ivan's own eyes that he had the eyes of the architect plucked out so that he would never again build anything to compete with the cathedral's splendor.

Ivan the Terrible showed no loyalty—not to his advisors, not to the people he ruled, not to his wives. Nobody remained at Ivan's side for long. He was loyal only to his metal-pointed baton—an instrument of torture that was always at his side. Unlike other despots, Ivan did not shout out orders and have his minions carry out the deeds. Ivan enjoyed torturing people.

And yet, the people supported their czar. Toward the end of the year, Czar Ivan secretly left his kingdom and announced that he was abdicating the throne. The people were frantic. They called for his return; they wanted their Ivan home where he belonged. It took the promise of absolute power before Ivan the Terrible would return to Moscow. Ivan had absolute power to torture, murder, and claim the property of anyone disloyal to the czar.

This was a tyrant's dream come true. The year was 1565. Ivan assembled a band of men, dressed them in black, and had them sit atop black steeds. These men, all of whom swore allegiance to their leader, were called Oprichniki. They raped, pillaged, plundered, and murdered. They disrupted church services, killing and kidnapping priests and slaying worshippers. Ivan was so good to his Oprichniki, so indulgent, that one day he allowed them to enter a village, strip the women naked, and use them for target practice.

Then Ivan turned this ruthless band of murderers into monks in a monastic-like order, in which he was the abbot. The Czar of Russia was a man given to extremes. Suddenly he was performing his own masses that included removing the ribs from the chests of men by using piercing-hot pincers. The masses were followed by orgies and uncontrolled drinking. Then Ivan would throw himself down on his own altar so violently that his forehead would bleed and be covered with bruises.

In 1572, Ivan abruptly disbanded the Oprichniki. That same

year he once again decided to abdicate the throne, only to return to power one year later.

Ivan married eight times. His first wife was his true love, chosen from all the beautiful princesses and noblewomen in his kingdom. Her name was Anastasia Romanovna. Together they had six children, but only two survived infancy. Anastasia had a calming influence on her husband, and when she died Ivan lost control. The Ivan of old was unleashed with a vengeance. He blamed the people closest to him for her illness, claiming his wife had been poisoned. Advisors were tortured and killed. Anger, depression, sadism, and paranoia ruled.

Ivan's second wife, Maria Temriukovna, was reputed to be a beauty, but Ivan found her boring. Two years after his second wife's death, he married wife number three. It's barely worth mentioning her name because two weeks after the nuptials, she, too, was dead. But for the record, her name was Martha Sobakin.

Wife number four was Anna Koltovskaya. Ivan had her sent to a convent.

Number five was Anna Wassilchikura, who was very quickly followed by Wassilissa Melentiewna.

Number six must have had a death wish. The wife of one of the most powerful, cruelest, most barbaric, and emotionally disturbed men in history had an affair. Before Wassilissa was booted off to her convent, she saw her lover being impaled.

Wife number seven would have gotten off lucky if all Ivan did was send her to a convent. Alas, Maria Dolgurukaya was drowned. She was not the virgin Ivan presumed her to be.

Maria Nagaya was the name of wife number eight.

The latter part of Ivan's reign was even more despotic than the early years of his rule. There were internal attacks and counterattacks, killing many of Russia's prominent personalities and leading figures. He instituted laws preventing peasants from moving from place to place. Those are the laws that set in motion the process that would create serfdom. What a legacy!

Ivan's moods swayed from gluttony to asceticism, from great joy to pensive sadness. He was never modulated; everything was in the extreme. His passions were ferocious. His heavy drinking was legendary. He had massive sexual orgies. He did not accept no for an answer. During the last years of his reign, Ivan was particularly out of control.

Ivan always got along with his eldest son, also Ivan. Ivan the father took Ivan the son on special field trips. In 1570, the son watched as his father and his band of murdering marauders decimated the town of Novgorod, burning it down because the czar distrusted the townspeople. The people themselves fared no better than their houses. They were all massacred. Some were mutilated; others were impaled. Some were tortured; others were burned. Ivan the son watched, amused.

In one of his frequent and fierce emotional outbursts, Ivan unleashed his terror upon his son's wife. He beat his daughter-in-law because she was, to his thinking, improperly dressed. She was pregnant. Her life was spared, but she lost the baby. When Ivan's son discovered that his father had stricken his wife and killed his unborn child, he ran to confront his father. They fought. Ivan the Terrible brandished his metal-pointed baton and bashed his son in the head.

Ivan murdered both his grandson and his son. It was the near-total ruination of his own legacy. He had almost ended his own blood line to the throne. Sadly it is believed that not a single direct relative of the czar survived his personal torment.

The appellation "terrible" that is attached to Ivan's name has a deeper meaning than Ivan the Awful or Ivan the Monster, the Demon, the Despot, the Devil. Yes, Ivan was a tyrannical thug. But we must remember that he was a Russian thug.

In Russian, Ivan was called Ivan Grozny. Grozny implies awe-inspiring as well as fear- and terror-inspiring.

Ivan was all of those.

2

ALEXANDER III
His Father's Son, His Son's Father

Born: 1845
Died: 1894
Ruled: 1881–1894

Alexander never believed he would rule. He was the second son of Marie and Czar Alexander II. He was the spare heir. His older brother, Nicholas, was being groomed as the perfect successor, leaving Alexander free to enjoy the status of royalty with none of the responsibility.

The difference in education between the future czar (or heir to the throne) and the grand duke (the heir's brother) is tremendous. An heir apparent is instructed in the ways of government, administration, language, power, control, and history. His brothers learn whatever they choose to learn. Grand Duke Alexander enjoyed his life of power with no pressure.

But when Nicholas became ill and was on his deathbed, he exacted a promise from Alexander. Not only would Alexander ascend the throne and one day rule the Russian kingdom as Nicholas had expected to do, he would rule with princess Dagmar of Denmark at his side, just as Nicholas had intended to do.

Alexander did as promised and wed Dagmar on November 9, 1866. He took over the empire on March 14, 1881.

From 1865—the year of Nicholas's death—until he became czar in 1881 after his father's death, Alexander attempted to stay out of politics. He spent his time catching up on the studies of a future czar. And the more he studied, the more he realized that when his day came, he would make many changes in the way Russia was ruled.

Alexander II attempted to institute reforms and even to empower certain segments of the population. Alexander III disagreed; he was disdainful of his father's liberalism. Even before he ascended the throne, the son made his feelings known. It became a source of conflict between the generations. When he came to power, Alexander III immediately let it be known that his power was absolutely absolute. He was ruthless in protecting his administration and putting down revolutions. There were to be no insurrections. Not in his Russia.

The conflict between the generations came to a head during the Franco-Prussian War of 1875–1879. Alexander II sided with the Germans; Alexander III sided with the French. The heir was far more philo-Russian than his father or his government. When he came to power, it became evident that the most striking and dictatorial element of the reign of Alexander III was the concept of Russification.

Alexander III more than resented—he actually despised—the outside influences that were affecting Russia. He felt that Russian culture was superior to all others and that there was no need to adopt or integrate any other cultures or languages.

When he came to power, Czar Alexander III set down a series of laws to that effect. There was to be one culture, one religion, and one language. That went for Russia proper and all the regions that were captured by Russia. Alexander's was an abusive regime that attempted to stymie all things that were not pure Russian. Particularly vile to Alexander were the cultures of Germany and Poland.

Alexander III set his government to work. There was to be a single national administration. He put an end to autonomous regions with different laws and different rules for governing. The Russian language was to be spoken even by the Germans, Poles, and Finns under his rule. Russian Orthodoxy was to be practiced. Jews were to be persecuted, and remnants of other cultures were to be destroyed. He wanted and demanded total allegiance.

Simple in many ways, this Alexander was principled. He fought for peace. He wanted to make certain that Russia did not go to war, but he was constantly prepared for war. Even under pressure, he did not go to war with Russia's little brothers, the Bulgarians. And even though Prince Bismarck of Germany was taunting him constantly, the czar maneuvered around, maintained his diplomatic distance, and averted a confrontation in the battlefield.

He was a brute. He was ungainly. He was strong of will and body. He was a Russian dictator—not a popular monarch.

Czar Alexander III was the target of many assassination attempts. Captured in the aftermath of one such attempt was a man by the name of Alexander Ulyanov—the brother of Vladimir Ilyich Ulyanov, a.k.a. Valdimir Lenin.

3

NICHOLAS II
The Naïve and Inept Czar

Born: 1868
Died: 1918
Ruled: 1894–1917

Boney M put it to music: "Rah, Rah, Rasputin, lover of the Russian queen." That would have been Queen Alexandra, wife of Czar Nicholas II.

Nikolai Aleksandrovich Romanov and his beloved and trusted wife were blessed with four daughters: Olga, Tatiana, Maria, and Anastasia. And then finally, a boy was born. He was Duke Tsarevich Alexei Nikolaevich—Alexei for short. Alexei was the apple of his father's eye. He was doted upon by his mother. The people rejoiced; the emperor had a son. But there was something not quite right.

Alexei was ill. The palace tried to keep it quiet, but there is no stopping the rumor mill—especially the royal rumor mill. The boy suffered from a blood-clotting disease called hemophilia. Any injury, be it an open wound or a bruise, put the boy at risk of bleeding to death. There was only one person who knew how to stop the bleeding and his name was Rasputin. Queen Alexandra became a devoted follower of the man who repeatedly saved her only son's life. She was enamored of him. Most other people were distrustful.

Rasputin was a mystic. He had the power to calm the boy and in that way, stop the bleeding. Rasputin, it turned out, calmed the boy not through his mystical powers, but through the science of hypnosis. Quite simply, the boy relaxed and the bleeding stopped. By the time the truth about Rasputin's powers came out, it was too late for Queen Alexandra. She had already put so much faith, so much trust, in Rasputin that she had been consulting him not only about matters concerning her son but about matters of state. Rasputin's advice was, in many ways, influencing national policy.

If the mystical treatment that Rasputin practiced had been divine, it would have been perfectly acceptable to the palace and to the people. It was the actual science he practiced that was unacceptable. Rasputin was banned from the palace, but the palace could not shake the Rasputin rumor.

Throughout Russia, rumors about Rasputin and Queen Alexandra flowed freely: his influence, his closeness, magical spells he had cast on the family, his romance with the queen.

On December 16, 1916, Rasputin was assassinated by a group of noblemen. He was poisoned. Then he was shot several times all over his body. He was beaten terribly by all the conspirators. Finally, he was thrown into the river and drowned. He survived the entire ordeal, succumbing only to the freezing cold river.

But for Queen Alexandra, too much damage had already been done.

Nicholas II was the czar of Russia, the king of Poland, and the Grand Duke of Finland. And he failed miserably in all three roles. Call him an idealist; call him a fool. The last emperor of the modern period hammered the nails in his own coffin.

The fall of Nicholas II from power marked the end of a lifestyle and style of rule that had been debated since the Enlightenment began in the seventeenth century. The questions surrounding the divine rights of kings were answered with Nicholas's demise. The Romanov family's three-hundred-year rule in Russia came to a close. It was a devastating blow to the family that dated its leadership to Julius Caesar. The appellation czar is actually derived from the name Caesar. The argument for and against the monarchy was the clearest expression of the inner conflict in Russia during Nicholas's reign. It was obvious to most people that freedom and the rejection of kingship were preferable to servitude. And yet those people who advocated for the monarchy were advocating for someone else to make their decisions. It was their safety net.

The Russian monarchy was a society of law and order. Deviants and criminals were dealt with harshly. Courts were somewhat corrupt, but they worked. Bureaucracy was notorious and revolt was inevitable, especially as the Russian Empire under Emperor Nicholas II continued to fail internationally and militarily.

His parentage is a mosaic of European geography and history. The father of Nicholas II was Alexander III, whose father was Alexander II. Nicholas's mother, Maria, was the princess of Denmark. His grandmother was Marie of Hess, which is on the Rhine.

Nicholas fell in love with—and chose for his wife—a German woman. Her name was Alexandra of Hess. His parents were against the match as Germans were considered outsiders. Alexandra's parents were Louis the IV, the Grand Duke of Hess, and Princess Alice from England. In other words, Nicholas's grandmother-in-law was Queen Victoria, ruler of the entire Commonwealth of Great Britain.

While Nicholas was born into royalty, he was not bred to rule. Nicholas would not have been his father's choice of successor, but the monarchy had little choice. Alexander III died in 1894 at the young age of forty-nine. Nicholas was the heir apparent.

Until the empire was thrust upon his shoulders, Nicholas was just the average son of a czar. He traveled and partied. Once the crown was on his head, however, he assumed the responsibility of governance and matured with the position.

For advice, Nicholas relied extensively on his wife, Alexandra. And she was relying heavily on the mystic Rasputin.

The Russian-Japanese war was a terrible psychological defeat for Nicholas and the royal family. Not knowing how to handle the situation, Nicholas sought the counsel of his advisors. In the end, the Russians were humiliated. Then matters got worse: A group of petitioners, marching to the czar's winter palace, were shot upon by the czar's soldiers. In another miscalculation, the czar relocated to his country palace after the shooting, not thinking that anything would come of the march. The people were one step closer to revolution.

But the real failure was World War I.

The general assumption is that World War I began with the assassination of Archduke Franz Ferdinand of Austria. The archduke was killed by a Serb named Gavrilo Princip, a member of the Serbian nationalist association Black Hand. The reality was far more complex. That assassination set in play a series of events that caused the war, but unrest and disillusion had been simmering for a long time.

Nicholas had created a series of treaties to protect Serbia. The assassination so angered the Austrians and Germans that they wanted to invade Serbia. Nicholas was not in favor of invasion; he could not afford to go to war, but neither did he want to abandon the Serbs. So Nicholas II of Russia, protector of Serbia, and Kaiser Wilhelm of Germany exchanged a series of communiqués hoping to reduce tensions and avoid a war across Europe. These notes are called the "Willy-Nicky Correspondence." Good plan on paper, but poor planning in actuality.

For the Russians and the Germans, it was all or nothing. Neither country had the mechanism to conduct a partial war. So a very reluctant Nicholas went to war. And Russia was, once again, badly bruised and beaten.

In his classic style of micromanagement, Nicholas took it upon himself to personally rally the troops and invigorate the war effort. He traveled to the front and assumed the position of commander in chief of the army. Until the well-intenioned but misdirected czar stepped in, that position had been held by Nicholas's more experienced and far better-trained cousin Nikolai Nikolaevich.

Why Nicholas thought that his presence would raise the morale of the soldiers is a question only he could have answered. He was not a general. He was not a military man. And by leaving his palaces for the front lines, Nicholas II left the empire and all the decisions necessary to run an empire up to his wife, Alexandra—a German.

Aside from the fact that his beloved wife could not govern well, the subtlety and inanity of the situation was lost on Nicholas. Russia was at war with Germany, and a German was ostensibly ruling Russia. It was a fatal combination. Compounding it all were the stories about Rasputin. Alexandra, who had always been an unpopular monarch, was now rendered even more powerless and ineffective in the eyes of her subjects.

The war was a military disaster. Internal affairs of the empire were in absolute disorder. It was the perfect time for a revolution.

On March 15, 1917, a date according to the Georgian calendar known as the Ides of March—the very date on which Julius Caesar was assassinated—Nicholas II was forced to abdicate his throne. (The abdication occurred at the end of the February Revolution according to the old Russian calendar, and on March 2 according to the Julian calendar.) It was an ironic end to a dynasty that traced its lineage back to Julius.

When he abdicated, Nicholas II thought it was all over. But one of the greatest mysteries of the modern era was just beginning. At first, the royal family was confined to their palace outside of St. Petersburg. Then they were moved east to Siberia for their own safety, and remained there through the Bolshevik revolution. At some point in November of 1917, all six members of the house of Romanov, plus servants and other relatives, were brought to Bolshevik-controlled areas in Yekaterinburg.

On July 17, 1918, the family disappeared. They just disappeared. According to Yakov Yurovsky—a watchmaker from the town of Perm—they were moved out of fear that a Czech force was there to liberate them. As units from the Czech legion approached the town of Yekaterinburg, the royal family—all except for Anastasia—was executed.

According to legend, the bodies of Nicholas II and his family were soaked in acid, burned, and thrown down a mine shaft. Then they were removed from the mine shaft and transported on a truck. When the truck broke down, the bodies were finally buried on the roadside.

The Romanov story—particularly the mysterious end of Grand Duchess Anastasia—has been the inspiration for numerous books and movies. There have even been imposters claiming to be Anastasia. We still do not know exactly what happened to the Romanovs. What we do have is very telling DNA evidence found in a sealed pit twelve miles from Yekaterinburg. In the pit were five skeletons of people related to each other and four skeletons of people not related to anyone. DNA research has revealed that three of the related skeletons are of the same immediate family; two of them are adults. One of those adults is a relative of England's royal family, and the other is related to Grand Duke George Alexander.

Two skeletons were not found: Alexei, the hemophiliac and heir to the throne, and his sister Anastasia.

Before power and the throne were thrust upon Nicholas II—when he was still a young man and the only title he carried was that of tsarevich, the son of the czar—he traveled to the Empire of Japan. While there, a man with a sword lunged at the future emperor. Nicholas's life was spared by his cousin, Prince George of Greece, who fended off the attacker. Nicholas was left with nothing to show for the attempt on his life but a scar across his forehead.

Once upon a time, Czar Nicholas II of the House of Romanov was a lucky man.

4

VLADIMIR LENIN
The Ideologue With a Goatee

Born: 1870
Died: 1924
Ruled: 1917–1922

His real name was Vladimir Ilyich Ulyanov. He later changed it to Lenin, which was one of the many pseudonyms he used. Why Lenin? No one really knows. But everyone knows of Lenin.

Vladimir Lenin was the ideologue who created a practical form of Marxism. Karl Marx came up with the concept, but it lacked the realist's approach to a society and government. Lenin was the realist. He built on Marxism and made it Leninism. He created a practical methodology for applying Marxism to a country in the modern world, or a "world of imperialism."

Lenin was born in Russia in the city of Simrisk. His parents were liberals. In nineteenth-century Russia, liberalism meant that you worked toward an important cause. In the case of Ilya Nikolaevich

Ulyanov and his wife, Maria Alexandrovna, the cause was free education for everyone.

Ilya and Maria were not purebred Russians. In those days, cultural exchanges due to wars and border shifts were constant and common. Russian society was a mosaic. Even the nobility was filled with cultural combinations introduced through arranged marriages from all over Europe. His father's side was Russian and Kalmyk. His mother's side had German ancestry. Lenin's maternal grandmother was a German Lutheran. His Jewish-born maternal grandfather converted to Christianity and was baptized in the Russian Orthodox Church.

Two dramatic events occurred in rapid succession in the life of Vladimir Lenin. They were events that forged deep impressions on Lenin's life, character, and ideology. In 1886, when Lenin was sixteen years old, his father died of a cerebral hemorrhage. In 1887, his older brother, Alexander Ulyanov, was executed. He was hung for participating in a failed assassination attempt on the life of Czar Alexander III. Ulyanov was an anarchist who saw evil in all forms of government, especially in Russia's czarist government.

As a young student, Vladimir excelled in the study of Greek and Latin and the classics. He became very interested in Marxist ideology after his brother's death. Years later, when Lenin and his philosophy of governance ran the country, the story of Ulyanov's actions and death became a pivotal part in Soviet education and lore. The story is taught to every Soviet child much the same as the story of George Washington and the cherry tree is retold in classrooms across the United States.

A very famous painting by the artist Belousov is reprinted in

Soviet textbooks. The artist depicts Lenin and his mother mourning Ulyanov's death. The caption reads, "We will follow a different path." In Soviet Russia, art was political. There was no room for misinterpretation. A painting of this magnitude required a caption to make certain that it was properly understood. Ulyanov chose anarchism; Lenin chose Marxism. Ulyanov chose an individualistic method of expression; Lenin chose a popular, or for-the-people, method of expression.

Despite being arrested for student protests and expelled from school for political activities, the future leader of the Soviet people studied, took the exam for the bar, and became a lawyer. But rather than practice law, he moved to St. Petersburg and settled into a career of politics—a very dangerous career path in czarist Russia that led to his arrest and exile to Siberia. He met a kindred spirit along the way named Nadezhda Krupskaya and they married. In 1889, while in Siberia, he wrote and published a work called *The Development of Capitalism in Russia.*

Exile ended in 1900, and Lenin began to travel. He lived in Paris, Austria, Switzerland, Czech, Germany, and even London.

He wrote more books and founded a newspaper. Lenin was writing constantly, using many aliases. It was during this period of his life that Vladimir Ilyich found the name he would use for the rest of his life: Lenin.

Then the February Revolution began. Czar Nicholas II had been deposed. Lenin wanted to be back home in Russia, but it was 1917, and World War I was in full swing. For Lenin to get train passage from his whereabouts in Switzerland back to Russia was not an easy feat to accomplish. But he did it.

Lenin was granted permission to travel through Germany on his way to Sweden. From there he would catch a ferry to the city of St. Petersburg, which had been renamed Petrograd. There was one condition: He could neither see nor be seen while en route. Kaiser Wilhelm did not want Vladimir Lenin in Germany for fear he would cause a serious disturbance. So it was agreed that Lenin and his entourage would travel in a sealed train with blacked-out windows. Lenin arrived in Petrograd on April 16, 1917. He became a leading figure within the Bolshevik movement. His co-leader and co-ideologue was Leon Trotsky. Lenin believed that workers could run the factories, and that factories should be governed by workers' committees. Those committees were called soviets.

His ideas were written up in a revolutionary pamphlet and entitled *State and Revolution*. The pamphlet was released after Lenin returned from Finland, where he fled after an unsuccessful workers' uprising.

After the revolution, Lenin became chairman of the Council of the People's Commissars. He had an ambitious set of goals. He wanted literally to electrify Russia and the rest of the Soviet states— to supply them with real electric power and technology. And he wanted to realize his parents' goal of free education to the masses.

World War I ended for Russia with the signing of the treaty of Brest-Litovsk on March 3, 1918, but the Russian Revolution raged on.

The struggle to form a Soviet democracy and a government of workers was enormous. The process of reeducating people after three hundred years of czarist thinking was proving very difficult. The workers state and the factory committees were not proceeding with enough speed. Resocialization was slow and awkward work.

Pressure and violence were raging. It was Reds against Whites—the Reds were the Bolsheviks, and the Whites were the czarists.

The Whites had the support of Germany, France, Japan, and the United States. But the Reds were better organized, more determined, and more committed. The Bolsheviks had their government and the *cheka*—their secret police. Everything was in place. It all came to a head on August 30, 1918.

Lenin had just finished addressing a meeting of the Socialist Revolutionary Party in Moscow and was heading toward his car. Fanya Kaplan—a well-known member of the party—called his name to ask a question. Lenin turned around to answer, and Fanya took aim. Bullets flew. She hit her mark.

One shot hit Lenin in the shoulder, the other in the lung. A third shot missed entirely. He was rushed to the Kremlin, avoiding hospitals for fear that other assassins were lying in wait. The response of Lenin and the Bolsheviks was to embark on a huge campaign to kill and arrest as many anti-Leninists as possible. It was the beginning of a long history of Soviet human-rights abuses.

The Bolsheviks joined forces with comrades around the world and created Communist International. The name was later changed to the Russian Communist Party. After a long, harsh struggle, the Reds beat the Whites. It was 1920. Bolsheviks ruled. The country was decimated.

Towns were destroyed, property was stolen, and anyone who complained was arrested in the name of Communism. Farms were burned to the ground. Resistance was met with executions and arrests. It was a society of mass intimidation and terror.

The bullets were never removed from Lenin's neck and shoulder—the procedure was thought to be too dangerous. He never regained full strength, and in May of 1922, Lenin suffered his first stroke and was left partially paralyzed. He had another stroke seven months later and resigned from political life. A third stroke came in March of 1923. Lenin died on January 21, 1924.

Three days after his death, the city of St. Petersburg was renamed Leningrad. The name reverted back to St. Petersburg or Petrograd after the fall of the Soviet Union. When he died, Lenin's brain was removed. Neurosurgeons from Germany and Russia studied the brain in an attempt to determine the exact reasons for Lenin's genius. In 1929, Oskar Vogt actually published results concluding that Lenin's cerebral cortex was extremely large, and that was the reason for his genius. The results have been rejected. Lenin was embalmed, and his remains lie in a glass case in front of the Kremlin in the middle of Red Square. The embalming fluid is changed regularly, and people come from Russia and around the world to view the body of Vladimir Lenin.

All of Lenin's writings were censored and corrected after his death. His supporters never wanted their leader to be accused of having made a mistake in either his understanding or his predictions.

After Lenin's death, his successor, Josef Stalin, practically turned him into a god. How ironic. Lenin created a society that rejected the idea of God, and his successor thought to turn him into a god.

5

JOSEF STALIN
Short, Paranoid, and Insecure

Born: 1878
Died: 1953
Ruled: 1924-1953

Stalin is not the given name of the most famous dictator of the Soviet Union. It is the name he chose for himself. Stalin, in Georgian, means "the man of steel."

Stalin's real name was Iosif Vissarionovich Dzhugashvili. From photos, he has a Ronald Reagan-esque look about him—Reagan with cropped hair and a full mustache. And much shorter.

He was actually only five feet two inches tall. It was his cult of personality that created the image of a man who towered over other men—over mere mortals. His presence was not dissimilar to the galvanizing presence of a Russian czar. After all, how could the great leader of the Soviets be so short? If he is perceived as short, he will be seen as weak. So every statue and portrait of Josef Stalin depicts him as towering over everyone and everything.

In brief, Stalin successfully took over and ruled the Soviet Union after the death of Vladimir Lenin. He did it by totally outflanking and outmaneuvering the entire competition. First he publicly and politically destroyed his enemies. Then he really finished them off: he eliminated, arrested, exiled, and even executed them. Stalin's long list of enemies included some people who had once been close friends. They were people with whom he and Lenin had stood side by side, shoulder to shoulder, leading the revolution

His rule is best defined as a cult of Stalin. He politically and publicly proved that he was Lenin's best successor. Then he transformed the ideals that Lenin had imbued in Soviet society, shaping them into his own model. Soviet society no longer belonged to Lenin; now it was his—Josef Stalin's—society.

Stalin rose to power according to a perfectly designed plan. He was the editor of the major Communist paper, *Pravda*. Since most other leaders of the revolution—including Lenin—were in exile, *Pravda* was the most important tool they had for communicating messages to the people. At certain times, Stalin took the liberty of refusing to print Lenin's pieces because Stalin believed they favored the first revolutionary government under Krensky. Lenin did not favor Krensky and his provisional government.

After Lenin died there was a huge debate as to who the rightful successor should be. The two major contenders were Stalin and Trotsky. Trotsky favored a continual and international revolution. He was very close with Lenin and was the ideological leader of Leninism. That was his biggest problem.

Trotsky was an ideologue—not a politician. Stalin was a politician. In direct contrast to Trotsky's proposals, Stalin proposed focusing inward and creating a Communist society from within. In the end, Trotsky lost and met the fate of all Stalin's enemies: he was exiled. That wasn't good enough for Stalin. Trotsky was still alive and living in Mexico, which made him a perceived potential threat to Stalin's power. In 1936, Stalin had Trotsky brutally assassinated while he was in his apartment. Leon Trotsky, by the order of Josef Stalin, was hacked to death with a hatchet.

In August of 1939—before the start of World War II—Stalin and Hitler made a pact. Together, they were to squeeze Poland and then divide it. Hitler attacked the Soviet Union in June of 1941, abrogating the treaty.

In the end, the Soviets were able to help the Allies defeat Germany, but it was very costly for the USSR. About 8.6 million Red Army soldiers and about 20 million Soviet civilians were killed in the war. On the other side, 4 million German prisoners of war were never heard from after they were captured by Stalin.

It wasn't only Stalin's enemies who suffered his brutal, demonic wrath. Stalin purged anyone who might challenge him in the future. A colleague one day was an enemy the next. He turned on people immediately; they never had a chance. Even the people who carried out his orders—his exterminators—were done away with. Stalin was not a man who took personal risks.

To this day, his policies and the number of deaths those caused are discussed and debated. It seems clear that Stalin is responsible for the severe and successive famines that ravished Russia from 1932–1934, famines that directly resulted in the deaths of five million to ten million farmers and peasants. Not only did he confiscate the crops of farmers who could not meet the required minimum growth standards he had set, but he punished them. He took away their seed for the next year. The punishment so far exceeded the crime it set the country into a backslide. He arrested and executed so many farmers there there were almost no farmers with experience left to cultivate any crops. That was Stalin's way.

He blamed the agricultural disaster on the farmers who resisted collectivization. He also came down very hard on the wealthier farmers—those who met the standard and so by definition were the most successful. They were the landowners, and as such they were the opposite of his worldview and philosophy. But squashing them would destroy the entire agricultural economy. Stalin's ideological correctness was more important than the economy of the entire Soviet Union.

But Stalin did have economic plans. The Warsaw Pact was the engine that drove industrialization of the Soviet Union. It was the five-year plan that forced the Soviets to modernize. Stalin forced the Soviets out of the Middle Ages and drove them into the Industrial Age.

Science, art, and literature all fell under the rubric of ideological Communist control. One of Stalin's great successes was his scientific program, but even that was severely hampered by Communist ideology. Stalin wanted to work toward nuclear energy and nuclear arms, yet he refused to permit the use of theories that came out of the West like quantum physics and relativity. He believed using Western-originating theories was against the principles of Communism.

It took a lot of persuading before scientists were permitted to progress with their work. And despite it all, in the 1950s the Soviets were able to create the Sputnik program and launch a spacecraft. It was Soviet advances in the sciences that were responsible for propelling the United States into a competitive space program.

It is hard to imagine, but under the oppressive rule of Stalin, the Soviet Union was turned into a country so powerful that it rivaled the United States. A country so powerful that it posed the only threat to the United States.

When Stalin died, he was embalmed and his body was placed in a glass case outside the Kremlin walls right next to the case containing the body of Lenin. In 1961, Stalin's successor, Nikita Khrushchev, buried the body in a state cemetery. The real Stalin and his Stalinism, Khrushchev said, were a blight on Lenin's memory. The transfer of the body was part of a process of national purging and healing that took place in the Soviet Union after Stalin's death.

Stalin was born and educated far from Moscow. He was a Georgian from the town of Gori. His father was a cobbler who, for a time, had his own store. After going bankrupt, Stalin's father found employment in a large factory in the town of Tiflis.

Stalin was known among friends and family as "Soso"—the diminutive form of Josef. Soso was sent to religious school. Though the school's population was largely Georgian, Russian was the spoken language there, and the teachers made fun of the local boys' Georgian accents. Even so, Stalin did very well in school, which pleased his mother very much. Stalin's mother always wanted him to be a priest. She persisted in that wish even after her son became premier of the Soviet Union. (There is a Jewish joke in there, somewhere.)

When Soso was still young, his mother, Ekaterina, did house

cleaning for a Jewish man in Gori named David Papismedov. This Jewish man would give Stalin books to read. He encouraged the boy to pursue ideas and concepts and became a positive educational role model for Stalin. He even gave Stalin money whenever the boy came and helped his mother. Meanwhile Stalin's father had abandoned the family and was probably killed in a bar fight in Tiflis.

Years later, Papismedov came to the Kremlin to see Stalin. To the shock of everyone around, Stalin not only received the Jewish visitor but was seen with him publicly and looked to be obviously enjoying himself in the old man's company, laughing and joking.

Stalin was an avid reader. In Georgian literature, there was a mountain ranger who dedicated his life to fighting for Georgian freedom and independence. His name was Koba. Stalin had found his fantasy hero. Koba was to become one of Stalin's most important underground names.

Stalin graduated and went off to religious seminary. He went there not because he was religious but because he wanted an education, and there was no university in his region. The despot responsible for the persecution of millions of his countrymen paid his way through religious school with a small scholarship and a stipend he received for singing in the choir. During this period, he began his group activities in Communism. He became active in the Leninist cause. He attended the 1907 conference in London of the Russian Social Democratic Labour Party. His fame rose within the party. Leadership at the national level began to take note of him because of the innovative way he raised money for the cause: he robbed banks.

Family life was not going that well. Stalin married a woman

named Ekaterina, just like his mother. She died only three years after their marriage, straddling him with a young son—Yakov. Ekatrina had been a calming influence on her husband, and Stalin spoke well of her. Only she could mend his heart, he would say.

Father and son did not get along. Yakov was so miserable that at one point he tried to shoot himself. He missed. His father's response to what could have been the loss of his son was straightforward and chilling. Hearing the news, Stalin said, "He cannot even shoot straight."

Having survived his suicide attempt, Yakov joined the army as a lieutenant and was captured by the Germans. The Germans told Stalin they would gladly exchange his son for a German general being held by the Soviets. Stalin's response: "A lieutenant is not worth a general."

According to sources, Yakov committed suicide while in a prison camp. This time he ran into an electrified fence and clung to the wires. It worked.

Stalin's second wife, Nadezhda Alliluyeva, shot herself in 1932. They say she committed suicide after an argument with her husband. They had two children. Their son, Vassili, died of alcoholism in 1962, and their daughter, Svetlana, moved to the United States in 1967. There is some reliable information about another child that Stalin had in the Gulag. There are also stories of a grandchild—Yuri Davidov—who would have to be the grandchild of Stalin and his common-law wife, Lida.

Stalin's mother died of natural causes in 1937. He did not attend her funeral. He did send a wreath.

On March 1, 1953, Stalin fell and had a stroke. A cerebral hemorrhage. It probably happened soon after he returned from a night of partying with cronies. Stalin had ordered his staff never to disturb him. And so he lay, with no medical attention, until the following evening. He died four days later on March 5, 1953. There have been claims that he was assassinated by means of rat poison. We will never know.

In total, Josef Stalin probably executed several million people. Historians can't come to an exact number of millions, but it's somewhere over fifteen million and could climb as high as fifty million.

Stalin was one of the greatest murderers of the twentieth century. He also merits a place of honor among the greatest murderers in the history of the world.

6

JOSIP BROZ TITO
From Partisan to Dictator

Born: 1892
Died: 1980
Ruled: 1943–1980

Tito was the leader of Yugoslavia from the end of World War II until his demise in 1980.

There is a discrepancy about his birth date. He was probably born on May 7, 1892, but during his underground fighting days against the Nazis he had forged papers. Those papers listed his birth date as May 25—the date of a failed Nazi assassination attempt against him. Tito took May 25 as the date of his rebirth.

He was one of those leaders who did not do well in school. Tito failed the first grade and flunked out of school at age thirteen.

Originally named Broz, he was a classic example of the combination of what made Yugoslavia. His father was a Croatian, and his mother was a Slovenian. While forced into a single country, the two communities were dramatically different cultures.

There is some speculation as to the origin of the name Tito. Some speculate the name was put together on the battlefield. When under pressure, the leader would shout out curt commands. Command part one was "ti" ("you" in Croatian). Part two was "to" ("that" in Croatian). So he would point at a person and say "you" and then to a task and say "that." Another theory is that the name was chosen for its roots in ancient Croatian culture. It was probably his code name in the underground. But it really just comes from the Roman emperor Titus. Tito is the Croatian form of the name.

His professional direction led him to be a mechanic's assistant, where he became exposed to the idea of labor movements and unions. Mechanics celebrated May Day, or Labor Day, which was to honor dedicated workers' contributions to world culture.

Tito joined the union in 1910 in the metal workers division. He found work in the Daimler and Benz factories of Germany, Yugoslavia, and Austria.

He was drafted during Word War I but spent most of his time running from the authorities or in prison for antiwar activities. Eventually, he joined the Red Army.

That was an army he could fight for. The Soviet army represented the vision that Tito thought most appropriate for him as well as the world.

The Germans were having many successes in an eleven-day battle; Belgrade fell on April 17, 1941. Then Bosnia and Herzegovina, as well as parts of Serbia and Slovenia, were occupied by the Nazis and their allies.

But in 1941, the Germans invaded Yugoslavia. Tito made a clear pronouncement that everyone should fight the Fascist Nazis. A large-scale program of sabotage began, and Tito was at the center.

Kids were blowing up small vehicles, and resistance organizations planned much larger sabotage programs including blowing up trains and bridges.

Tito was the most prominent and most vocal member of the organization that led the resistance. This led the way to his assuming positions as marshal and then leader of Yugoslavia, which he became on December 4, 1943.

Tito declared the government of Yugoslavia independent and free, and did it while still occupied by the Germans. This particularly angered and frustrated the Germans. They were trying to capture Tito as a symbol of the resistance and defiance against the Nazis. On one occasion, he was shot and wounded. He was actually saved because of his dog.

Tito received tremendous support for his resistance fighters from the United States and Great Britain, especially after the major war conferences in Malta and Teheran in 1943. But there was significant tension. Tito was very close to the Soviets, and the Soviets were not friendly with the United States and Great Britain. This came to a head in 1945 when Tito signed a treaty with the Soviet Union granting them entry into Yugoslavia. The Soviets were the impetus necessary to oust the Germans. And indeed, together with Tito's forces, the Red Army successfully repelled the Germans.

A provisional government was established after the war, and Tito was at its head. National elections were soon held, and, as expected, Tito won an overwhelming majority. He was the prime minister as well as the foreign minister.

Now things got very ugly—even nastier than during the war. Tito and his forces, together with the Soviets, imprisoned or murdered their opponents. Some were even deported to prison camps in the Soviet Union.

But Tito was his own man. He created his own form of Communism. Stalin actually called it Titoism. There was significant tension between Tito and Stalin; Yugoslavia was thrown out of Stalin's Communist association in 1948. The rift between Tito and Stalin was the subject of much discussion and debate. Principally, could a Communist entity survive outside the umbrella of Stalin's power and protection?

In 1961, because of that rift with Stalin, Tito helped create the Non-Aligned Movement. Together with Nasser of Egypt and Nehru of India, Tito created an organization of countries that were not aligned with the Soviets or the United States. The idea was that there were many other countries that were not part of the Cold War and whose interests were not being considered in the conflict. They had to unify and force their agenda onto the world's stage.

Tito's model seemed to work. There were many economists, especially European economists, who actually believed Tito blended the best parts of the West and the best parts of Communism. Because Yugoslavians were permitted to travel freely, there was much exchange of ideas and culture, as well as investments from abroad. Yugoslavians had a higher standard of living and seemed to genuinely be better off.

But even a benevolent dictatorship is still a dictatorship. In 1976, a new constitution was passed proclaiming Tito president for life.

He died on May 4, 1980. He was eighty-eight years old. His funeral was attended by dignitaries from around the world.

Internally, the Yugoslavians, who have a long history of subjugation under demonic rulers, might write a very different history of Tito.

7

ZOG
Son of the Palace Cook

Born: 1895
Died: 1961
Ruled: 1928–1939

King Zog of Albania was quite a character. He sported a small waxed mustache. He smoked about 150 perfumed cigarettes every day. He liked playing poker—with his sisters. He adorned himself with medals. He wore his royal cap at a jaunty angle.

Zog's given name was Ahmed Zogolli—a proper Muslim name. Ahmed later shortened Zogolli to Zogu, which means "hawk" in Albanian. He then further shortened his name to Zog. Powerful. Masterful. Zog.

Officially, Zog was elected president of Albania. He was also Albania's prime minister. But a European-style government with a president, rather than a monarch, was a concept that many Albanians simply did not understand. It was the people of Albania who first proclaimed their ruler king of the Albanians. He was then proclaimed field marshal of the Royal Albanian Army. And then Zog himself proclaimed a constitutional monarchy similar to the regime in Italy. His family members were given royal titles: His mother became the queen mother and his siblings became prince and princess. Still unmarried at the time of his coronation, King Zog appointed his nephew, a boy named Tati, His Highness, Prince of Kosovo.

Zog's mother had another, more informal title and position. She was in charge of food and beverages. She managed the royal kitchens. For Zog, it wasn't an issue of taste; it was a matter of trust, or in this case, distrust. Zog was afraid of being poisoned, and he made his mother his watchdog.

King Zog had good reason to fear—he was hated. History records over six hundred blood vendettas against Zog.

In Albania, blood vendettas proceeded according to tradition. During Zog's time, a wounded party was permitted to take revenge because of an intentional or perceived insult or violation of pride (like breaking off an engagement). One of the more colorful vendettas against Zog centers around his own broken engagement. Zog was betrothed to the daughter of Shefqet Bey Verlaci, but that was before he became king. Once he became king, the engagement was off and the vendetta was on. Obviously, Zog survived.

He survived over fifty attempted assassinations.

In one of the more creative attempts, assassins chose to kill Zog in Vienna as he was about to attend a performance of the opera *Pagliacci*. As Zog exited his car the assassins opened fire. Zog shot back, even after he had been hit, using the revolver he always carried. Had they waited until the performance was in progress, the noise of their shots might very well have gone unnoticed by opera-goers listening to the orchestra.

In 1923, even before his election to the presidency, Zog was shot at and wounded while attending a session of parliament. A year later, he went into exile with six hundred of his allies after one of them was successfully assassinated.

In tribute to Zog, Albanian nationalism was the model for all rising nationalism in the late nineteenth century. Every national independence movement would say, "If the Albanians can have a country and be in charge of their destiny, then certainly we can do the same." He brought stability to his country. He modernized the military and instituted an educational system. He outlawed cruelty to animals. Even though he was a Muslim, he outlawed the wearing of the veil by Albanian women.

Zog became governor of his parents' *bey* when he was sixteen years old. *Bey* is a Turkish word describing the region controlled by a lord. It is a set of villages run by serfs.

During World War I, Zog took sides with the Austro-Hungarians while the rest of Albania sided with Turkey and Eastern Europe. It was an unpopular move, and it resulted in Zog being detained in Vienna and in Rome. And he liked it. He liked the Western lifestyle he was exposed to, and he liked the women he met. But by 1919, the future ruler was back home in Albania. The relationship he forged with Rome during this early period in his career was to prove very useful later when he most needed them.

In the 1920s Zog became the leader of the reformist party in Albania. He served as foreign minister, defense minister, and interior minister; he was climbing the ladder of success. His popularity was rising, and in January 1925, he was elected president of the Constituent Assembly.

President Zog set out to modernize a Muslim state that was still stuck in the Middle Ages. Albania was a country where almost nobody had heard of the industrial revolution. He tried to Europeanize Albania using Italy as his role model and investment banker. Italy assumed a tremendous amount of Albanian defense costs. In return, Zog allowed the Italians to have a tremendous amount of influence in his decision making and policies, especially as those policies pertained to Albania's interactions with Germany, England, and Russia.

For the first time in hundreds of years, Albania was becoming an independent state. Corrupt and backward, but independent.

Zog was a monarch who looted his own treasury and hoarded his country's jewels to support his own lifestyle. It is said that his own expenses totaled 2 percent of the nation's wealth. The joke goes that as he was checking into a hotel in London, the bellmen who were schlepping his suitcases asked what was in them that made them so unusually heavy. He responded that they were filled with gold. The joke was on the people of Albania.

Zog was the ultimate egotist and megalomaniac. He developed his own salute. He asked all Albanians to take their right hand and salute their heart. It was called the "Zog salute"—a salute to the heart. He was always surrounded by bodyguards.

When he was sworn in as king, he held the ceremony in the parliament. He swore an oath of allegiance on both a Bible and a Koran in order to try to bridge gaps in his country. Zog wanted to instill parliamentary strength and make certain there would be some sense of stability that would remain in Albania even after his demise. In contrast to other monarchies, his constitution made it illegal to marry royalty from any other country—a practice that was widely followed throughout Europe. And no member of the royal family could be prime minister or a cabinet member. He tried to bring Albania into the twentieth century in education as well as government. It was a Herculean task.

The depression of the 1930s was a blow to the fledgling economy of Albania. The country became even more dependant on Italy, which was under the Fascist rule of Benito Mussolini. Italy stepped in ostensibly to help, but in reality it took control. The only way Zog could oust his one-time supporters was by nationalizing Roman Catholic churches and schools. He sent his Italian advisers home and booted out his Italian police. By April of 1939, the Italians were back. This time it was Zog who was booted out.

Zog was not alone in exile. In April of 1938, he had finally married. He broke his own rule—his wife was a Hungarian-American aristocrat. Her name was Countess Geraldine Apponyi de Nagy-Apponyi. A year later their son, His Royal Highness Crown Prince Leka Zogu, was born. Two days later Italian troops invaded Albania.

The family first moved to Egypt. Then they took their heavy suitcases and moved to England, but the European royals would have nothing to do with Zog. So it was off to America. In 1951, the Zogs thought to set up a castle in the United States. They bought an estate in upstate New York for $102,800. There are rumors that the one-time king of Albania paid for his sixty-room estate not with cash but with precious gems, with rubies and diamonds. The castle was sold in 1995. The family had never moved in. By the time Zog sold the mansion it had been vandalized by thieves hoping to find hidden treasure. Zog had hoped to set up a kingdom-in-exile, complete with an entire entourage. Immigration officials had other plans and granted him only about twenty of the more than one hundred visas he applied for. Zog had actually attempted to bribe officials to permit his staff entry.

Despite his passion for fine food and couture fashion, Zog's real objective had been to advance the independence of Albania and modernize a backward society. And he was somewhat successful. The man who transformed Albania from a series of feudal territories into a twentieth-century community lived out the rest of his life on the French Riviera. He died in a French hospital and is interred in a Parisian cemetery.

8

NICOLAE CEAUSESCU
Strong-Arm Father of Romania

Born: 1918
Died: 1989
Ruled: 1965–1989

It happened in Bucharest. One hundred thousand people gathered outside the Romanian Communist Party headquarters in Republican Square. The date was December 21, 1989. Organized by his own people, Ceausescu was expecting a rally. He was expecting to hear thousands of voices chanting his name. He had arranged for the gathering to be broadcast, live, on Romanian television. With cameras rolling, the crowd took up a chant.

But the people came not to praise Ceausescu; they came to ask for his head. There were no accolades for the Romanian head of state, the head of Romania's Communist Party, the chairman of Romania's Socialist Democracy and Unity Front, the head of the armed forces of Romania, the president of Romania's National

Council for Working People, the chairman of the Supreme Council for Economic and Social Development in Romania.

As Nicolae Addruta Ceausescu stepped out on the balcony, his loyal wife Elena at his side, the crowd started chanting, "Down with the murderers!" *Tomisoara.* "Down with dictatorship!" "We are ready to die!" It wasn't a rally. It wasn't even a protest. It was a lynch mob.

The live broadcast was stopped, but not before the people of Romania saw their leader visibly shaken. The crowd grew larger throughout the night. The next day, Ceausescu attempted to address them one more time. And then Nicolai and Elena Ceausescu fled for their lives. Their helicopter was at the ready, waiting on the roof of their building. Reports say that Romania's minister of defense, Vasile Milea—the man who refused to heed the decree of the Romanian leader and order the army to shoot to kill the masses of people—was executed.

Ceausescu and his wife were found in an armored personnel carrier in Cimpulung about eighty miles north of Bucharest.

On December 25, Nicolai and Elena Ceausescu were tried by a special military court and convicted of mass murder. That same day, they were sentenced to death and shot by a firing squad. Across the nation, the people of Romania turned on their television sets to view the dead bodies—and to breathe a collective sigh of relief. The Ceausescus were buried in unmarked graves. In 1992, the site of their burial was discovered, and a granite headstone was placed over the stones, courtesy of the Communist Party.

Like most of Europe during World War I, the inter-war years, and World War II, Romania was caught up in arguments about the future. It was Communism versus nationalism. The future was all about ideology.

It was during this period of passion and politics that Ceausescu met Elena Petrescu. He was a serious Communist, making them kindred souls. He was arrested and imprisoned again and again, and all the while she stood by his side. He was labeled a Communist organizer by the authorities.

Then good fortune shined on Ceausescu. In 1940, he was sent to a concentration camp at Tirgu Jiu. His cell mate, Gheorghe Gheorghiu-Dej, was the leader of the Communist movement in Romania. Other than his wife, this was the most important friendship ever forged in the life of one of the worst dictators in the modern world. Ceausescu's relationship with Gheorghiu-Dej changed the course of Romania's history; it forever changed the face of Romania.

Meanwhile, Romania had entered World War II on the side of the Germans. Germany had a hard time keeping hold of Romania. Ceausescu escaped just as the Soviets were about to occupy his country. He was named secretary of the Union of Communist Youth and promoted to the rank of brigadier general. When the war was over, almost one million Romanians were dead. The good news for Ceausescu was that Romania was behind the Iron Curtain; the Communist Party had won. And Gheorghiu-Dej saw to it that his protégé and understudy was voted in as a member of the Romanian Parliament, the Grand National Assembly.

By 1950, Ceausescu was a major general and deputy minister of the army, the Communist Party had taken control of the government, and Romania had been renamed the Romanian People's

Republic. He was climbing high, assuming position after position. When Gheorghiu-Dej succumbed to pneumonia in March of 1965, Ceausescu grabbed the reins of power and became leader of Romania's Communist Party. The country was renamed again; now it was the Socialist Republic of Romania.

The new leader, following in the footsteps of his mentor, set about challenging the authority of the Soviet Union. Ceausescu wanted Romania to be independent; the Soviets wanted to shorten the leash, reigning Romania in tighter and tighter. Romania condemned Soviet intervention in Czechoslovakia in 1968 and was critical of the Soviet invasion of Afghanistan in 1979. The ruler of Romania was spunky. He was very creative and was making significant attempts to break away from Soviet influence. But his penchant for extremism and totalitarian thought and leadership was showing through.

New laws were put into effect. All contact with Russian and Soviet professionals was forbidden. Anyone in the army or any position of leadership who was married to a Soviet was told to divorce, step down, or send his wife back to the Soviet Union. In 1967, just to irritate the Soviets, Ceausescu established relations with East Germany and Israel. The Soviets were so upset that they amassed troops on his border and threatened to invade. But they didn't. The bold and daring Ceausescu became the darling of the West.

Richard Nixon visited Romania in 1969, and in 1975 the United States actually granted Romania the coveted status of most-favored nation. Romanian imports to the United States were not taxed, and the nation of Romania was assisting the United States in its efforts around the world. Romania joined the International Monetary Fund, the World Bank, and the Non-Align Movement. They were building very strong relations with China and North Korea. It was the Golden Age of Ceausescu.

And then the personal pendulum of Ceausescu started to swing in the other direction. Gone was liberalism. Gone were human rights.

He began to apply huge limitations on the press and on freedom of expression. He used the press almost exclusively to promote himself and his own personality cult. He promoted his version of nationalism—a nationalism centered around Nicolae Ceausescu. He instituted a repopulation policy. People were heavily taxed if they did not have children; childless couples were labeled deserters and unsupportive of the state. Abortion and contraceptives were illegal. Sex education was outlawed. The population of Romania increased by 50 percent. Also increased were child mortality, birth defects, and child abandonment. Children were left to rot in filthy, decrepit, institutionalized orphanages.

U.S. secretary of state George Shultz called Ceausescu the person with "possibly the worst human rights record in Europe."

Ceausescu created the Securitate. It is pronounced like the Italian Securitateee. It was the biggest internal security force in all of Europe with the power to investigate and arrest anyone at any time. Romania was a police state. Everyone was afraid of the secret police, and the secret police were everywhere.

Elena was becoming one of the most powerful people in the country. She was head of the politburo. She was in charge of employment for the entire nation.

Almost everyone holding any important position in Romania was either a protégé or a relative of the head of state. Romania under Ceausescu was a system of government totally controlled by one person and his cronies. He was involved in training the PLO. He trained the Syrians and the Libyans in their fight against the West and the Soviets. Ceausescu wanted unrest in the world in order to empower the weak.

The Genius of the Carpathians failed miserably as an economic leader. In his attempt to control economics, he fell into debt. He very severely reduced services, including electricity and even food. Everything was exported. The people of Romania were left to starve and to freeze. The austerity programs Ceausescu initiated in order to pay national debts resulted in the starvation of fifteen thousand to twenty thousand people per year.

Resentment was building quickly. He warned people against pushing the limits of free speech. The world was beginning to turn its collective back on Ceausescu, and he didn't even notice. The people of Romania were turning on their leader, and he never saw it coming. He was too wrapped up in himself and his own genius. They were starving; he was feasting. They were freezing; he wore cashmere and minks.

The protests began in 1987 in Iasi, near the Moldova border. They moved to Brasaov. In March of 1989, a letter from six party members was sent to the Voice of Free Europe. It became known as "The Letter of Six." The letter was a challenge to the power of the Romanian regime. On December 16, 1989, a protest broke out in the western part of Romania called Timisoara. Protesters marched on Communist headquarters the next day, and Ceausescu ordered the army to open fire. Four thousand protesters were killed. The next stop was Bucharest.

Ceausescu was the son of a rural farmer. At age eleven he became a shoemaker's assistant. Elena was the daughter of a share farmer. Two peasants. One despotic regime.

9

SLOBODAN MILOSEVIC
The Ethnic Cleanser

Born: 1940
Died: 2006
Ruled: 1988–2000

Slobodan Milosevic has the distinction of being one of the greatest murderers of the twentieth century. That is a very difficult clique to break into.

He was charged and tried by the United Nations in The Hague at the International Criminal Tribunal for Former Yugoslavia for crimes against humanity in Kosovo. At the outset, he was charged with violating "the laws or customs of war" and with "grave breaches of the Geneva Conventions." But as the trial dragged on for a year and a half, new evidence was quite literally uncovered—hundreds of thousands of murdered Bosnians were found buried in various sites. The charges were amended to include genocide in Bosnia.

He used intimidation, murder, and mass-media manipulation

to achieve his ends. He was so committed to his goals that it did not matter if it meant murdering friends and allies.

Milosevic was born in Serbia during World War II when Yugoslavia was under Nazi occupation. Yugoslavia was a federation; it was a country of different societies with different cultures, languages, religions, and allegiances all lumped together and expected to get along. His parents separated when he was a child, each one committing suicide during his adult years. Milosevic's father, a deacon in the Serbian Orthodox Church, killed himself in 1962. His schoolteacher mother hung herself in 1974.

His most important political exposure came when he went to law school at Belgrade University. While there, he became the leader of the Student Communist Party. He also made a new friend: Ivan Stambolic, nephew of the man who had been the president of the Serbian Executive Council—the Serbian equivalent of prime minister. That entrée into the political arena transformed Milosevic's life.

Stambolic, without knowing it, was about to pave the way for Slobodan Milosevic. He would carry him on his coattails until Milosevic no longer needed him. And then Milosevic would orchestrate his patron's demise. .

Milosevic became ensconced in the Communist Party. Wherever Stambolic went, Milosevic went—only one step behind. Stambolic left a position and Milosevic stepped right in. At the Technogas company. As head of the Beobanka bank. In Belgrade city politics. And when Stambolic became the president of Serbia, his protégé became the new leader of the Serbian Communist Party. Milosevic won the position with the narrowest margin in the party's history.

Stambolic may have been a fan, but most party members were not.

Then Slobodan Milosevic, the man who owed his career to Stambolic, masterminded the president's deposition from office and replaced him as president of Serbia. He did it through deception and manipulation—two activities Milosevic excelled in. In the year 2000, twelve years after Milosevic wrestled away the presidency, Stambolic was kidnapped. The body was found three years later.

Milosevic was a powerful speaker, and he manipulated the media to convince the masses of his causes and purpose. From his speeches and by his actions, it was hard to determine if Milosevic was a staunch nationalist or a believer in Communism. But it made no difference. He had the power and he had the people.

He had been a member of the Communist Party but was never a Communist extremist. He broke from the party with relative ease and no visible angst. His actions were those of a strong nationalist, but there was very little in his terminology or expressions to identify him as ultranationalist. In European political life, there was no such animal as an unaffiliated leader. He was certainly not a Fascist; he didn't fit the mold. He was Milosevic.

He was mean. He was callous. He was dangerous. He was ruthless. But what turned Slobodan Milosevic into a genocidal mass murderer? Yugoslavia was a state thrown together after World War I. It had a long history of tensions, quarrels, unrest, and even periodic oppression. One ethnic group was always going at it with another. On March 16, 1991, Serbian president Milosevic, leader of the largest of all ethnic groups in Yugoslavia, declared the total dissolution of Yugoslavia. In June, the leaders of Slovenia and Croatia did the same thing. Macedonia did it in September. Bosnia and Herzegovina followed along in March of 1992. Gone was the central government. It was every group for itself. Power and control would go to the victor. The strongest and most ruthless was the first to take control.

Milosevic was a Serb. The Serbs wanted all the Croats and Bosnians out. They began with massive dislocations. Then came forced removals. Milosevic now had a political excuse for unleashing his pent-up anger and frustration. He cleansed away his soul— if he had one—through the most extreme of political and human actions: ethnic cleansing.

In Milosevic's mind, ethnic cleansing was the best long-term solution to the inner-group problem. This thinking was not dissimilar to the way Hitler approached his "final solution." But the style was very different. Hitler created a machine for death: death camps that were factories for murder. Milosevic's program was a page out of nineteenth-century humiliations: medieval brutalities and murders. His style was fitting to the region and to the tensions. It was barbarism not experienced anywhere else in the twentieth century. It was called the Croatian War.

Milosevic's new state was called the Republic of Serbia Karjina. During his trial for war crimes, Serbia Karjina was described as a "joint criminal enterprise," the goal of which was "the forcible removal of the majority of the Croat and other non-Serb population from the approximately one-third of the territory of the Republic of Croatia that he planned to become part of the new Serb dominated state." Milosevic believed in a policy of all Serbs in one state. All other nationalities were to be removed.

Because of his initial successes in cleansing Serbia, Milosevic widened his scope, removing unwanted populations from their homes even in nontraditional Serbian areas. Bosnia and Herzegovina were at war with Milosevic even before they declared independence in 1992. Bosnian-Serb forces captured most of the country, expelling or murdering hundreds of thousands of non-Serbs.

The Croatian War came to an end in 1995. Because of NATO air strikes run by the United States, the Republic of Serbia Krajina was on the brink of collapse. The war forced Croatian-Serbs out of Croatia and into exile. The conflict was officially ended with the Dayton Agreement.

The agreement did not grant immunity for war crimes. Milosevic never asked for that clause to be included—not for himself or for his henchmen. Instead, Milosevic signed on behalf of the Serbs. He was so aggressive and confident, nobody would guess that only a short time later, Milosevic would be charged and tried for war crimes. Media coverage of the signing even painted Milosevic as the hero and one of the main movers behind the agreement.

There was no time to rest after signing the Dayton Agreement. Another conflict was breaking out—a rebellion in Kosovo against Serbian rule. More pent up anger; more violence. The Kosovo Liberation Army started attacking Serbian and Yugoslavian forces. This time Milosevic was more restrained in his retaliation. Only hundreds of people were killed, and a mere one hundred thousand Kosovo Albanians were made homeless.

Meanwhile, Milosevic's two terms as president of Serbia were coming to an end. He was not permitted a third term. Because of the breakdown of the central government and the continued frac- tionalization, he turned his attention inward to his native power base: the diminished, dwarfed Yugoslavia. He ran for president of the Federal Republic of Yugoslavia, which by then consisted only of Serbia and Montenegro. And he won.

On May 27, 1999, Milosevic was indicted for the crimes he committed in Kosovo. But it was not until Saturday, March 31, 2001—after a long standoff outside his heavily armed and fortified castle—that he gave himself up. The Yugoslavs had charged him with corruption and abuse of power. He was turned over to the United Nations and brought to The Hague. Milosevic was officially accused of war crimes on January 30, 2002, and the trial began February 12, 2002.

There were many people aiding Milosevic's defense, but in the beginning, the law-school graduate chose to defend himself. His defense was partly successful because the Serbian defense establishment was supplying its president with a steady stream of secret documents and recorded interrogations that justified Milosevic's actions.

Milosevic understood international law very well—probably better than his prosecutors did. He knew it was not good enough for the prosecution to simply show that he was the head of a state and that atrocities were committed. He knew his accusers needed to prove that he, as head of the state, had a hand in those atrocities—that he had prior knowledge and ordered them to happen. Or at least that he did nothing to prevent them once he knew about the intended atrocities. Guilt of any kind had to find itself somewhere along that continuum.

As the trial proceeded, Milosevic's popularity among Serbs and Yugoslavs rose. They were appalled that their leader had to suffer the indignities of imprisonment and trial. Many key players from the Western world were not entirely convinced that Milosevic was a mass murderer guilty of war crimes and refused to testify against him. Nikolai Ryzhkov, the former Soviet prime minister, even testified on his behalf.

Milosevic became ill. The diagnosis was high blood pressure and a severe case of the flu. He had been in prison for five years; the trial had lagged on for two years. There were only fifty hours of testimony left. And on March 11, 2006, Slobodan Milosevic died in his cell of a heart attack.

At the time of his death, Milosevic thought he was winning his case. No one knows what would have happened had he lived out the trial. No one knows what the results would have been. But we do know that had Milosevic been exonerated it would have been a green light for tyrants and terrorists and mass murderers.

10

ALEXANDER LUKASHENKO
Dangerous and Very Paranoid

Born: 1954
Died: Still living
Ruled: 1994–present

Alexander Lukashenko. Year after year that name tops the list of the world's most despotic despots and the most tyrannical tyrants. He is one of the most notorious thugs alive.

Alexander Grigoryevich Lukashenko has been the president of Belarus since 1994. Belarus is a former Soviet republic that maintains a loose relationship with Russian and other Soviet republics.

To call Lukashenko an oppressive ruler is to minimize his reign of power and fear. The White House calls his government "an outpost of tyranny." Other Western countries have called Lukashenko "the last dictator." While, unfortunately for the keepers of freedom and democracy, the tyrant of Belarus probably will not be the last of Europe's dictators, he might very well be the worst.

There are no mass executions in Belarus. The people are not

starving to death. They are being strangled intellectually. The rogue regime of Alexander Lukashenko rules by stripping away individual rights and outlawing individual freedoms.

He was born to a single mother in a poor, small village in what was then the Byelorussian Soviet Socialist Republic. The people of his village made their living tilling the land. These are not trivial facts. Lukashenko's early life had a tremendous impact on the person he would become. He served in the army and in 1982 became the deputy chairman of a collective farm. After graduating from the Belarussian Agricultural Academy, he became director of a state farm and construction materials plant. Lukashenko had his personal and professional roots not merely in agriculture but in collective agriculture.

Today it is illegal to own a private farm in Belarus. It is illegal to farm for profit. Villagers live in cottages built for the collective. There are no bathrooms or outhouses. The roads leading to farming villages are pitted or unpaved. The people of Belarus today work the land just as their fathers and grandfathers worked the land. That is the way Lukashenko wants it. It is the way he grew up, and Lukashenko is a self-described man of the people. His own home has running water and electricity, but he still enjoys having official photos taken of himself on the farm, driving a tractor or harvesting the fields.

Creativity and individual thought is stifled from a very early age in Belarus. There may be no threat of war right now, but should there be, Belarus will be prepared. The Belarus army is large— very large. Boys are required to register for the army at sixteen years old. At forty-three years old, men are exempt from serving. For twenty-seven years, every male in Belarus knows that he can, at any time, be called into active duty. The only exemption to military service is enrollment in an educational institute—a state-run, state-controlled educational facility. There are still a very few private universities in Belarus, but Lukashenko is closing them down on ideological grounds. Study of the Bible is forbidden. Only the Russian Orthodox Church is sanctioned by the government.

Lukashenko entered politics in 1990. After the Soviet Union dissolved in 1991, he became even more politically determined and proudly claimed to have been the only deputy of parliament who voted against dissolution of the Soviet Union. In 1993, he was elected chairman of the anticorruption committee of the Belarus parliament. He might not have been aware of it at the time, but that election was his ticket to success. He ran every future campaign on anticorruption platforms; it became his calling card, his signature, his political motto. It was "out with the corrupt leaders, in with me, Alexander Lukashenko."

He was a gifted and persuasive speaker. He still is. He was so successful that when this newcomer to national politics ran for president, he won against five other seasoned candidates. In the first round of the election, he won 45 percent of the vote. The other candidates, including the speaker of the parliament, did not make it past the single digits. In the second round, he won 80 percent of the vote. He was Russia's man and he was in office. By 1994, Lukashenko was president of Belarus—a remarkable achievement even in a country of only ten million citizens.

Lukashenko did not want to liberalize Belarus's economy or privatize the large factories. Instead, he doubled the minimum wage.

The International Monetary Fund and the World Bank stopped lending money to Belarus; they saw his actions as irresponsible. He concocted the position Deputy Director of Ideology and ordered that there be a representative in each place of business. He set prices. He took control of the banks, and the result was a run on the banks.

His greatest success was getting Russian oil at a discount price. Russia's oil line was Belarus's lifeline. And even though the line was built and paid for by private business, Lukashenko claimed it for his own. Belarus could not survive without it—the country has no oil and no pipelines of its own. In his defense, it must be pointed out that there has now been some economic growth in Belarus. Relative to neighboring countries, Belarus is growing at a steady rate. Unemployment is down to 2 percent. Post-Soviet breakdown hurt the lowest and weakest sector of society in Russia and the Ukraine, but in his own way, Lukashenko seems to be taking care of his poor. They don't get paid much, but they get paid on time.

In the summer of 1996, a parliamentarian petition was circulated to impeach the president on charges that he had violated the constitution. Lukashenko called in his troops, his allies from the former Soviet Union, and the issue of impeachment was dropped. In November, a new constitution was passed giving the president even more power. Lukashenko used that power. He dissolved the parliament of Belarus and replaced it with 110 personally picked supporters and cronies. He renewed his term of office and added yet another, a policy followed by many dictators until they are either assassinated or finally elect themselves presidents for life. What happened to the original members of parliament? They resigned. Some were imprisoned. Many have disappeared. Dissenters, opposition members, anyone whose voice is raised in disagreement with the president is dealt with. The KGB exists in Belarus. Today there are mass arrests and even death squads. Lukashenko is a nineteenth-century dictator living in the twenty-first century.

On September 12, 1995, three hot air balloons—part of the Coupe Gordon Bennett hot air balloon race—entered Belarus air space. When they filed flight plans months earlier, race organizers informed the Belarus government about the race. Under orders from their president, the Belarus air force forced the balloons down. Actually, they shot down one of the balloons and killed two citizens of the United States. The occupants of the other balloons were fined for entering Belarus without a visa and then let go.

The West, especially the United States, has repeatedly called for Belaraus to be internationally isolated. Lukashenko is a known supporter of terror. In the 1990s, Belarus irritated the West by selling weapons to some of the most unsavory nations on the globe. It sold $400 million in arms to Iran, Iraq, Sudan, and Yugoslavia. Lukashenko was extending a helping hand to a growing number of anti-U.S. nations.

But there was nothing the United States could do. All the weapon transactions were properly registered and sold under the guidelines of the United Nations. The international community is convinced that Lukashenko sold as much illegally to the same countries as he did legally, but no one has been able to prove it. At the very beginning of the current Iraqi war, several high-level Ba'athist leaders sought by the West escaped capture with the help of passports issued by Belarus. Not only did Lukashenko supply the Iraqis with antiaircraft missiles, he supplied them with passports.

In 1998, the Central Bank of Russia stopped trading in the Belarus ruble. Lukasahenko responded by taking over the Belarus Central Bank and blaming foreign governments for every problem that existed in his country, from the economic turmoil to bad foreign relations. He blamed them for anything that would deflect his own responsibility for the deplorable situation.

According to the Vienna Convention, diplomatic residences are off limits, verboten, to host countries. The president did not care. He threw the ambassadors of France, Germany, Great Britain, Italy, Japan, and the United States out of their residences. The ambassadors have since returned, but Lukashenko continues to speak out against the West in his state-controlled media empire.

Is there anything positive to be said about Alexander Lukashenko? He likes sports. He likes sports so much that he appointed himself chairman of the Belarussian Olympic Committee. According to the rules of the International Olympic Committee, government leaders are not allowed to be members of Olympic Committees—a meaningless detail to the dictator.

But Lukashenko does not like being called a dictator. He prefers to be called an authoritarian.

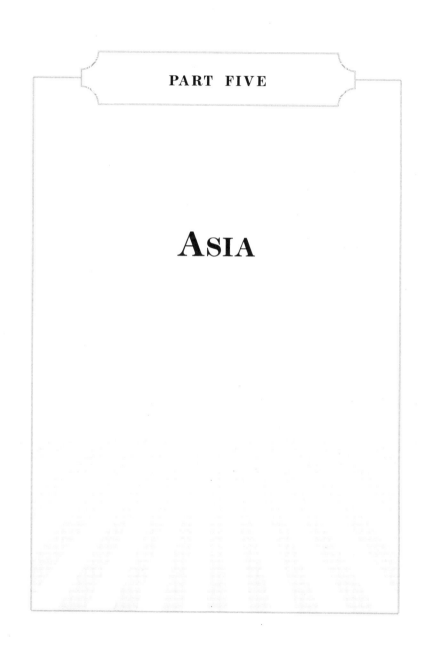

PART FIVE

ASIA

Asia is the largest land mass on the earth. About one-third of all the world's land lies there, and 60 percent of all the world's people live there. China and India alone compose more than half of the world's population. And there is almost no democratic rule in all of Asia.

Asian culture is thousands of years old and deeply steeped in tradition and religious life. In ancient Asia, people lived their lives according to a hierarchy. In many parts of Asia that has not changed. Social class continues to be stratified; there is very little movement. Classic Asian societies do not encourage change and do not welcome different cultures. The differences in each society force them apart rather then bring them together. Leaders, especially autocratic leaders, take advantage of those differences. Even in modern times, most of Asia is lacking the basic tools needed to modernize. It is the perfect environment for thugs.

Historically, there was no crossover of cultures between Asia and Europe. The distances were too vast, the cultures too different, the languages too difficult to understand. Modern times have changed all that. The world is now a more convenient place to navigate, but its societies, for the most part, are still separate and distinct. Modern times have brought modern cultural clashes. Why, for example, would the leaders of China or North Korea adopt Western values of freedom when the West is constantly attacking them?

The West has its reasons, but Asian peoples do not know them. Asian leaders work hard to convince their own people of the need to stay right where they are—right where they have been—and not move forward.

If Eastern Europe lagged years behind Western Europe in political thought, then ancient Asia lagged centuries behind. Asia's political thugs like it that way.

GENGHIS KHAN
Conqueror Not Barbarian

Born: Circa 1165
Died: 1227
Ruled: 1206–1227

Contrary to popular belief, Genghis Khan was not a mythological monster. He was a real-live monster.

Genghis Khan ruled Mongolia during the twelfth century. He was one of the most ruthless leaders in all of history, and it was his ruthlessness that was of mythological proportion.

Genghis Khan is not a name but a title. It means "universal ruler" or "emperor of all emperors." It was bestowed upon a man named Temujin. He was the leader of a destitute clan that fought against and conquered rival clans. Temujin organized these illiterate Mongol tribes into a confederation called Mongolia. As a thank you for his success, in 1206 the people made Temujin their genghis khan. He was the ruler of all the clans. Genghis Khan may be remembered by the greater world for being a ruthless warlord, but the people of Mongolia have marked his place in history and herald him as a great figure and unifier of the Mongolian people.

After conquering and consolidating the local clans, Genghis Khan and his confederation took their show on the road, conquering other lands. With all due respect to his barbarism, he was an enormously gifted general and a quick learner in applying new strategies of war as circumstance and the terrain changed.

In the beginning, the tools of war for Khan were almost exclusively horsemen and cavalry. Then his repertoire grew. He began using sieges and catapults to conquer cities while on campaign. After he conquered a city, he would destroy it. Khan's reputation was built on his destruction of cities; it was well-deserved.

He would raze cities, burning them entirely to the ground, and would kill everyone inside. Khan was feared, and that fear was one of his most effective tools in battle. He was ruthless. He destroyed the fields of his enemy. He destroyed their water sources. He destroyed their irrigation systems.

In less than ten years, Genghis Khan captured Northern China and took over most of Muslim-controlled Central Asia. Then he set his sights on Russia and Iran. Khan ruled from the Caspian Sea to Korea. He had more power over more of the world than any other conqueror in any period of history.

And the funny thing is, he matched his ruthlessness as a conqueror with his benevolence as a ruler. The people under the domain of Genghis Khan actually had freedom of religion.

2

CHIANG KAI SHEK
Transplanted Tyrant

Born: 1887
Died: 1975
Ruled: 1948–1975

Chiang Kai Shek was more than a ruler. He was a legend.

He was the leader of China, but in just two years it became clear that wasn't going to work out. After his forced resignation, Chiang moved to Taiwan and became leader over there.

Before he could rise to a position of national leadership in China, Chiang needed to crush the power of the warlords. He had to forge a single nation out of a large series of clans and tribes. And he succeeded, despite a critical error in judgment.

In 1931, the Japanese were encroaching upon Manchuria at the same time the Communists, led by Mao Tse Tung, were revolting. Chiang had to make a choice: Where would he turn his attention and center his efforts? He chose to deal with the Communists before the Japanese. He failed. He could not contain the Communists, and six years later, he had to reach out to them for help when war broke out with the Japanese. After the war with Japan, China continued with its own civil war. Chiang was tough but not successful. He had already suffered tremendous losses against the Japanese, and the Communists were exacting a toll of their own. Negotiations failed, and he resigned. Chiang and loyal nationalists ran away to Taiwan.

In Taiwan he was much more successful. Chiang benefited heavily from support in the form of both investments and direct aid that he received from the United States. Under his dictatorship, Taiwan became one of the most vibrant economic forces in the world. But there were very few freedoms, including economic freedoms. In the parliament, freedom of speech was protected. On the streets and in the media, it was severely limited. Even economic freedoms were limited.

He established a very interesting blend of government. When Chiang came to Taiwan, there was a constitution. But that did not stop him from creating an entirely authoritarian state. The leadership he chose was almost exclusively from the mainland—they were not Taiwanese but exiles from China. He set up this new government—he called it "temporary provisions"—to create a foundation that would support an overthrow of the Communists on the mainland.

Chiang had a monopoly on power, and no opposition was permitted. He got away with it by explaining that this extreme form of government was the only route to survival because the country was still at war with the Communists. He declared that a state of emergency existed that required total unity and no distractions. What it really meant was that the nationalists were taking over education, imposing their culture and history on the entire school system. Local language and traditions were forbidden in media and other places. Anyone who advocated alternative views on Taiwan or China was jailed. If you supported Communism, you were jailed. If you supported Taiwan independence, you were jailed. If you advocated for local culture, you were jailed.

Despite term limits in the constitution, Chiang was reelected four times. It is true that he created a vibrant Taiwanese economy, but it's just as true that he did it at the expense of democracy. Chiang Kai Shek died from a massive heart attack in 1975. There was a month of mourning in Taiwan—the Taiwanese wore black armbands, and all celebrations were banned. Even color television was abolished. Everything was in black and white. In mainland China, his death was hardly noted. A simple headline read "Chiang Kai Shek Has Died."

3

MAO TSE-TUNG
His *Red Book* Rocked the World

Born: 1893
Died: 1976
Ruled: 1945–1976

To say that Mao Tse-Tung was a Communist leader in China is to understate the obvious. He was *the* Communist leader of China—the most populated country in the world. That would make Mao the Communist leader of the world.

Mao came to power as a result of a civil war between the nationalists and the Communists. The nationalists were led by Chiang Kai Shek; the Communists were led by Mao. Mao won.

The man who brought the People's Republic of China into being was more than a party leader. He was also a poet. His poetry was a combination of pragmatism and utopian vision and belies the ruthless character of its author.

In 1961, Mao wrote a poem reflecting his thoughts on a photo of the Cave of Gods:

At bluegreen twilight I see the rough pines
Serene under the rioting clouds.
The Cave of the Gods was born in heaven,
A vast wind-ray beauty on the dangerous peak.

The poem holds perfectly to traditional Chinese poetic style.

Mao realized early on in his career that the power of China was with the peasants. He knew instinctively that if he could harness the strength of the peasants, he could revolutionize his society—and maybe the world. But the strength of the peasants was not harnessed with poetry. It was harnessed with force. Mao's philosophy of rule is best expressed by one of his own favorite and often-repeated expressions: the power of the barrel of the gun.

As a child, swimming was Mao's greatest love. Years later as Chairman Mao, leader of the Chinese People's Republic, he created a national swimming policy. Swimming would strengthen the people's bodies and clear their minds. He even wrote a poem about swimming.

Mao was known to swim in the stormy ocean in the north of China. It was very hazardous, but Mao was a very strong swimmer. He liked to float on his back. He had a private swimming pool in one of his villas, but the place he most preferred to swim was the very heavily polluted and dirty rivers in the south of China. He would drift downstream with the current for miles and then turn around and swim back on his back.

Mao was totally unfazed by the human waste and globs of other unthinkables drifting alongside him. When he would ask subordinates to join him, they would react more normally to the waste in the water. Mao would taunt them: "What are you afraid of? Maybe you are afraid of sinking? Don't think about it. If you don't think about it, you won't sink; if you, do you will." Welcome to the world of Mao Tse Tung.

The leader of the most populated country in the world never brushed his teeth; he rinsed his mouth with green tea. He never bathed; he preferred to be rubbed down with towels. Mao really had no idea what was going on with the people. When he traveled, he took a private train and all other train service was halted. When his agricultural plans failed, special fields were planted for him along his travel routes so that he could look out the window and admire the flourishing earth.

In February of 1957, he delivered a very long and very rambling speech titled, "The Correct Handling of Contradictions Among the People." The book that most influenced his life and thinking was *Communist Manifesto*. He was egocentric and paranoid and had tasters taste his food before he ate anything. But politically, first and foremost, Mao was a Marxist.

Mao truly believed that everything stemmed from revolution. He also truly believed in empowering the peasants, as long as they remained as peasants. The army was called the Revolutionary Army of the Workers and Peasants. The country was called the People's Republic of China. This was no accident. It was a Communist state, and that state belonged to the people first and foremost. Mao was so good to his soldiers that he even produced heroin to raise money for the Red Army.

Like Stalin, Mao embraced the concept of a five-year plan for economics and development. The first plan set the stage for the second plan, which was called the Great Leap Forward and lasted from 1958 to 1961. The plan was to focus on heavy industry and move China into the modern industrial world.

But reality set in. The shift in markets and the movement to industry probably resulted in the starvation of thirty million people. There was a 15 percent drop in grain output the first year. It was devastating. The second year, 1960, yielded an additional 10 percent drop. The goal might have been for China to move forward, but it seemed like China was drifting backward. And fast. By 1961, the policy of the Great Leap was abolished.

He married four times, had many mistresses, and even more one-night stands. His fourth wife was a character. She had great influence on her husband both in terms of thought and in state policy. Her name was Chiang Ch'ing (1914–1991). She was an actress whose first big part was in Ibsen's play *A Doll House*. Together they had eight children. During Mao's lifetime, his wife was protected; but after he died she was arrested and imprisoned for acts against the people.

Legend has it that every single liquor store in Beijing was out of booze the day she was arrested. Everyone was toasting her imprisonment.

4

POL POT
Despot of the Killing Fields

Born: 1925
Died: 1998
Reign: 1975–1979

The place where people go in but never come out." That's what was said about the most famous of all Pol Pot's interrogation centers: S-21. Located in an abandoned school in Phnom Penh, it was where political prisoners took their last tortured breaths. There were rules. Everyone would confess—man, woman, child. Everyone was a traitor. Electric shock. Hot metal prods. A gallows. Almost fifteen thousand people murdered. S-21 was how Pot Pol ruled Cambodia.

Pol Pot spent twelve years building up his party. It was called the Khmer Rouge, and though he did not create it, he certainly was the embodiment of it. *Khmer* means "Cambodian"; *rouge* is French for "red." It was the party of the Communist Cambodians. Pol Pot became Brother Number One. His identity was concealed from the Cambodian people—no one knew who was leading the country. No one knew who was leading them down the road, forcing them to dig their own graves, and then pushing them in.

Pol Pot was dictator for only four years. In that time, according to reliable estimates, he murdered four million Cambodians. That's one out of every two Cambodians. Even conservative estimates put the death total at one-quarter of the population. Millions of people were murdered, starved, beaten, and executed. It was genocide.

His objective, even before being appointed senior tyrant of Cambodia, was to return to what was called "year zero"—a time when everyone would be equal. Everyone would be working the land. There would be no divisions of property or class. Cambodia would be purged of capitalism. So he abolished money and closed schools. Foreigners were expelled. Police, teachers, Christian clergy, and Muslim believers were executed. He went after anyone who was educated (wearing glasses was a sign of education). Anyone with an infirmity was persecuted and killed.

Villages turned into ghost towns. Cities were empty. The entire population of Cambodia was relocated to agricultural communities—now known as the killing fields. One and a half million people either starved to death, died of disease, or were executed for breaking the law. What did Pot Pol and his cronies envision for their country? Rice. They wanted to increase their production of rice.

Everything was communal. Homes were intentionally burned down so there was no place to return to; only the communities would be home. People were marched out to the communities at gunpoint. Hospitals were emptied; patients were sent to the communities, condemned to slow and painful deaths.

Bullets were not to be wasted on the people of Cambodia. The bullets were too valuable. And who were Pol Pots perfect soldiers? Land mines. He left them scattered about the countryside.

Wearing jewelry was against the law. Complaining was against the law. Grieving the death of a loved one was against the law. Parents and children were separated. Children spied on parents. He was teaching independence. He was making people strong. He was a monster.

He was so sure that he would become prime minister that he prepared a death list. After toppling the existing monarchy, he executed every name on that list, including Cambodia's most influential politicians and leaders.

He decimated Phnom Penh, was tried in absentia for the crime of genocide, and sentenced to death. It was the Vietnamese who ousted Pol Pot from power. Even after he was stripped of the title prime minister of the Khmer Rouge, Pol Pot refused to give up. He spent years fighting guerilla wars with a small army of loyal supporters.

Who was this man Pol Pot? He came from a wealthy family and went to Catholic school. He received a scholarship to study radio electronics in Paris, got sidetracked by Marxism and Communism, never finished the degree, and was asked to return the scholarship money. But is the trivia of such a life worth knowing? Is it important to know that his first wife went insane? (Maybe that's worth knowing.) That he subsequently married a much younger woman? That he had children of his own? None of that changes anything. He was a demon disguised as a despot.

His body was cremated on a heap of old car tires dumped near a public latrine.

5

FERDINAND MARCOS
Dutiful Husband, Deluded Dictator

Born: 1917
Died: 1989
Ruled: 1965–1986

Ferdinand Marcos was president cum dictator of the Philippines for twenty-one years. He was a despot and a murderer. But more than that, he was an embezzler. Marcos was one of the greediest leaders of the twentieth century.

During his tenure as president of the Philippines, Ferdinand and his wife, Imelda, embezzled about $60 billion for private use. On top of that, the president was paid handsomely, legitimately receiving hundreds of millions of dollars for filling the top post in the Philippine government.

Ferdinand Edralin Marcos learned the art of politics at his father's knee. His mother was a teacher; his father was a politician. Young Ferdinand chose to pursue a law degree, and from the very start it became apparent that he did not play by the conventional rules of the game. In 1933, he played a role in the murder of one of his father's political rivals. Six years later—while still in law school—he was arrested, tried, and convicted for the crime. The future president of the Philippines completed his legal studies while serving time in prison on a murder charge.

He studied well. In 1940, the jailhouse lawyer represented himself, appealing his case in the Supreme Court of the Philippines. And he won. His conviction was overturned, and he became a trial lawyer based in Manila.

Ferdinand took time out from his practice during World War II to join the army. He was an officer and claimed to have played a significant role as leader of a guerilla unit fighting against the Japanese. He made it up, but it did not hurt either his military or his legal careers.

Marcos returned to Manila after the war, resumed his law practice, and in 1947, was tapped to become an assistant to Manuel Roxas, the first president of the Philippines. It was the beginning of a long and bumpy political career that would take him all the way to the presidency.

In 1949, Ferdinand Marcos became the youngest member of Parliament in the history of the Philippines. He won the election as a Liberal Party candidate representing his home province. In 1953, he was reelected. And on May 1, 1954, Ferdinand married Imelda Romualdez. It was the perfect match. Imelda was as cunning, greedy, and power savvy as her husband.

His star was rising. By 1959, Ferdinand Marcos was no longer a member of the House of Representatives. He was a member of the Senate and was the opposition leader in Parliament. By 1963, he was president of the Senate. Through a series of failed promises and political switches, Ferdinand Marcos, a member of the Nationalista Party, was elected president of the Philippines in 1965. His winning platform promised improved living conditions and land reform.

Four years later, Marcos made Philippine history once again. He was the first president in modern Philippine history to be re-elected for a second term. And that is when the turbulence and the violence that marked most of Marcos's reign as president began.

Economic growth slowed almost to the point of a complete halt. The Communist Party was making serious strides. A large part of the support for the Communist Party came through the growth of their military wing, the New People's Army (NPA). The NPA was a violent radical group that attacked at will. At the same time, on the Island of Mindanao, secessionist members of the Moro National Liberation Front (MNLF) were striking out at the establishment. The MNLF was a Muslim terrorist group that rejected the entire concept of Philippine-Catholic control over their island.

Communists, Muslims, students—they were all clamoring for control, instigating violence, and acting in defiance of the Philippine president. By 1970, terrorist bombs were destroying cities. An attempt was made to storm the presidential palace in January. And in August of 1971, Marcos suspended the right of habeas corpus. It was a foreshadowing of his suspension of democracy. On September 21, 1972, Marcos declared martial law.

The Philippines more closely resembled a dictatorship than a democracy, and Marcos was the undisputed ruler. Newspapers were shut down. Massive numbers of people were arrested—members of the opposition, students, journalists. Many were killed, gunned down on the streets by the army.

Marcos began to appoint family and friends to top government positions. His inner circle was composed exclusively of close, personal allies. His military chief of staff was a friend from childhood. His wife, Imelda, became the governor of Manila and a minister in the government. Cronies from the army were appointed to head private corporations. The army itself was expanded from 60,000 soldiers to 140,000. Between 1971 and 1977, the Marcos government arrested 60,000 political prisoners. Many were tortured; some just disappeared.

A new constitution was written in 1973, giving Marcos undisputed control of the country and the ability to remain president as long as he wished. The leading advocate for freedom and democracy, Benigno Aquino (Marcos's nemesis), was arrested in 1977 and tried in a military tribunal on the charge of subversion. He was convicted and sentenced to death. However, Aquino was not executed; Marcos was probably afraid of the backlash.

In 1980, Aquino was released from prison and brought to the United States for medical treatment. He remained in the United States until 1983, receiving treatment and successfully creating an organization dedicated to the overthrow of President Marcos. Aquino was head of the opposition in exile.

Finally, on January 17, 1981, Marcos suspended martial law. The country ran to an election. Ferdinand Marcos was handed an overwhelming victory, but the election was rigged. On August 21, 1983, Benigno Aquino, after three full years in exile, returned to the Philippines.

As Aquino disembarked from the plane he was shot in the head, assassinated. Marcos claimed it was the work of the Communists. A committee convened to investigate the murder and discovered a plot by the army to kill the opposition leader. Suspects were arrested and then released. Aquino's funeral turned into a massive demonstration. Hundreds of thousands of supporters and mourners rushed to the streets. This groundswell of solidarity paved the way for the creation of the People's Power Movement, which was led by Corazon Aquino, the widow of Benigno.

On February 7, 1986, a presidential election pitted Corazon Aquino against Ferdinand Marcos. Eight days later, the official announcement hailed Marcos as the victor. But not everyone agreed with the announcement.

The Catholic Church joined with the opposition saying that the results were rigged. The defense minister and the vice chief of staff of the military claimed that the results giving Marcos victory were fraudulent. A rebellion was brewing.

On February 25, Ferdinand and Imelda Marcos escaped with their lives—and with suitcases carrying jewels and billions of dollars worth of gold looted from the people of the Philippines. The couple flew to Hawaii, leaving a country in turmoil, economic despair, and debt. From there, Ferdinand Marcos began to plan his return to power.

In 1988, Marcos was indicted by the United States government and prepared to stand trial on charges that included racketeering, mail fraud, and obstruction of justice. On September 28, 1989, before being brought to justice for any of his crimes, Ferdinand Marcos died of a heart attack. He was still in Hawaii.

The embalmed body of Ferdinand Marcos was brought back to the Philippines in 1993 and put on display in his home town. In 2003, $650 million taken from frozen Swiss bank accounts belonging to Marcos was handed over to the government of the Philippines. Then in 2004, Transparency International, an international organization that fights corruption, named Marcos the second-most corrupt world leader of the past twenty years. A nationwide poll taken in the Philippines in 2005 ranked him the best of the country's last five presidents.

6

IMELDA MARCOS
The Devil Wore Prada, Jourdan & Magli

Born: 1929
Died: Still living
Ruled: 1965–1986

Imelda Marcos did not have 3,000 pairs of shoes. She only had 1,060 pairs. At least, that's what she said. Only her servants would know for sure.

Imelda's biggest claim to fame was her shoes. Then came her position as the first lady of the Philippines, wife of Ferdinand Marcos, the authoritarian tenth president of the Philippines. Ferdinand ruled. Imelda ruled through extension. And then came her role as beauty queen. The holder of the beauty title "Rose of Tacloban" organized the first Miss Universe pageant in the Third World.

When Ferdinand Marcos was hospitalized with kidney ailments, his wife took the reigns of government. Imelda, always a powerful and aggressive woman, became the public face of the Marcos government and the decision maker. Her husband trusted her.

In 1972, President Marcos declared martial law over the Philippines. He was free to name anyone he pleased to any position he pleased. His wife pleased him a lot. She was an ambassador, a government minister, and a member of committees. She orchestrated the opening of diplomatic relations with China, the Soviet Union, Libya, and Cuba.

Her husband knew how to keep his wife happy. He sent her shopping in New York. She could handle the $750 million price tag on the Empire State Building, but the building itself was a little too ostentatious for her taste. It was more in the style of Leona Helmsley. But Herald Center suited her perfectly. She also collected art. Michelangelo. Botticelli. And gems. When a new beach was opened in the Philippines, Imelda imported white sand from Australia for the opening ceremony. Imelda even had specially made bullet-proof bras.

In a country of abject poverty, the Marcoses lived a life of utter extravagance. And they paid for it. In 1986, Ferdinand's regime was toppled and the family fled to Hawaii. The new president, Corazon Aquino, launched an investigation to determine the source of the great wealth amassed by Ferdinand and his wife. The Marcoses had embezzled and hidden close to $30 billion for their personal use. Only about $600 million was returned to the nation.

Ferdinand Marcos died in exile, and President Aquino refused to allow his remains to be returned to the Philippines. But Imelda was allowed to return home and promptly ran for president. She lost her bid for the presidency, but in 1995 she won an election to become Congresswoman Marcos, representing a district in her home province.

Imelda Marcos was a character. When asked about her unusual wealth, she said she had married a wealthy man. When asked about her extravagant lifestyle, she said it was her duty to be a star for the poor. "Never dress down for the poor," she said. "They won't respect you for it."

7

THAN SHWE
Myanmar? Where is Myanmar?

Born: 1933
Died: Still living
Ruled: 1992–present

Than Shwe is the leader of Burma. Officially, the country is no longer named Burma. Shwe renamed it Myanmar, but only a small handful of people in the world have made the connection between the two names.

Burma, or Myanmar, holds the dubious honor of having more child soldiers than any other country in the world. Than Shwe lowered the conscription age to eleven. He did not personally enter the army until he was twenty years old, serving in the unit specializing in psychological warfare. Senior General Than Shwe has spent his adult life implementing and improving upon the methods of psychological warfare he learned in his early years in the military.

Coups are not rare in Burma. While others fell from power, their careers destroyed, Than Shwe kept climbing the ladder of success. With each coup, he climbed another rung, including a seat on the central executive committee of the ruling party. And when bloody protests resulted in the creation of the State Law and Order Restoration Council, Than Shwe was one of its twenty-one members.

He became the right-hand man of Burmese ruler General Saw Maung. When Saw Maung very unexpectedly resigned his position claiming health problems, Than Shwe stepped right in. He had reached the top of the ladder. He was chairman of the Council, head of state, secretary of defense, and commander in chief of the armed forces.

Burma relaxed. It looked as if Than Shwe was going to be more open and less oppressive than his predecessor. Optimism was in the air. The new leader liked to play golf. He began the process of writing a new constitution. He invited the Red Cross and Amnesty International into his country. He cracked down on government corruption and graft. He freed political prisoners. It looked as if Burma was in for a kinder, gentler rule.

Today, under Than Shwe's government, using a fax machine or a modem without a license is a crime punishable by fifteen years in prison.

The real Than Shwe emerged. Restless, ruthless, sullen, the master of psychological warfare. The new constitution was never finished. He created a campaign to force out a quarter of a million Muslims. He told them to flee to Bangladesh. There is no freedom of the press, and journalists who criticize his regime are blacklisted, imprisoned, and tortured.

Win Tin, a seventy-five-year-old journalist, still sits in a Burmese prison. He's been there since 1969.

In 1990 when Nobel Peace Prize-winner Aung Suu Kyi won 80 percent of a general election, the regime cancelled the vote and Aung Suu was placed under house arrest.

In the name of national unity, the Burmese military junta under Than Shwe has divided Burma's fifty million people into subgroups and gone about cleansing the nation. The once simple and straightforward soldier is now a paranoid, power-hungry, corrupt dictator.

Like her husband, Daw Kyaing Kyaing is not what she seemed. Burma's first lady used to accompany her husband as he delivered gifts to Burmese soldiers. Her children rode to school in simple army vehicles rather than luxury sedans. Now she has been implicated in bribery scandals.

In a recent landmark legal case, California oil company Unocal Corporation forced the Burmese government to pay damages for the pain it suffered when the Burmese army forced it to become slave labor working on the oil pipeline. Unocal employees were raped, beaten, and tortured.

Finally, there was a little justice for a few of the victims.

8

ISLOM KARIMOV
One-Half Uzbek and One-Half Tajik

Born: 1938
Died: Still living
Rules: 1991–present

Islom Karimov likes to drop people in vats of water and boil them to death.

He is the president of Uzbekistan. The United Nations has labeled Karimov's particular brand of torture "institutionalized, systematic, and rampant." In fairness to the Uzbeki leader, it must be pointed out that his government is, after all, fighting against Islamist rebels intent on wresting away control of his secularist government.

Islom Abdug'aniyevish Karimov, the man who was democratically elected by 86 percent of the vote in 1991 and by 91.9 percent of the vote in 2000, is an ally of the United States and the West in the war against al-Qaeda terror. As an aside, the opposition candidate in the 2000 election said that he, too, voted for Karimov.

His name was on the ballot only to make it look like a democratic election.

Karimov's term is over in December 2007, but nobody expects to see him leave office.

The details of Karimov's early life are simple. He was born of an Uzbek father and a Tajik mother and raised in a Soviet-run orphanage. Bright enough to get noticed and sent to university, he studied engineering and economics before joining the Communist Party.

On March 24, 1990, Islom Karimov became president of the Uzbek Soviet Socialist Republic. On August 31, 1991, he declared Uzbekistan independent. And now he fights an internal war against Islam. The leaders of the Islamic Movement of Uzbekistan have been sentenced to death in absentia. Supporters of Islam still in Uzbekistan are regularly arrested and tortured.

After 9/11, the United States and Uzbekistan joined a strategic alliance. U.S. forces were stationed in Uzbekistan despite the tremendous criticism leveled against President George W. Bush for supporting the regime of an acknowledged human-rights abuser.

The war against terror creates some strange bedfellows. This is a perfect case in point. Karimov is a despotic ruler. But Uzbekistan had great intelligence in Afghanistan, and Karimov has the motivation to fight the terrorists. The United States, however, must keep a check on the methods Karimov uses to fight his war against al-Qaeda.

He doesn't disapprove of all terror, mind you. Just Islamic terror.

9

SAPARMUT NIYAZOV
Comic Book Demon

Born: 1940
Died: Still living
Reign: 1991–present

If you were writing a comic book about a despot, your character would be modeled after Saparmut Niyazov. Unfortunately, he is real.

Niyazov is the president of Turkmenistan and has held that position for more than a quarter century. One of the first things he did after taking office was make water, gasoline, and electricity free to all citizens. He also outlawed lip synching. And he outlawed makeup for TV news anchors because it is hard for him to distinguish the male anchors from the females.

The president of Turkmenistan is a kook. But he is the ruler who declared Turkmenistan free from the former Soviet Union.

He is also the author of *Rukhnama*, or *Book of the Soul*. His work is required reading for all students—and for the entire nation. He is a thinker. Niyazov redefined the stages of growth. Children go from birth to 12 years old. Adolescents are 13 to 24 years old. Youths are 25 to 35 years old, and maturity lasts from 36 to 48. At 49, you are prophetic, at 61 inspirational, wise at 73, old at 85, and Oguz Khan-like from 97 on up. Oguz Khan is the legendary founder of the Turkmen nation who died at 109.

How did Niyazov become president? He is truly self-made. Niyazov was orphaned at a very young age and raised in an institution. His father was killed during World War II, and the rest of his family was lost in an earthquake when he was eight years old. He joined the Communist Party and quickly rose through the ranks. While still an adolescent, at the age of twenty-two, he became president of the Communist Party. That was in 1962. In 1991, Niyazov was elected the first president of Turkmenistan after supporting the coup against Mikhail Gorbachev.

Niyazov's role model is Kemal Ataturk, father of the Turks. According to law, the president of Turkmenistan had to retire at age seventy, but that won't happen to Niyazov. Like so many other dictators, he has proclaimed himself president for life.

He has arrested masses of people thought to be part of an opposition. He has severely limited freedom of the press. After an attempt on his life on November 25, 2002, his government clamped down hard on human rights. Critics of the president say the attempted assassination was a ploy—an excuse to arrest the opposition.

He banned opera, claiming it was unnecessary and not culturally Turkmeni.

He banned young men from wearing beards or sporting long hair, and women must wear modest clothes.

If a foreigner wants to marry a local it will cost $50,000.

He renamed bread. It is no longer called *chorek* but is named after his mother. He dedicated the year 2003 to her as well.

He renamed cities, schools, days of the week, and months of the year. They were all named after him.

And after he personally quit smoking, Niyazov outlawed smoking in all public places.

Despite his eccentricities and authoritative style, Saparmurat Niyazov is loved by many of his countrymen. To them, he is Serdar Saparmurat Turkmenbashi the Great, the great leader of the Turkmen.

10

KIM JONG-IL
Maniac with Platform Shoes and High Hair

Born: 1941
Died: Still living
Ruled: 1994–present

N orth Korea is on the verge of becoming a serious nuclear threat to the free world. That's scary. The leader of North Korea is Kim Jong-Il. He's scary.

Kim Jong-Il looks more like a caricature than a dangerous and powerful leader. He styles his hair so that it shoots straight up. He wears four-inch-high clogs to conceal his height. He is five feet two inches tall—short even by Korean standards. But in this case especially, appearances can be deceiving.

His birth is cloaked in intrigue. Soviet historical records have him born in Siberia while his father was the captain and commander of the Soviet Rifle Brigade. But his official state biography has him born in a log cabin high atop one of North Korea's most sacred mountain peaks. It also says his birth was announced by the appearance of a double rainbow, a bright star, and a swallow descending from heaven.

His father, Kim Il Sung, appointed him as his successor in 1980. And when his father died in 1994, Kim Jong-Il became the new dictator of North Korea. It was the first time in the history of Communism that a son succeeded his father in leadership. While not unusual in other forms of dictatorships, it is highly unusual in Communist dictatorships. It smacks of monarchy—the antithesis of all that is Communist.

The United Nations, Human Rights Watch, and the U.S. State Department have all marked North Korea as a serious problem. North Korea has consistently been on the top of the list of human-rights abuses for nearly three decades. And Kim Jong-Il has done absolutely nothing to change his country's image.

On the contrary, under his highly secretive and militaristic administration, well over two million people have died of malnutrition and starvation in North Korea. In January of 2005, Kim cut the daily food ration from 300 grams of cereal to 250 grams. That's half the minimum daily caloric requirement for survival.

North Korea is divided into groups. There is the "hostile" group: people who are not permitted to live in the capital, who are given the worst jobs, and who get the worst housing. But they are not the lowest strata of society; there is a group below them. Those people all live in prison camps. There are over a quarter-million North Koreans in prison camps, and they aren't even criminals. They are the relatives of criminals. Their crime is being related to a no-goodnik. Kim Jong-Il still applies the law his father passed. The law stipulates that three generations of criminals shall be imprisoned.

Many North Koreans suffer for the crime of being born into the wrong family.

Prison camps are a step above the fate that awaits other sinners: public execution.

It is actually a criminal offense in North Korea to let a picture of Kim Jong-Il or Kim Il Sung gather dust or be creased, wrinkled, or dog-eared. The punishment is jail time. Televisions and radios are permitted, but they are preprogrammed to receive only state stations. The people are permitted no outside information. Only the government is permitted information.

Kim Jong-Il has planted spies everywhere. There is no escaping the informants. They are in places of work, in neighborhoods, and on the streets. There is no freedom even at home—phones are tapped. About 30 percent of the population is employed in the security or defense fields—soldiers or spies.

Traditionally, North Korea is and has been a very closed society. But Kim Jong-Il seems to be opening up diplomatically—at least a little—with South Korea. As of the year 2000, Kim has allowed his administration to participate in a series of talks with the South Koreans—his country's former nemesis.

On other issues he remains stubborn and unbending. Kim signed his name to the Nuclear Non-Proliferation Treaty. But he repudiated it on January 10, 2003, and expelled the international inspectors. There is no doubt that he is working hard to develop nuclear energy and nuclear weapons. On July 4, 2006, he tested four short-range nuclear missiles over the Sea of Japan. A fifth missile spun out of control within seconds of takeoff.

On October 9, 2006, Kim Jong-Il claims to have tested his first nuclear bomb underground. Was it really a nuclear bomb? Doubtful. It was probably a ploy to attract the attention of the West. Air tests picked up no unusual radiation, and the explosion seemed too small for a real nuclear bomb. But he's trying.

Kim Jong-Il likes little girls. He has been married three times and has at least thirteen children from mistresses. He has young girls—girls in middle school, just eleven and twelve years old—selected to "service" his high-level officials.

He has a penchant for movies, so in 1978, he kidnapped Shin Sang-ok, a South Korean filmmaker, and Choi Un Hui, his ex-wife and a famous actress. Kim forced them to produce, write, and star in propaganda movies. He said it would prop up the North Korean film industry.

He has a wine cellar with ten thousand bottles of wine. He loves good scotch and brandy, reportedly spending $700,000 a year just on Hennessey. (The average yearly salary for a North Korean is $900.) And he loves golf. According to official sources, he has shot a hole in one five times.

Kim Jong-Il is hoping to be succeeded by one of his sons.

CONCLUSION

So what now? How are we to respond to the thugs of the world? We could shake our heads in disbelief of their horrors or chuckle at their follies or simply throw up our hands in surrender to a world held hostage by such characters. But the fact is, we are a better world today because of the legacy of horror and brutality these rulers left, and are continuing to leave, behind.

Without defending or justifying their actions, I simply say that because these thugs pushed the societies over which they ruled—and ruled absolutely—to one extreme, we push our societies to the other extreme. Balance and counterbalance. Thugs deny freedoms; we valiantly protect freedoms. Thugs place little value on human life; we cherish human life. Thugs act to protect their own narrow self-interests; we fight for the interests of others.

Our societies—societies that embrace justice and freedom and the rights of the individual—stand in direct contrast to the dictator and the authoritarian leader. It is because we value freedom that we must understand the role tyrants played in history. We must understand the impact they had on their societies.

Our freedom has become a foil against their evil. What many of them represented was a power localized in a single individual, whether that person was a dictator, a king, a czar, a pharaoh, a kaiser, a caesar, or a president for life. No matter the period in which they lived or the rules by which they played, the reality is that the systems they set up were created exclusively for the purpose of pleasing only themselves—the leaders. Democracy and freedom are exactly the opposite of those systems.

Without leaders who wielded ultimate control over every aspect of their subjects' lives—from birth through death and burial—there would have been no recoil. Our sense of power and justice and our recognition of the importance of social responsibility emerged only because of the immoral and inappropriate leadership displayed by the thugs of world.

The ancient Hebrew prophets—especially Isaiah, Hosea, Amos, and Micah—understood it best. They attempted to convince the Israelites and Judeans that even though God created evil alongside good, good was better. The benefits of doing good far exceeded the benefits of cowering in fear. They attempted to empower the people by imparting to them the advice that with the proper perspective, a unified front, and the right force, a group can impact society and even topple an oppressive regime.

Historically speaking, the free world owes a lot to these despots, dictators, absolute rulers, and human demons. So to the reigning and ruling thugs of the world: thank you for showing us how not to act, how not to govern, how not to rule. Thank you.

And thank you for the good you left behind. Thank you for the architectural triumphs you built, even if they were mostly to glorify yourselves. Even though they were built on the backs of slaves. Even if your people lived in poverty while you amassed the wealth to afford these marvels. Thank you for bringing the world closer by conquering other nations far away from home. By imposing your will and your order on nations with different customs and cultures. By sealing deals and closing treaties with rival nations with the promise to marry your enemies' daughters. Thank you.

All leaders do some good. Well, almost all. Idi Amin and Pontius Pilate might be two good exceptions. Yes, I chose leaders who were a cut above everyone else for their guile and brutality. But I also chose to profile people because of their contribution to the world.

Hitler is the best and worst example from our time of good resulting from evil simply because he was so totally, purely evil. His justice was evil. His science was evil. His culture was evil. So what do we do with this? We analyze it and understand it for what it is. Hitler experimented on unwilling and defenseless humans. Much of his experimentation was predicated on proving his personal racial theories. Some of the science was bad and tainted, but some of it was also valid. How do you handle the valid science? Hitler's work on hypothermia was part of a set of experiments that today helps save lives. Do we discard the scientific findings because in order to get them his scientists froze, drowned, and murdered Jews? We do not. We have not. We should not. Even the most horrific leaders have contributed to our lives and to our world.

This is not to simply say, for example, that under Hitler's influence the trains ran on schedule. It is to say that because of the atrocities under Hitler's fascist regime, an entire new Germany emerged. A Germany that rose up from the ashes and created the foundation for one of the most formidable economies of the twentieth century. Hitler was not good and the immediate results of his evil were not positive. But even out of Hitler's evil there eventually came some positive advances. Had it not been for him, the world would not be what it is today. The entire concept of genocide and holocaust is understood in a very different light today because of what transpired in the fuhrer's Germany.

Hitler reshaped the twentieth-century world just as Herod reshaped the ancient world. Just as Siad Barre reshaped the twenty-first century in Somalia. Not to see that is not to understand history and the impact that leaders and the events they precipitate have on their own small worlds, on the world at large, and for generations to come.

It was Stalin who taught us to be careful of secret societies. It was because of the fate meted out to the shah of Iran that we know to resist security forces and to lend aid to the people who stand up against authoritarian hierarchy. It was Caesar and his many conquests that taught us to guard our borders and protect our boundaries. It was Saddam Hussein who taught us that individual rights and international guidelines cannot be waved aside and dismissed.

Democracy and freedom are the natural outgrowth and response to an authoritarian style of leadership. It is not good enough to simply say that a dictator was a dictator. Or to say that during this despot's reign, what happened simply happened. Or to say that the wanton disregard for human life under their rule was simply a way of life.

No.

It was wrong. It was awful. It was barbaric. It was inhuman. And it is a historical reality. We learn from history. The suffering and the authoritarian rule, the styles of leadership, and the impact the actions of despotic leaders had on their populations became essential tools for us to use in creating better leaders and better societies. These many men—and the few women who made it into their league—are our forefathers too.

Freedom is about seeing authoritarian leadership and responding to it. Even the United States of America was created by throwing off the tyranny of England. Without authoritarian leaders there would be very little conflict and very little revolution.

Some of these leaders were mad. Others had supercharged egos. Some had complex personalities; others were plain and simple. Some were to the manor born; others fought hard to attain their position. In the end, many of them got what they gave. They were deposed, decapitated, beaten, assassinated. Others died gracefully of natural causes. No matter the period in which they lived, the society they ruled, or their style of leadership, they were all thugs.

Thug. Tyrant. Despot. These are all words to describe incredibly bad people who led their societies by doing incredibly bad things. We often tend to use these terms indiscriminately and interchangeably. We could just as easily call them licensed murderers, persecutors, or molesters. We know they did it all for their own pleasure, glory, and gain, but what really, historically, defines these thugs?

Dictator. Czar. Kaiser. King. We may tend to think of these titles as characters in a story. They are the uncomplicated villains we see in theater and on television. But on the stage of life, these titles, like many of the men who wore them proudly, were not entirely one-dimensional. Sometimes the title defined the ruler. Just as often, the ruler defined the title. And every once in a while, it was a case of self-fulfilling prophecy.

Way, way back, rulers would choose titles for themselves. A sovereign would look for a title that had positive connotations, and only later would that same title come to mean something different—something evil, something reflective of the man who bore the title. Sometimes, in their naivety, rulers would take on a name that so appropriately represented their leadership role it was shocking. Sometimes the title was inherited at birth or imposed by country, constitution, or religious dictate.

How do we differentiate between royalty and absolute monarch, between dictators and despots? What makes a president different from a president for life? Who is the benevolent ruler and what makes someone a benevolent dictator? How did one become a pharaoh? An emperor? A czar? There is truly a unique history and etymology behind each of these words.

benevolent dictator. Also called a benign dictator, this is a concept rather than a title. Enlightened despotism, benevolent despotism, and benign dictatorship all refer to a style of governance and leadership. The original concept had it that the monarchies of Europe should institute certain changes as a result of the influence of the Enlightenment. Reforms were enacted influencing the major issues of the day—leadership, economics, religion, and tolerance. The principles of the Enlightenment suggested that everyone had rights, that everyone was fundamentally the same, and that everyone was entitled to the same exact system of rights. This concept held that people were indeed created equal. The term *benevolent dictator* is still in use today; it is a title often bestowed by democratic countries on nondemocratic but kinder, gentler absolute leaders.

caesar. The title means supreme leader. It is the only title that actually comes from the given name of a dictator and then becomes synonymous with other titles for authoritarian leaders. Caesar is actually the family name of dictator for life Julius Caesar. The name becomes a title after Julius. From Augustus to Hadrian, the appellation caesar is added to every single ruler of

Rome, including every Holy Roman Emperor. In Latin, *caesar* means "to cut." It was thought that Julius Caesar was given the name because he was removed from his mother's womb by surgical operation—what we today call a caesarian section, or c-section. If medical practitioners of the day already knew how to perform the surgery, didn't they have a name for the surgery? They did, but legend has it that the operation was performed slightly differently in the case of this birth. Unlike previous cases in which babies were removed after their mothers' deaths, this surgery was performed on a live woman. The idea was to save the mother and the baby. Highly unlikely, but certainly a nice story.

The word *caesar* in Latin also means "to pause." The famous dramatic Latin expression in theater is *caesura*, which means "a break or a pause in the middle of a line for dramatic purpose." Today we would call it a dramatic pause or—remember the legend—a pregnant pause. The ancient world was a world filled with plays, drama, theater and games. And in that world—the world that spoke ancient Latin and Greek—*caesura* was a very common expression.

Some have suggested that caesar also means "the hairy one." This argument appears far less compelling to me. Especially so after looking at images of the great—and very bald—Emperor Julius Caesar.

czar. Spelled with a *c* or a *t*, depending on how you choose to transliterate it from the Slavic languages, the word has a life of its own. In Old Slavic, the word is *cesari,* clearly taken from the name caesar. From there the title czar makes its way into the leadership circles of Russia and the culture of Eastern Europe. The obvious link to caesar is the foundation point, but when the Holy Roman emperors assumed the title it became even more powerful. The title czar resonates with the ideas of the past and the power of supreme leaders dating back to Julius Caesar. Czarism is the system of government based on the total control of the government by the authoritarian ruler.

When the Holy Roman Empire fell in 1453, the Russian Orthodox Church saw the Russian monarchy as a potential role filler for their Christian empire. And so, in 1547, Ivan IV became the first Russian king to be crowned czar. While in reality the czar was limited in power in the Russian church, the title continued to be used. Finally, frustrated by his inability to control the Russian church, Peter I in 1721 changed the official title of all Russian leaders from czar to "Emperor of All Russia."

czarevitch. This was the name given to all first born sons of the czar. There is no single word in English that is a real equivalent to czarevitch. Prince means any son of the king. The closest we can come to capturing the essence of czarevitch is heir to the crown or heir to the throne. The title grand duke was also often used to describe the heir to the throne of Russia.

demon. The word *demon* refers to the character of a person rather than to the role or position that person held. Labeling someone a demon is very different from calling them a dictator, tyrant ,or thug. Interestingly, both Latin and Greek have very similar words for demon: *daemon*. We see the same word in French, and this definition of character has thoroughly made its way into English. The word *daemon* in Greek mythology refers to the strata of secondary creatures or beings who hovered between the gods and men. What it really means is having the character traits of the devil. It means someone who does evil things and is possessed by the desire to inflict horror on people.

despot. The word comes from the ancient Greek: *despotes* means the master or lord. It was a title that, in different places and in different times, referred to rulers. The rulers of ancient Byzantium were called despots. In the Greek Orthodox Church bishops are referred to as despots. Despots are leaders with absolute power.

dictator. The word is originally Latin: *dicere* means "to speak." The idea behind the title is that the word of the dictator is "the final word." Originally, the dictator was a magistrate. The magistrate was in power and position for a specific amount of time and only in a time of emergency. The Roman dictator was appointed for a limited period of either six months or the length of the crisis. The magistrate/dictator had extraordinary legal powers and was appointed by the consul. By definition the dictator had power over all other magistrates and, of course, over everyone and everything else. He made all the decisions. The situation changed, however, in 300 BCE. The power of the dictator was significantly limited and no dictators were chosen after 202 BCE.

The exception to the dictator rule is Julius Caesar. Then again, Julius Caesar broke all the rules and that is what most marked his place in history. Caesar's form of dictatorship was different in action and in deed from those who came before him. Caesar was appointed dictator for life just before he was murdered. This was no coincidence of history.

Fascist. The word comes from the Latin and Italian words *fascis*. To understand the term we must go to ancient Rome, a culture and a society that understood justice. In ancient Rome the symbol for justice was the *fascis*—a bundle of wood. The bundle of wood was wrapped around a hatchet. Symbolically, the image represented the idea of submitting to the authority of society. The original Italian Fascists grabbed on to the theme and made it their own. Fascism came to mean a rigid one-party system in which everyone is wed to a single tyrant and all allegiance is dedicated to a single power source. The symbolism and nuance is very important. Italian Fascists distorted the original Roman imagery of allegiance to justice and superimposed an allegiance to a greater good. Italian Fascists determined that good could only be achieved if you first submitted to the leader.

kaiser. The spelling and pronunciation of kaiser are local German. This is one of the most obvious grammatical moves we have demonstrating the transformation of a word from Latin to medieval German to modern German. The use of the term is unequivocal. *Kaiser* means "ultimate leader." Like czar, kaiser has a clear and direct link to caesar. This is a title that has made its way from Julius to the emperors of the Holy Roman Empire into the leadership of Germany.

In Medieval Europe, the concept of meshing the kingship with the church was important because it had allowed for valuable political and military advantages. The pope and his army were in Rome; the contributing forces were the Christian kings of Europe. These kings saw themselves as leaders and heads of their national churches. They were not to be outdone by the pope in either theology or in war.

king. The word definitely originates in the ancient cultures of the Near East. In Assyriac, the language of ancient Assyria, we find use of the word *cyning,* which comes from the root *cyn,* meaning "kin." From there the word makes its way to medieval English as *kynge,* to German as *konig,* and finally into our modern language as *king.* King is probably the most common of all the titles used by authoritarian leaders throughout the ages. King has been around for a long time and has crossed over various traditions and cultures and continues on its way even in some cultures today. The role of the king is now not always authoritarian; at times it is purely figurative, but the courtesies due a king remain in place.

An alternative explanation for the meaning of the word *king* is that it comes from the concept of kin. *Kin* means "head." *King* then means "the head of the noble leader's son." This definition places strong reference on the concept of the primogenitor. The firstborn son of the king will succeed and carry on the leadership of the nation, tribe, country, or clan.

pharaoh. Anyone who has read the Bible is familiar with the term *pharaoh*. Some people think that pharaoh is actually the given name of one or more Egyptian ruler. Actually, the word *pharaoh* means "the king of Egypt." In the Bible, the word is a proper noun and no additional name was added. In ancient Egyptian, *p'ro* means "king." The word is very similar in Hebrew: *paro*. Greek and Latin also have similar versions pronounced with a soft ph sound. It is from the Greek and the Latin that pharaoh comes into translations of the English Bible.

president for life. The title president for life, or leader for life, crosses over several historical periods and geographical locations. Those ancient leaders who were declared gods certainly were leaders for life, and for that matter, they were leaders even after their demise. The people appointed Julius Caesar dictator for life. And many modern dictators have declared themselves to be leaders for life. Today, when a leader chooses that title, we can assume with confidence that he is an abuser of human rights and has no fear of ever standing trial for those abuses and violations.

thug. The word comes from Hindu, meaning "someone who robs or swindles." Very similar in Prakrit and in Sanscrit, the term was coined because of a religious sect in India that practiced thuggery. They robbed, stole and murdered, all in worship of their god, Kali, the god of destruction. The term thug changes the culture of the analysis. Today the term *thug* is not the least bit connected to the Hindu culture. It simply means "a person who uses brute force to achieve unrighteous ends."

tyrant. The word comes from the Greek: *tyrannos* means "an absolute ruler or someone who took control without the authority." There is also a Latin equivalent: *tyrannus*, "a usurper." In either language the meanings are very similar. But the difference is that in the Greek, the position was illegally seized, not merely immorally taken.

ANCIENT NEAR EAST

HAMMURABI

Bryant, Tamera. *Life and Times of Hammurabi.* Mitchell Lane Publishers, 1995.

Davies, W. W. *Codes of Hammurabi and Moses.* Kevin Neeland Press, 2006.

Harper, Robert Francis. *Code of Hammurabi, King of Babylon.* University Press of the Pacific, 2002.

RAMESES II

Petras, Kathryn. *Mummies, Gods and Pharaohs.* Workman Publishing Company, 2000.

Thomas, Susanna. *Rameses II: Pharaoh of the New Kingdom.* Rosen Publishing Group, 2003.

Whiting, Jim. *Life and Times of Rameses the Great.* Mitchell Lane Publishers, 2005.

DAVID

Finkelstein, Israel, and Neil Asher Silberman. *David and Solomon: In Search of the Bible's Sacred Kings and the Roots of the Western Tradition.* Free Press, 2006.

Kirsch, Jonathan. *King David: The Real Life of the Man Who Ruled Israel.* Ballantine Books, 2001.

McKenzie, Steven L. *King David: A Biography.* Oxford, 2002.

CYRUS

Briant, Pierre. *From Cyrus to Alexander: A History of the Persian Empire.* Eisenbrauns, 2002.

Kirwin, C. J. *Dawn of the Greatest Persian: The Childhood of Cyrus the Great.* Authorhouse, 2003.

Wiesehofer, Josef. *Ancient Persia.* I. B. Tauris Press, 2001.

Darius

Abbott, Jacob. *Darius the Great: Ancient Ruler of the Persian Empire.* Lost Arts Media, 2003.

Wiesehofer, Josef. *Ancient Persia.* I. B. Tauris Press, 2001.

Cleopatra

Higgs, Peter, and Susan Walker, eds. *Cleopatra of Egypt: From History to Myth.* Princeton University Press, 2001.

Shakespeare, William. *Antony and Cleopatra.* Folger Shakespeare Library. Edited by Barbara A. Mowat and Paul Werstine. Washington Square Press, 1999.

Weigall, Arthur. *The Life and Times of Cleopatra, Queen of Egypt: A Study in the Origin of the Roman Empire.* Chautauqua Institution, 1924.

Herod

Josephus. *Life of Herod.* Phoenix Press, 1998.

Perowne, Stewart. *The Life and Times of Herod the Great.* Sutton Press, 2003.

Sandmel, Samuel. *Herod: Profile of a Tyrant.* Lippincott, 1967.

Pontius Pilate

Carter, Warren. *Pontius Pilate: Portraits of a Roman Governor.* Liturgical Press, 2003.

Mills, James R. *Memoirs of Pontius Pilate: A Novel.* Ballentine Books, 2001.

Strenski, Ivan. *Pontius Pilate.* Translated by Charles Lam Markman. University of Virginia Press, 2006.

MODERN MIDDLE EAST

Adbullah I

Satloff, Robert B. *From Abdullah to Hussein: Jordan in Transition,* (Studies in Middle Eastern History). Oxford University Press, 1994.

Wilson, Mary Christina. *King Abdullah, Britain and the Making of Jordan.* Cambridge Middle East Library. Cambridge University Press, 1990.

Farouk

McBride, Barrie St. Clair. *Farouk of Egypt: A Biography.* A. S. Barnes, 1967.

McLeave, Hugh. *The Last Pharaoh: Farouk of Egypt.* Tower Books, 1969.

Stadiem, William. *Too Rich: The High Life and Tragic Death of King Farouk.* Carroll & Graf, 1991.

Gamal Abdel Nasser

Aburish, Said, K. *Nasser: The Last Arab.* Thomas Dunne Books, 2004.

Jankowski, James. *Nasser's Egypt, Arab Nationalism and the United Arab Republic.* Lynne Rienner Publishers, 2001.

St. John, Robert. *The Boss: The Story of Gamal Abdel Nasser.* Arthur Baker, 1961.

Idi Amin

Foden, Giles. *The Last King of Scotland.* Vintage, 1999.

Ingram, Scott. *History's Villains: Idi Amin.* Blackbirch Press, 2003.

Jamison, Martin. *Idi Amin and Uganda: An Annotated Bibliography.* Greenwood Press, 1992.

Anwar Sadat

Finklestone, Jos. *Anwar Sadat.* Routledge, 1996.

Karsh, Efraim. *Heroic Diplomacy: Sadat, Kissinger, Carter, Begin and the Quest.* Routledge, 1999.

Sadat, Anwar. *Anwar El Sadat: In Search of Identity, an Autobiography.* HarperCollins, 1978.

Siad Barre

Clarke, Walter, and Jeffrey Herbst, eds. *Learning from Somalia: The Lessons of Armed Humanitarian Intervention.* Westview Press, 1997.

Fitzgerald, Nina J., ed. *Somalia: Issues, History and Bibliography.* Nova Science Publishers, 2002.

Roberts, Craig, and Ed Wheeler. *Doorway to Hell: Disaster in Somalia.* Consolidated Press International, 2002.

Ben Ali

Borowiec, Andrew. *Modern Tunisia: A Democratic Apprenticeship.* Praeger Publishers, 1998.

Long, David E., and Bernard Reich, eds. *The Government and Politics of the Middle East and North Africa.* 4th ed. Westview Press, 2002.

Reich, Bernard, ed. *Political Leaders of the Contemporary Middle East and North Africa: A Biographical Dictionary.* Greenwood Press, 1990.

READING LIST

AL-BASHIR

Anderson, G. Norman. *Sudan in Crisis: The Failure of Democracy.* University Press of Floriday, 1999.

Lesch, Ann Mosely. *The Sudan-Contested National Identities.* Indiana University Press, 1999.

Petterson, Donald. *Inside Sudan: Political Islam, Conflict and Catastrophe.* Westview Press, 2003.

MOHAMMAD REZA PAHLAVI

Ghani, Cyrus. *Iran and the Rise of the Reza Shah: From Qajar Collapse to Pahlavi Power.* I. B. Tauris, 2001.

Kapuscinski, Ryszard. *Shah of Shahs.* Vintage, 1992.

Kinzer, Stephen. *All the Shah's Men: An American Coup and the Roots of Middle East Terror.* Wiley, 2003.

SEYYED RUHOLLAH KHOMEINI

Khomeini, Ruhollah. *Islam and Revolution: Writings and Declaration of Imam Khomeini.* Translated by Hamid Algar. Mizan Press, 1981.

Martin, Vanessa. *Creating an Islamic State: Khomeini and the Making of a New Iran.* I. B. Tauris, 2003.

Moin, Baqer. *Khomeini: Life of the Ayatollah.* Thomas Dunne Books, 2000.

Taheri, Amir. *The Spirit of Allah: Khomeini and the Islamic Revolution.* Adler & Adler Publishers, 1986.

HAFEZ ASSAD

Maoz, Moshe. *Syria Under Assad: Domestic Constraints and Regional Risks.* Edited by Avner Yaniv. Palgrave Macmillan, 1986.

Pipes, Daniel. "The Word of Hafez al-Assad." *Commentary*, October 1, 1999.

ALI KHAMENEI

Gheissari, Ali, Vali Nasr. *Democracy in Iran: History and the Quest for Liberty.* Oxford University Press, 2006.

Hitchcock, Mark. *Iran: The Coming Crisis; Radical Islam, Oil and the Nuclear Threat.* Multnomah, 2006.

Keddie, Nikki R. *Iran: Religion, Politics, and Society: Collected Essays.* Taylor & Francis, 2005

Reading List

Fahd ibn Abdul Aziz al-Sa'oud

Fahd Bin Abdul Aziz. *Kingdom of Saudi Arabia*. Falcon Press Production, 1981.

Henderson, Simon. "After King Fahd: Succession in Saudi Arabia." *Policy Papers, No. 37*. Washington Institute for Near East Policy, 1994.

Rasheed, Madawi al-. *A History of Saudi Arabia*. Cambridge University Press, 2002.

Yasser Arafat

Karsh, Efraim. *Arafat's War: The Man and His Battle for Israeli Conquest*. Grove Press, 2004.

Rubin, Barry, and Judith Colp Rubin. *Yasir Arafat: A Political Biography*. Oxford University Press, 2006.

Rubinstein, Danny. *The Mystery of Arafat*. Translated by Dan Leon. Steerforth Press, 1995.

Muammar Ghadaffi

Cooper, Paul E. *Libya: The Dream or Nightmare*. The Quiet Leaf Group, 2004.

Kikhia, Mansour O. el-. *Libya's Qaddafi: The Politics of Contradiction*. University Press of Florida, 1998.

Vandewalle, Dirk. *A History of Modern Libya*. Cambridge University Press, 2006.

Bashar Assad

Darraj, Susan Muaddi. *Bashar Al-Assad*. Major World Leaders. Chelsea House Publications, 2005.

Lesch, David W. *The New Lion of Damascus: Bashar al-Asad and Modern Syria*. Yale University Press, 2005.

Leverett, Flynt. *Inheriting Syria: Bashar's Trial by Fire*. Brookings Institution Press, 2005.

South, Coleman. *Culture Shock! Syria*. Culture Shock! Guides. Graphic Arts Center Publishing Company, 2001.

Saddam Hussein

Aburish, Said K. *Saddam Hussein: The Politics of Revenge*. Bloomsbury, 2000.

Coughlin, Con. *Saddam: His Rise and Fall*. HarperCollins, 2005.

Coughlin, Con. *Saddam: King of Terror*. Thorndike Press, 2003.

Karsh, Efraim, and Inari Rautsi. *Saddam Hussein: A Political Biography*. Grove Press, 2002.

READING LIST

WESTERN EUROPE

ALEXANDER THE GREAT

Cartledge, Paul. *Alexander the Great.* Vintage, 2005.

Gergel, Tania, ed. *Alexander the Great: The Brief Life and Towering Exploits of History's Greatest Conqueror.* Penguin, 2004.

JULIUS CAESAR

Caesar, Julius. *The Conquest of Gaul.* Translated by S. A. Handford. Penguin, 1983.

Fuller, J. F. C. *Julius Caesar: Man, Soldier and Tyrant.* Da Capo Press, 1991.

Kamm, Antony. *Julius Caesar: A Life.* Routledge, 2006.

HENRY VIII

Hutchinson, Robert. *The Last Days of Henry VIII: Conspiracies, Treason and Heresy at the Court of the Dying Tyrant.* William Morrow, 2005.

Ridley, Jasper. *Henry VIII.* Penguin Books Ltd., 2002.

Weir, Alison. *Henry VIII: The King and His Court.* Ballantine Books, 2002.

LOUIS XIV

Goubert, Pierre. *Louis XIV and Twenty Million Frenchmen.* Vintage, 1972.

Levi, Anthony. *Louis XIV.* Carroll & Graf Publishers, 2004.

Lewis, W. H. *The Splendid Century: Life in the France of Louis XIV.* Waveland Press, 1997.

MAXIMILIEN ROBESPIERRE

Andress, David. *The Terror: The Merciless War for Freedom in Revolutionary France.* Farrar, Straus and Giroux, 2006.

Jordan, David P. *The Revolutionary Career of Maximilien Robespierre.* University of Chicago Press, 1989.

Scurr, Ruth. *Fatal Purity: Robespierre and the French Revolution.* Metropolitan Books, 2006.

LEOPOLD II

Fowler, Amy M. *The Visual Rhetoric of Colonization: A Historiography of Representations of the Congo Free State.* ProQuest/UMI, 2006.

Hochschild, Adam. *King Leopold's Ghost: A Story of Greed, Terror and Heroism in Colonial Africa.* Mariner Books, 1999.

READING LIST

IOANNIS METAXAS

Mazower, Mark. *Inside Hitler's Greece: The Experience of Occupation, 1941–44.* Yale University Press, 2001.

Petrakis, Marina. *The Metaxas Myth: Dictatorship and Propaganda in Greece.* International Library of War Studies. Tauris Academic Studies, 2005.

Vatikiotis, P. *Popular Autocracy in Greece, 1936–41.* Routledge, 1998.

ADOLF HITLER

Fest, Joachim C. *Hitler.* Harcourt, 2002.

Rosenbaum, Ron. *Explaining Hitler: The Search for the Origins of His Evil.* Harper Perennial, 1999.

Toland, John. *Adolf Hitler: The Definitive Biography.* Anchor, 1991.

BENITO MUSSOLINI

Bosworth, R. J. B. *Mussolini's Italy: Life Under the Fascist Dictatorship, 1915–1945.* Penguin Press HC, 2006.

Mussolini, Benito. *My Autobiography.* Dover Publications, 2006.

Smith, Denis Mack. *Mussolini.* Phoenix Press, 2002.

FRANCISCO FRANCO

Ashford Hodges, Gabrielle. *Franco: A Concise Biography.* Thomas Dunne Books, 2002.

Ellwood, Sheelagh. *Franco: Profiles in Power.* Longman Publishers, 2000.

HENRI PHILIPPE PETAIN

Bruce, Robert B. *Petain: Verdun to Vichy.* Potomac Books, 2007.

Webster, Paul. *Petain's Crime: The Complete Story of French Collaboration in the Holocaust.* Ivan R. Dee, 1991.

Williams, Charles. *Petain: How the Hero of France Became a Convicted Traitor and Changed the Course of History.* Palgrave Macmillan, 2005.

EASTERN EUROPE

IVAN IV

De Madariaga, Isabel. *Ivan the Terrible.* Yale University Press, 2005.

Payne, Robert. *Ivan the Terrible.* Cooper Square Press, 2002.

Waliszewski, K. *Ivan the Terrible.* Nonsuch Publishing, 2006.

READING LIST

ALEXANDER III

Naimark, Norman M. *Terrorists and Social Democrats: The Russian Revolutionary Movement Under Alexander III.* Harvard University Press, 1983.

Zaionchkovskii, Petr Andreevich. *The Russian Autocracy Under Alexander III.* Edited by David R. Jones. Academic International Press, 1993.

NICHOLAS II

King, Greg. *The Court of the Last Tsar: Pomp, Power and Pageantry in the Reign of Nicholas II.* Wiley, 2006.

Lieven, Dominic. *Nicholas II: Twilight of the Empire.* St. Martin's Griffin, 1996.

Radzinsky, Edvard. *The Last Tsar: The Life and Death of Nicholas II.* Anchor, 1993.

VLADIMIR LENIN

Fiehn, Terry, and Chris Corin. *Communist Russia Under Lenin and Stalin.* Hodder Murray, 2002.

Lenin, Vladimir Ilyich. *Essential Works of Lenin: "What Is to Be Done?" and Other Writings.* Dover Publications, 1987.

Remnick, David. *Lenin's Tomb: The Last Days of the Soviet Empire.* Vintage, 1994.

Service, Robert. *Lenin: A Biography.* Belknap Press, 2002.

JOSEF STALIN

Montefiore, Simon Sebag. *Stalin: The Court of the Red Tsar.* Knopf, 2004.

Radzinsky, Edvard. *Secret Archives.* Anchor, 1997.

Service, Robert. *Stalin: A Biography.* Belknap Press, 2005.

JOSIP BROZ TITO

Barnett, Neil. *Tito.* Haus Publishers Ltd., 2006.

Djilas, Milovan. *Tito: The Story from Inside.* Phoenix Press, 2001.

Vuksic, Velimir. *Tito's Partisans 1941–45.* Osprey Publishing, 2003.

ZOG

Braunlich, Phyllis, Deloris Gray Wood, and Thomas D. Braunlich. *Stone Pillows: An American Christian Missionary in the Moslem Land of King Zog.* Xlibris Corp., 2003.

Fischer, Bernd Jurgen. *King Zog and the Struggle for Stability in Albania.* East European Monographs, 1984.

Tomes, Jason. *King Zog.* Sutton Publishing, 2003.

NICOLAE CEAUSESCU

Pacepa, Ion Mihai. *Red Horizons: The True Story of Nicolae and Elena Ceausescus' Crimes, Lifestyle, and Corruption.* Regnery Publishing, Inc., 1990.

SLOBODAN MILOSEVIC

Doder, Dusko, and Louise Branson. *Milosevic: Portrait of a Tyrant.* Free Press, 1999.

LeBor, Adam. *Milosevic: A Biography.* Yale University Press, 2004.

Milosevic, Slobodan. *The Defense Speaks: For History and the Future.* Ramsey Clark, 2006.

ALEXANDER LUKASHENKO

International Business Publications. *Belarus: President Alexander Lukashenko Handbook.* World Political Leaders Library.

ASIA

GENGHIS KHAN

Gabriel, Richard A. *Genghis Khan's Greatest General: Subotai the Valiant.* University of Oklahoma Press, 2006.

Rice, Earle. *Empire in the East: The Story of Genghis Khan.* Morgan Reynolds Publishing, 2005.

Whiting, Jim. *The Life & Times of Genghis Khan.* Mitchell Lane Publishers, 2005.

CHIANG KAI SHEK

Ch'En Chieh-Ju. *Chiang Kai-Shek's Secret Past: The Memoir of His Second Wife, Ch'En Chieh-Ju.* Edited by Lloyd E. Eastman. Westview Press, 1994.

Fenby, Jonathan. *Chiang Kai Shek.* Carroll & Graf Publishers, 2004.

Furuya, Keiji. *Chiang Kai-Shek: His Life and Times.* Edited by Chun-Ming Chang. St. John's University, 1981.

MAO TSE-TUNG

Chang, Jung, and Jon Halliday. *Mao: The Unknown Story.* Knopf, 2005.

Li Zhi-Sui. *The Private Life of Chairman Mao.* Random House, 1996.

READING LIST

MacFarquhar, Roderick, and Michael Schoenhals. *Mao's Last Revolution.* Belknap Press, 2006.

POL POT
Short, Philip. *Pol Pot: Anatomy of a Nightmare.* Owl Books, 2006.
Kiernan, Ben. *The Pol Pot Regime: Race, Power, and Genocide in Cambodia under the Khmer Rouge, 1975–79.* Yale University Press, 2002.

FERDINAND MARCOS
Celoza, Albert F. *Ferdinand Marcos and the Philippines: The Political Economy of Authoritarianism.* Praeger Publishers, 1997.
De Morga, Antonio, E. H. Blair and J. A. Robertson. *History of the Philippine Islands, Volume 1 and 2.* BiblioBazaar, 2006.
Hedman, Eva Lotta. *Philippine Politics and Society in the Twentieth Century: Colonial Legacies, Post-Colonial Trajectories (Politics in Asia).* Routledge, 2001.
Schirmer, Daniel B., and Stephen Rosskamm Shalom. *The Philippines Reader: A History of Colonialism, Neocolonialism, Dictatorship, and Resistance.* South End Press, 1987.

IMELDA MARCOS
Day Romulo, Beth. *Inside the Palace.* Putnam Adult, 1987.
Navarro Pedrosa, Carmen. *Imelda Marcos: The Rise and Fall of One of the World's Most Powerful Women.* St. Martins Press, 1987.

THAN SHWE
Taylor, Robert H. *Burma: Political Economy Under Military Rule.* Palgrave Macmillan, 2001.
Doral, Francis, and Clare Griffiths. *Insight Guide: Burma/Myanmar.* Insight Guides, 2000.

ISLOM KARIMOV
Karimov, Islam. *Uzbekistan on the Threshold of the Twenty-First Century: Challenges to Stability and Progress.* Palgrave Macmillan, 1998.
Pyati, Archana. *Karimov's War: Human Rights Defenders and Counterterrorism.* Edited by Neil Hicks. Human Rights First, 2005.

Reading List

Saparmut Niyazov

Gale Reference Team. "Turkmenistan: Saparmurat Niyazov." *APS Review*, October 2, 2006.

Stein, Pam. "Turkmenistan: Premier Saparmurat Niyazov." *APS Review*, July 28, 2005.

Kim Jong-Il

Becker, Jasper. *Rogue Regime: Kim Jong Il and the Looming Threat of North Korea*. Oxford University Press, 2006.

Kim, Sung Chull. *North Korea Under Kim Jong Il: From Consolidation to Systemic Dissonance*. State University of New York Press, 2006.

Lintner, Bertil. *Great Leader, Dear Leader: Demystifying North Korea Under the Kim Clan*. Silk Work Books, 2005.

ACKNOWLEDGMENTS

I had an idea. Lynne and then Joel and then Alice and then Julie turned it into this book.

Lynne Rabinoff, my literary agent. Lynne has class; she has style; she has integrity. And she is boldly, brutally honest. Exchanging ideas with Lynne is an intellectual treat. I trust Lynne's instinct implicitly and am honored that she trusts in me.

Joel Jeremiah Miller, my publisher. Joel is every author's dream come true. His insight was invaluable. His judgment kept me honest. His sense of humor is keen. I thank Joel for honing my historical concept and for allowing my literary voice to ring true.

Alice Sullivan, my senior editor. Alice took this manuscript and turned it into a book. Her calm and equanimity swept this work, as if effortlessly, through the perilous process of publishing. I am grateful to Alice for so gently paving the way.

Julie Foster, my editor. Julie's keen and critical eye was essential in fine-tuning this book. Her literary understanding and professionalism brought this book to its conclusion. I am lucky that this book was placed in Julie's guiding hands.

Thank you, Thomas Nelson, for connecting the dots.

Micah D. Halpern
2007

INDEX

INDEX

Index